"EFFECTIVENESS OF SOCIAL NETWORKING FACEBOOK FOR TEACHING SCIENCE"-A STUDY

2017

Acknowledgement

I am deeply indebted and highly grateful to my guide Dr. Rajshree S. Vaishnav, Professor & Head, P.G. Dep. of Education R.T.M.N.U., Nagpur who has guided and supported me from inception to completion of my work, it was just impossible to carry out and complete this study without her consistent encouragement and help through the work and will go a long way in my teaching career for which I shall remain ever indebted to her.

It is the result of her interest, sound knowledge and valuable guidance. She has always been a source of inspiration to me. I shall ever remember her commitment to research endeavour and her constant support to me in my research undertaking. I consider myself fortunate and proud having worked under such a talented and versatile personality.

I highly thankful to my Co- Guide Dr. Sanjay Barde, Janta college of Education, Chandrapur for their guidance right from inception a support during the completion of the research work, and Principal Dr. Ashok Jivtode, Janta College of Education, Chandrapur for allowing me to carry out this research work at their Center.

Thanks also goes to the Librarian, Janata College of Education, Chandrapur, Librarian, P.G.T.D. (Education), RTM Nagpur University, for their cooperation in making available the necessary literature for the study.

I am highly thankful to principal of Wonderland High school Nagpur, principal of Kendriya Vidyalaya Vayusena Nagpur, and Principal of Kendriya Vidyalaya Ambazari, Nagpur for permitting me to conduct this experiment in their schools.

I would also like to thank all students and parents who co-operated with me during my whole data collection process, it would have been impossible for me to reach to an authentic research conclusion without their sincere involvement.

I am highly indebted my father Mr. G. Singh, my mother Mrs. Sheela Singh for helping me to understand and appreciate the importance of learning and for planting the educational seed that enabled me to complete this work. I also extend my thanks to my brother Mr. Mukesh Singh, sister-in-law Mrs. Pallavi Singh and my nephew Pranat singh.

My special thanks to my 10 years old son Kushagra for his patience, understanding and co-operation during the tiring times of software development, late nights of studying and writing.

Ms. Vandana Singh

CONTENTS

LIST OF TABLES

LIST OF FIGURES

CHAPTER – I

INTRODUCTION

1.0.0 The Present Study: Preview

The present study entitled "Effectiveness of social networking Facebook for teaching science"-a study, belongs to the area of educational technology i.e. use of social networking site (Facebook) for creating a rich content for the 21st century students, so that they are free to access it as per their own pace, time and suitability.

Social networking sites are now one of the most common types of online website found on the internet. Facebook site is the one of the most popular social networking sites. The accessibility and the reflective nature of Facebook site is appropriate to many learning and teaching application and convenient for the learners as well as for the teacher educators to use the website anywhere and at any time.

In the present study an attempt has been made to develop learning material using Facebook pages for teaching science to students of class IX "Central Board of Secondary Education". Facebook page was developed for the 15 chapters of science to find out the effectiveness of Facebook along with conventional teaching method in terms achievement of students and reaction of students towards developed Facebook page. The effectiveness of developed Facebook page is determined on the basis of comparison between the achievement score of students studying with only conventional method of teaching with those studying through Facebook with regular classroom teaching by taking intelligence and study habit as co-variate. The comparison between overall achievement of male and female students studying through Facebook along with conventional method was done.

In the developed learning material using Facebook certain features have been incorporated to make it more users friendly and convenient to achieve the multidimensional objectives of education and the personal communication between the researcher and student participants are been made through phone calls, e-mail, messages and face- to- face conversations. Their difficulties encountered, problem-solving strategies employed to achieve the multidimensional objectives of education.

These features include

1. Variety of tools with which to create, present and share content.
2. Forums and threaded discussions.
3. Quickly customize designs and include videos, photos and podcasts- it`s safe easy and secure.
4. Create a class and keep total control over student comments, monitor and moderate all contents.

1.1.0 Social Networking Sites

A social network is made up of individuals that are associated to one another by a particular type of interdependency. It could be ideas, values, trade, etc. Social networks operate on many levels. Initially social networking happened at family functions where all relative and friends would conglomerate under one roof. Social networking has always been prevalent; Earlier the process was long drawn, including a chain movement where in one person led to another through a web of social contacts, today the process is highly specialized.

Now days there are many online social networking sites where individuals provide information about themselves and their social networks. Social networking allows for like- minded people to communicate with each other.

Social networking is the necessity of this age. Social networks are formed when people sharing certain interests including hobbies, religion, politics, ideas, values etc., integrate into groups or communities.

To facilitate social networking, there are many websites. These social networking sites include Flickr, Face book, Myspace, Orkut, Twitter, Fropper, etc. Such sites help people to keep in touch with each other and also associate with long lost friends from school and college.

Though it began as a fad among the youth, people of all generations have caught the craze now. Membership can only be obtained through existing members who will admit you into the circle as their friend or family. People can upload photos and videos through these sites and share them with their group of friends.

Social networking sites also have a troublesome side. One has to be cautious about disclose personal information and sharing photographs with strangers. These can be used for threatening purposes and may lead to dangerous situations. There are many examples like In Mumbai, Adnan Patrawala, a wealthy youngster, was abducted and killed by some friends whom he met on Orkut.

Social networking comes in handy when one require a job. One can use their contacts to find good job opportunities. Advertisers also have found social networking sites a handy tool to get response on their products as people tend to believe their peers' opinions on certain products rather than an advertisement. This has led them to utilize such sites to promote their products.

In the social networking world, one can make a distinction of different kind of social networking sites. Basically there are three kind of differentiation.

1. **Professional Oriented:** Aim of Some websites like LinkedIn, Viadeo or Xing is to create a set of relationship and feedbacks on workers, so to help both the flexibility of employers, that can built their professional trustworthy with references and responses, and the workers recruiting of companies that can have an online easy approachable records of workers.

2. **Interests Oriented:** Some websites like Flickr, a Nobii, devian Art, Live Journal are usually linked by common interests as photography, Digital arts, writings, and one can think about the topic as the knot of the web around which conversation and interaction takes place.

3. **Socialize Oriented:** Some websites like Facebook, Myspace, Badoo, Netlog, Friendster sites can trace the activities of their friends, chat, have a look at their profile, share pictures with others, link music, post articles or videos and comment on people's profiles.

Of course, the boundaries among these three categories are blurred, as some site could have different uses as their original motive. Dating, for instance could be seen as a part of the Professional oriented group but on the other hand it is also part of the socialize oriented group. Some of the above mentioned socialize oriented Social Networking sites give the possibility to create group of interests or walls of conversation.

Social networking sites are attracting the attention of all the users in the world- like Students, high school kids, researchers, academicians, industrialists, celebrities, etc. Social networking websites are important not only to keep in touch with people but also beneficial for educational purposes in many various ways.

There are many educational benefits of using social networking sites for both teachers and students. Social networking sites like Orkut, Facebook, Multiply, Myspace, and Twitter etc. are used by all age people across the world to interact with others and for educational purposes like online sharing of education related topics, learning outside of school or college planning and more.

The attention of academic researchers has been captivated very much by the increasing popularity of social networking sites. Research also confirms that social networking sites have impacted student learning positively in various ways. Social networks focused on maintaining relationships among teachers and their students are used for educator professional development, learning, and sharing content.

1.1.1 Some Famous Social Networking Sites

1. Social Connections

Keeping in touch with friends and family members is one of the greatest benefits of social networking. Here is a list of the most widely used websites for building social connections online.

Twitter: Twitter was created in March 2006 by Jack Dorsy, Evan Williams, Biz Stone and Noah Glass and by July 2006, the site was launched. Twitter is an online. Twitter allows its users to make short, regular statement about their own experiences, as well as signposting followers of their newsfeed to other content, and re-produce other Twitter content of which they approve ("re-tweet"). Users access Twitter through the website interface, SMS or mobile device app. Twitter is now one of the ten most visited websites and has been described as the SMS of the internet.

Facebook: Currently Facebook is the most successful and popular social networking site. Facebook started life as a networking tool for US college graduates but has developed into a global platform. Facebook is increasingly diversifying to ensure that its members other social networking activity can be conducted within Facebook through "plug-ins".

Digg: Digg is a peer-ranking site which enables people to highlight content on the web through a bookmark "button" on their browser. Content is then aggregated through Digg and the relative popularity of particular content is used to signpost other Digg users.

Foursquare: Foursquare is one of most successful social media platforms to make use of the opportunities presented by mobile internet. Foursquare enables its users to "check-in" at particular locations. This data is then made available to their friends, as well as potentially to other foursquare users nearby. Foursquare remains most popular in the US, and has been seen as a major marketing opportunity for businesses to reward customer loyalty and create specific incentive schemes.

Friends Reunited: This social networking site predominantly used in the UK, Friends Reunited connected people with former classmates from school and university. The site was most popular in the early 2000s.

Google+: It is a social networking and identity service that is owned and operated by Google. Google's social networking has aimed to draw together the most successful elements of other social media, while also taking benefit of the vast number of people currently with a Gmail account. The site has launched in 2011, has yet to build up a critical mass of users in Europe. Google has described Google + as a social layer that enhances many of its online properties, and that it is not simply a social networking website, but also an authorship tool that connects web content directly with its owner/ author. LinkedIn sales revenue has grown by an average of 89% over the past year, and its net profit has grown by an average of 1.39% annually. The Verge Start-ups blog listed it as one of the most successful start-up companies by market capitalization, revenue, growth and cultural impact.

MeetUp: This website is like a tool which allows people to connect with others in their locality with shared interests. Meet

Up has been most successful in the US although it is also used elsewhere.

Tumblr: It is launched in 2007; most of its users are based in the US, although it also has some European users. It is another short-form blog, Tumblr enable users to post content and see content posted by other users they follow.

Orkut: Orkut is a social networking platform that is launched in 2004, although it never rose to prominence in the US or Europe, previously it was one of the primary social networks in both India and Brazil. Presently it has been discontinued.

2. Multimedia Sharing

Some social networking sites which are made specially to share video and photography content online. Some of the most popular sites for multimedia sharing are given below

Myspace: In the mid-2000s Myspace was the first social network to achieve global breakthrough. Initially started as a way for musicians to share their music for free. Myspace boomed to embrace a vast number of users who used it simply to communicate with their friends. Now with a smaller number of users, Myspace declined and Facebook emerged into vast usage.

Flickr: Flickr is a photo-sharing site, where people can share their own photographs, and comment on and in some cases make use of photographs posted by others.

Ning: Ning is a platform which permits users to interact through the different technical features available on the site, including sharing content and threaded conversations. Users can customize to a bigger range than on some other platforms, and pay for some services. Although it remains a relatively smaller platform than many other social networking sites.

Pinterest: It is one of the newest social networking sites. It enables users to collect images from online list, which they then "pin" to themed boards which can be watched by other users of the site. So far, the site has reached highest profile in the US, but is progressively popular in the UK and Europe, where it has become usually popular with designers and developers.

Vimeo: Vimeo is a film-sharing website. It has yet to arise to prominence compared to YouTube, but has a significant following from independent filmmakers in the US and the rest of the world.

YouTube: YouTube is made by three former PayPal employees in February 2005 and owned by Google since late 2006, and basically it is a video sharing website. Here users can upload, view and share videos. Currently this is the most popular video-sharing website on the internet, it also offers viewers the opportunity to comment on and catch with others' social media. Users of the website can rank others content with simple "like" and "dislike" buttons, as well as setting up their own channels for their own content, in fact, around half the videos on the site have been ranked in this way. Over 70% of their users come from outside the US. Most of the content on YouTube has been shared by individuals, but media corporations including CBS, the BBC, Vevo and other organizations offer some of their material via YouTube, as a part of the YouTube partnership program. Unregistered users can watch videos and registered users can share an unlimited number of videos.

Instagram: Instagram was created by Kelvin Systrom and Mike Krieger and launched in October 2010.It is an photo sharing, video sharing and social networking service that allows its users to take pictures and videos, apply digital filters to them and post them on a variety of social networking services such as Facebook, Twitter, Tumblr and Flickr. A distinctive feature is that it restricts photos to a square shape similar to Kodak Instamatic and Polaroid images in contrast to the 16:9 aspect ratio now typically used by mobile device cameras.

Picasa: Picasa is similar to Flickr, Picasa provides a way to organize and share photos. It is a Google product and so offers integrated tagging and sharing with Google+.

3. Professional

There are some social networking sites which are designed to provide opportunities for career related growth. Some of the websites are given below:-

LinkedIn: It is a social networking site for people in professional occupation. It was founded in December 2002 and launched on May 5 ,2003.one of the only social networks to explicitly connect itself with people's professional identities, LinkedIn carries most detailed information about users' career history and creates connections with people with shared backgrounds. It is the only male-majority social network. The site is available in 20 languages, including English, French, German, Italian, Portuguese, Spanish, Dutch, Swedish, Danish, Romanian, Russian, Turkish, Japanese, Czech, Polish, Korean, Indonesian, Malay and Tagalong.

Reddit: Another peer-ranking tool which allows users to post content of which they approve and then allows other users to rank the content "up" or "down".

4. Informational

Informational communities are made up of people seeking answers to everyday problems. These **websites** are usually content and design driven. A few examples are given below.

Super Green Me: It is an online community where those individuals communicate who are interested in adopting green living practices.

Do-it-Yourself Community: Social media resource permits doing it yourself enthusiasts to communicate with each other.

Answers.com: When anyone wants basic information about someone or something, try plugging the query into Answers.com's general search field, or browse the ever-expanding Directory of reference material. The information you pull up will contain dictionary definitions and encyclopaedia articles culled from resources licensed from a variety of publishers.

5. Educational

Educational websites are community for teaching or studying: Create, share, and explore high quality of content. Educational websites are popular within the educational system. Some of the websites are:-

National Geographic Kids: National Geographic Kids website provide the information related to nature. Kids can watch videos, play games, and best of all; learn about animals, nature and the world around them.

BrainPOP: Kids understand more about historical events, science and even the stock market, all with the help of a plucky robot and his friends.

EdX.org: Edx website is one of the world's leading MOOC platforms. MOOCs (massive open online courses) are offered for free to anyone who want to learn.

6. Hobbies

It guides to anything related to the hobby. Whether one is interested in stamp collecting, Gardening, flying model planes, pop art or cooking. The websites will interact a person to other, who also passionate about the hobby, that allow to share tips and receive suggestions and guidance.

discoverahobby.com: Here you can discover the information on how to initiate a new hobby, where to find lessons, online instructional videos and pictures, and the best beginners equipment, books, and videos. One should try new and different things to find what they really like.

Dance-Forums.Com: Dance-Forums is a site where those individuals can communicate who love music and dancing and share their interests. Everything you need to know even from beginners and seasoned professionals can be learned from this site. Forums are the best because you can interact with both beginners and advanced performers.

SportLemon.tv: SportLemon site is probably the biggest and most dependable of all the streaming sports websites out there. They carry all major sports and usually offer multiple links to make sure you find a working stream.

7. Academic

Academic researchers who want to share their research and review results achieved by colleagues may find academic specific social networking to be quite valuable. The most popular online communities for academics are:-

Academia.edu: Academia.edu is a platform for academics to share research papers. The company's mission is to accelerate the world's research. Academics use Academia.edu to post their research, monitor deep analytics around the impact of their research, and track the research of academics they follow.

Connote Collaborative Research: It is an online resource for scientists, researchers and clinical practitioners to find, organize and share useful information.

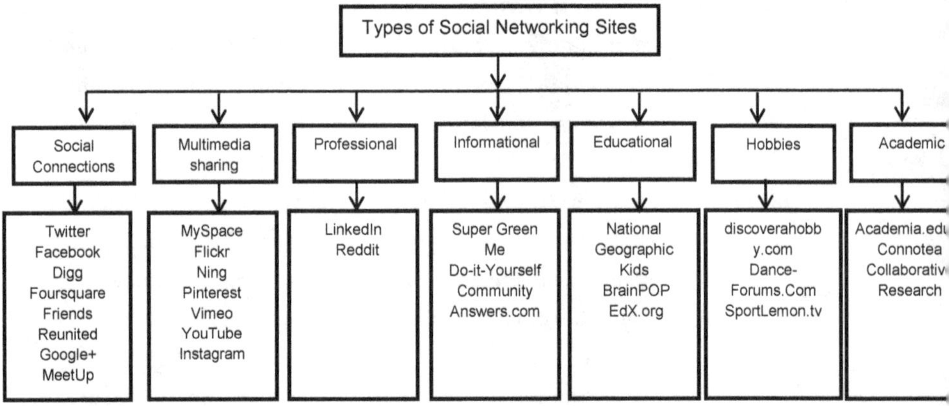

Flow Chart 1.1: Types of Social Networking Sites

1.1.2 Reasons to Use Social Networking Sites in Education

There are so many reasons why educators and school authorities need to seriously ponder about an effective policy of integrating social networking into the classroom. Here are in brief some of these reasons are stated

1. Social Media is not going away
2. When Kids are engaged they understand better.
3. Safe Social Media Tools are free available.
4. Replace online procrastination with social education.
5. Social Media inspires collaboration instead of cliques.
6. Users have a huge degree of control to share comments, photos, and videos at any time of day.
7. Communication is instant and minute-by-minute.

8. The union can target users who have common interests or experiences.
9. Communications can be managed locally, regionally, nationally and globally.
10. Communication reaches across socially diverse groups

Social networking is a recent discovery that has the Internet still at the edge of its seat due to its popularity with people. This is mostly because it really is for the people. Bringing every kind of social group together in one place and letting them communicate is really a big thing indeed. Everything about it lies on the uses and misuses of social networking, and what it can do for you.

1.2.0 Facebook

The social networking site known as Facebook that has gradually become more popular. People of all ages have made their own Facebook pages and use them for many different reasons. Facebook has been a dominant presence in our lives in the past several years and there is no evidence at the moment that it will stop being so. The debate about Facebook has only just started and academia has been fertile ground for exploring the possibilities that it presents as an educational tool. It has been a subject of conversation and exchange of arguments, with the balance of opinions favouring its use. There are, however, many who realize that we are jumping on the bandwagon very fast, and that there are many things about Facebook use and users that need to be understood before we use it as a tool that can be utilized for activities other than leisure and social interaction in a digital space.

According to Crook et al. (2008), Web 2.0 is a set of Internet services and practices that provide users a good opportunity to participate in various communities of knowledge building and knowledge sharing. With a step change from Web 1.0, Web 2.0 technologies offer an opportunity for user involvement in what makes up the Internet. They permit users to share and to be more involved in social networking communities which are different from Web 1.0 that was more a matter of downloading. Web 2.0 technologies offer interaction and data management resources that actively encourage new forms of collaboration and coordination of users. Consequently, with more involvement given and the easier way to stay connected with other people, Web 2.0 technologies have been widely used as a supplementary learning tool giving students independence in learning. In other words, these technologies promote a wider range of expressive capacity permiting students to express their interests or work collaboratively with teachers, peers, and authentic audience.

Facebook is a medium for communication, and yet very important part of life. At a glance, a user can learn everything from what gender a Facebook member is, to what religion they believe in, what school they attend, and their likes and dislikes, all with the click of a mouse. One writer notes how popular the site has become in a short time. She writes, "When Facebook launched in February 2004, American college students seized the opportunity to have a new social medium" (Ling, 2008). currently, millions of new visitors join the site every year, and people can search relatives, old friends, new friends, and much more as they surf the entries of neighbours, acquaintances, and classmates.

While many realize that Facebook is a new, trendy idea,and it is actually based on a Victorian university tradition, the "Freshman Facebook," that introduced the incoming class to students through the photographs. A researcher notes, "Like its relative the yearbook, the Facebook is a photographic document created by a community or individual for the purpose of visually defining community life" (Miller, 2007). Many colleges and universities still use the Facebook, and the web site's creators based their name and idea on that old college tradition, they just updated it for a younger, hipper, techie audience. However, compared to other social networking sites, like My Space, Facebook is far less chaotic, busy, and difficult to understand. The pages are neat, easy to navigate, and allow the information in an uncluttered, neat site that is pleasant to look at.

Some use their Facebook account for interacting with their friends and family. But some use it for interacting with new friends they have never met. Many people don't know how the things you post on Facebook like personal information; relationship status, photos and even status updates can be extended to millions of users on Facebook if you don't play with your privacy settings.

Facebook is designed to make it easy for one to post their information with anyone they want. Users need to decide how much information they feel comfortable sharing on Facebook and control how it is distributed through their privacy settings.

Privacy settings are important if one want to protect the privacy and security on Facebook. Privacy settings control the people who look at your status, photos and wall post. However some information like age, sex and name are mandatory for you to have a Facebook account. 98% of users have more information that just their age, name and sex. Many people post their Basic information like: Birthday, hometown, family members, relationship status, anniversary, likes, dislikes, hobbys and political and religious views also included favourite activities, personal interest, favourite music, movies, TV shows and something about them.

Due to the uprising of Facebook more social networks are working through Facebook and even require a Facebook login to be a part of their website (ex. Pinterest, Spotify, Instagram). Facebook has permitted other social networking sites to become more and more popular. The launch of Facebook has sparked so many ideas of web designers and creators to rise up and invent anything then share it with people all around the world. Sharing ones life, interests and ideas is what Facebook was built upon and the creativity of people has used Facebook to utilize their ideas and share it with others.

There are many reasons that make Facebook so popular. Some of the reasons are, its easy accessibility, the growing use of social networks, the means of connecting with friends, and the fact that people more inclined to use it. The obsessiveness of logging onto Facebook can be bad when one trying to get something accomplished. One can be easily distracted with such as new pictures people post, hilarious statuses, or people wanting to chat with you. All of these reasons combine into one big effect; Facebook is ridiculously main stream and that doesn't seem to be changing any time soon.

1.2.1 Evolution of Facebook

Facebook is one of the most influential social networking websites on the internet, Facebook.com is a comprehensive and encompassing clustering of networks based on universities and colleges, high schools, work places, and geographic areas. These membership networks are independent of one another but based on the same interface and systems of communication. Intersections and overlaps between each network are possible but they often have crucial and intentional hurdles to access in between. Facebook was founded by Mark Zuckerberg with his college roommates and fellow Harvard University students Eduardo Saverin, Andrew McCollum, Dustin Moskovitz and Chris Hughes.Started originally in February of 2004, Facebook hit its first tipping point in the late summer of that year with the introduction of groups and public posting 'walls.' A second surge in growth resulted from Facebook's introduction to the global public the site went from consistently floating around 14 million unique visitors per month to over 26 million (Lipsman 2007c). In the span of a little over 3 years - from 2005 to 2008—the user account has grown over 20 times in size. Facebook has grown in leaps and bounds over the years. They started out in September of 2005 with what seems like a mere 3.5 million members (Arrington 2005) and grew steadily as they added more college networks to eventually encompass them all. In the span of just half a year (July 2006 to February 2007) the site grew from 7.5 million registered accounts to nearly 18 million (Abram 2007). By May that spring they had hit 24 million and closed the summer with 39 million in September (Wakabayashi 2007).

As of May 2008 collectively Facebook declares over 80 million users and remains one of the fastest growing websites on the internet (Facebook Press Room 2008a). As of November 2010 Facebook declares more than 500 million active members, 50% of which log on to Facebook in any given day. The site has been ranked after Google.com as the second most popular website in the world. In 2011 Facebook reports the average member can express interest in over 900 million objects, and the average member follows 80 such pages.

As of September 2012, Facebook has over one billion active members, more than half of them using Facebook on a mobile device.

Facebook accessible almost everywhere and provides a more connected, interactive experience. The Facebook members experience the features that includes joining groups, becoming a fan, updating a personal status, and games (e.g. Farmville and Sorority Life). These features are accompanied by the basic social networking elements of sharing information, interacting with other members, uploading pictures, writing notes (blogs), and posting event invitations, all of which contribute to a more connective

The uniform format of all Facebook profiles challenges members to be more expressive and strategic to distinguish their identity. Facebook allows members of all ages, religion, interest and skills to actively socialize and participate with a minimal time investment to use the site; now lets see how Facebook has evolved and became a strong household presence with the development and availability of the Internet.

2003 Mark Zuckerberg releases Facemash, the predecessor to Facebook. It is described as a Harvard University version of hot or not.

2004 Mark Zuckerberg registers thefacebook.com domain and launches Facebook as a Harvard-only social network later on extended to other universities. In the same year Facebook accomplishes its one millionth registered members.

2005 Facebook obtains Facebook.com domain for $200,000 and launches a high school version of the website. It also launches its photos feature with no limitations on storage

2006 Facebook is open to everyone aged 13 and over, and with a valid email address. Facebook initiates a blogging feature known as "Facebook Notes". Facebook starts News Feed. The original news feed is an algorithmically generated and regularly refreshing summary of updates about the activities of ones friends. The concept is almost new at the time, with Twitter having started only a few months in advance.

2007 Facebook initiates m.facebook.com and officially declares mobile support. It also releases Facebook Platform for developers to make applications on top of Facebook's social graph. Facebook, for the purpose of permitting targeted advertisements and allowing members to send their activities with their friends Many activities on partner sites were published to a member's News Feed. On the Same day, Facebook launches Facebook Pages.

2008 Facebook announces a complete site redesign with options for tabbed redesign, and allows members to opt into it. Facebook initiates Facebook Credits in order to assist users to buy Facebook gifts and also activates the Facebook like button.

2009 Facebook launches a new feature whereby users can @-tag friends in their status updates and comments. Facebook claims that it has turned cash flow positive for the first time

2010 Facebook starts a redesign that emphasizes the most significant parts of someone's life, including one's biographic information, photos, education, work experience, and important relationships. It changes the tabs at the top of each profile page with links on the left side of the page.

2011 Google announces Google+, widely perceived as a competitor to Facebook. Experts admit that Facebook's subsequent rapid release of new features and advancements may have in part been expediated due to competition from Google+. Facebook partners with Skype add video chat and updates its website interface to make messaging more smoothly.. Facebook Messenger is started for Android and IOS. On 19th October, 2011 update makes the app available to Blackberry os. Facebook allows members to subscribe to non-friends and to set the extent to which they receive updates from their existing friends and members they are subscribing to. Facebook login page changes due to Facebook Timeline addition.

2012 **Facebook** initiates showing advertisements (called Featured Posts) in the news feed. The advertisements are generally for pages that one's Facebook friends have engaged with. Facebook claims 1 billion active members.

2013 Facebook starts Facebook Home, a member interface layer for Android-compatible phones that gives a replacement home screen and makes it easier for members to browse and post. Facebook announces a new timeline and stickers, initially only for its iOS apps in April, but later in July extending to its web version. Facebook also starts Internet.org in association with six cellphone companies (Samsung, Ericsson, MediaTek, Nokia, Opera, and Qualcomm).The goal of Internet.org is to bring affordable Internet access to everyone by increasing affordability, efficiency, and facilitating the development of new business models around the provision of Internet.

2014 Facebook launches Facebook Paper, a separate iOS app that provides a newspaper-like or magazine-like experience for reading on the phone, scheduled for announce on February 3. Facebook also initiates Facebook Creative Labs, an intracompany effort to have different teams working on different mobile apps that specialize in most of the aspects related to the Facebook experience, rather than trying to make alterations to Facebook's main web version, mobile version, or its iOS and Android apps, and intimates that Facebook Paper is the first product of Facebook Creative Labs. Facebook Paper receives mixed feedbacks, and some experts note its resemblance with Flipboard. Facebook announces Facebook Slingshot, an instant messaging software application for sending photos and videos with friends, for Android and iOS devices.

Facebook makes it simple for members to unfollow friends and pages they've liked, both while viewing pages in the feed and while reviewing summaries of the most prolific contributors to their feed. Facebook launches pseudonymous app Rooms, where Facebook members can make and participate in forums on any topic and do not need to disclose their real names

2015 Facebook acquires QuickFire Networks, a company that make a custom hardware and software platform for downsizing video file sizes and upload times. On January 8th The Wall Street Journal received the news, with confirmation later arriving on QuickFire's site. Facebook launches a free friend-to-friend payment service within its Messenger app. Facebook introduces a feature called Scrapbook that permits parents to provide their kids an official presence on Facebook even when they are too young to have their own accounts on the network by tagging them in photos. A Scrapbook can be possessed by two members who have revealed to Facebook that they are in a relationship. When the kids grow old enough and get their own accounts, they can take over ownership of the Scrapbook and replace the privacy settings thereof.

Facebook introduces an Android app called Hello to immediately match phone numbers of incoming and outgoing calls to Facebook profiles to view information about the caller/callee, block calls from commonly blocked numbers, and find out for businesses to call, with initial rollout in the United States, Brazil, and Nigeria.

Facebook introduces "Instant Articles" for Publishers. Publishers who use Instant Articles can opt in to have some of their articles presented to mobile users inside Facebook's app itself, without users having to leave the app and visit the customer's website. Facebook includs more features for pages to make it smoother for businesses to use them.

1.2.2 Creating Facebook Image

When creating a Facebook profile, it is an important to include several basic elements. First and foremost, the profile should include contact information, as well as the email address of the students.

Though there are many different features, the main backbone of the Facebook consists visible profiles that display an articulated list of friends, who are also members of the system. These visible profiles are the unique pages where member needs to enter the data on himself. Initially user needs to join the system. There are different ways of joining but the most commonly used is logging with the help of a valid email ID and creating a password. The valid email ID is a form of way of authentication from the Facebook for the users.

After logging, the user is directed to those visible pages where he is asked several questions. These questions typically include information regarding name, age, location, hobbies, etc. It basically ask questions to answer “about me” from the users.

1.2.3 Features of Facebook

Facebook members employ a number of features including notes (blog), games, chat, joining fan pages, starting groups, posting statuses, and writing on other’s walls. Through these experiences, members create their self-concept and affiliate identities to develop their image, and to produce their own spotlight through a micro celebrity experience on Facebook.

Credits

Facebook Credits are a virtual currency. members can use to purchase gifts, and virtual goods in many games and applications on the Facebook platform.

Share Pictures

The site also encourages members to share a picture though it's not compulsory. Facebook website also permits the members to develop or modify their profile page by certain themes or multimedia content so as to make it more attractive. Facebook also allows members to add applications totally developed by them. Once users have setup their Facebook profile they are ready to go public,

Privacy

With the passing of the time, people faced the privacy issues and various scams where member's detail was stolen and misused it to a tremendous level. Hence Facebook site was bothered about the privacy issues since the beginning.

In Facebook it is absolutely up to what profile pages users want to keep visible. Members can even keep them concealed in the system even if anyone searches for them. They have many more options even within the list of friends. Such approach is really professional one. Hence it is better for the users who are professionals and want to create professional network. But there are options to disable that too. Structural variations and access to profile pages are one of the main differences by which the social networking sites distinguish themselves. After becoming a member of the site, users are suggested to identify the relationships. There are many options in determining relationships. It starts with simple to mention close blood relatives to totally unknown people.

Friends

The most popular includes- Friends, Contacts, and Fans. Facebook website have need two way acceptance for the friendship, but for becoming a fan or a follower requires only one directional. The member technically finds his friend's network so as to make the network. One thing need to be noted here, when anyone finding for the friends, the member looks for his real friends or at least whom he knows. But the findings are not always the same. This is the one of the essential factors in the formation of the base of the site. The public display of connections or friends is a critical part of the site. The Friends list have links to each Friend's profile thus permiting the member to travel through the network of each friend's friends. Suppose one may have ten friends on their network but each of those friends has hundred friends. Hence one is virtually connected to 1,000 connections.

Wall

Facebook have another feature of sending the comments on the each other's profile, it is called "Wall". " It is a kind of short message for each other. Member can send reply on the comment and like this interact with each other. Members can select to which friends it can be set as private. Simultaneously, there is one more feature of sharing private messages just like a normal email. Facebook members can have live chat with their friends.

Share Videos

Facebook members can upload all the type of videos including music, sports, funny to personal videos. But while uploading the video, the requirement is that it should be in specific format. The objective behind it is for the compatibility with technical specifications of the site.

Timeline

Since December 15, 2011, a Timeline is the new virtual space in which all the content of Facebook members will be managed and displayed. In a Timeline the photos, videos, and posts of any member will be categorized according to the period of time in which they were uploaded or created. Posts and events are shown along a timeline that runs through the centre of the profile, ther is an option of adding events anytime,

Formation of Communities

Another important feature of the site is the creation of the various communities. Member need to have a particular reason and a purpose for the formation of a community. The owner plays an important role in the formation of the most of the community, and if he wishes he can add the moderators. The communities covers the light topics as well as the serious ones. Some of the examples of communities are "I like to Brad Pitt," 'I love my girl" to "Economy recession," etc. These are just couple of examples. One can never have the actual number of communities on site as almost every hour new communities are forming. There is also an option to have a picture for the community. The settings for joining a community varies. Some are open communities where any member can be associated just by clicking on join button. In such communities owner and the moderator are playing hardly any role.

There are some communities which are closed and need approval of the owner or the moderator before joining it. These communities are for a specific purpose and hence owner feels to make those as members who can share something valuable. Once a community is created, anyone can initiate a discussion on various topics. This is called as threads or discussion board. Mostly members of the community contribute useful knowledge in the discussion. Sevaral times owner of the community erase certain topics or discussions. Each Facebook profile has a static URL which makes providing a link to the profile like that each community have a link which can be shared with ayne by the owner or other members..

Profile Badge

Facebook has another feature known as profile badge that make a type of mini business card and is based on information from the profile and can be added to web sites.

Nearby Friends

Nearby Friends feature assisst the users to find which friends are nearby or on the go. If any member turns on Nearby Friends, they will occasionally be conveyed when friends are nearby, so one can connect with them and meet up. For example, when user going to the movies, Nearby Friends will notify if friends are nearby so he can watch the movie together or meet up afterward. Nearby Friends is not mandatory to choose but an optional feature. User can choose who can see if they are nearby (for example: your friends, close friends, or a specific friends list) and one can turn it on and off at any time. Sharing the location with Nearby Friends goes two ways — user and his friends both have to turn on Nearby Friends and choose to share with each other to see when they are nearby. Friends will only be able to see that who are nearby if share this info with them and vice versa. When Nearby Friends is on, one can see when friends are traveling if they're also using this feature and sharing. User will be able to see the city or neighbourhood they are in, including on their profile. When one see a friend visiting a place he has been, it's the perfect opportunity to send a recommendation for a great restaurant. One can also make last-minute plans to meet up with a friend who happens to be in the same place you're headed to.

A Look Back

A Look Back is another feature that assembles user's highlights since joining Facebook. Depending on how long he has been on Facebook and how much he has posted, one will see a movie, a collection of photos or a thank you card. Whenever user share movie, they use the dropdown audience in which selector choose who hey share it with. People who are in the viewers users select (ex: friends, public) will be able to see movie.

Keep in mind that if only few users are allowed to see the movie will now be able to see everything one included in his movie.

One can edit the movie to adjust what's included, and to choose the viewers to share it with. If user change his mind about who user would like to share his movie with, he can change the viewers from the activity log.

Paper

In Facebook another feature is Paper which help to explore and post stories from friends and the world around. Paper creates story telling more graceful with an captivative design, full screen and distraction-free layouts. Uers have also made it easier to craft and post interesting and attractive stories of their own. Paper is created of stories and themed sections, so one can pursue his favourite interests. The first section in Paper is Facebook News Feed, where one can appreciates new designs for photos, videos, and longer written posts. Users can adjust the Paper with more than a dozen of opions for other sections about various themes and topics—from photography and sports to food, science and design. Every section contains a rich mix of matter from emerging voices and well-known publications.

Storytelling and sharing have been reimagined in Paper to show stories at their best.

1. Everything responds to touch so can pick up or thumb through stories with simple, natural movements.
2. One can tilt phone to explore high-resolution panoramic photos from corner to corner, and watch faces and other valuable details up close.

3. Full screen auto play videos come to life and bring deep into the action.
4. Attractive detailed covers make it simple to spot articles from trusted publishers and decide what to read or see.
5. Articles unfold in the app and present full screen for a focused reading experience.
6. When one is ready to tell his own story, person will know exactly what the post or photo will look like because one can see a live preview before send it.

Trending

Trending surfaces interesting and relevant conversations in order to help you discover the best content from all across Facebook. To the right of your News Feed, you'll see a list of topics that have recently spiked in popularity. The list is personalized, including topics based on things you're interested in and what is trending across Facebook overall. Each topic is accompanied by a headline that briefly explains why it is trending. User can click on any headline to see the most interesting posts from friends or Pages that are talking about that particular topic.

Year in Review

Year in Review is a collection of biggest moments on Facebook from the past year. It is including life events, popular posts shared and posts to friends have tagged you in. User can see year in review at https://www.facebook.com/yearinreview.The individual stories contained in year in review are visible to the same audience as they were originally shared with.

Donate

Donate lets users contribute directly to participating non-profits through Facebook. The Donate feature will appear beside Posts in News Feed shared by participating non-profits and at the top of their Facebook Pages. When people click Donate Now they can choose the amount, enter their payment information, and immediately donate to that cause. They also have the option to share the non-profit's post with their friends. We hope this will help increase donations as people encourage their friends to donate to the causes that are important to them. Donate also gives non-profits an easier way to reach out and ask for help, both to support their everyday mission and in the wake of major disasters. And, with a community of over one billion people on Facebook, every local cause can become a global one — and every global cause can become a personal movement.

Facebook Live

On August 13, 2010, Facebook launched a new service called Facebook Live, a live streaming video channel that is intended to keep Facebook users updated to what is happening on the social networking site. The service, powered by Live stream, will feature videos from Facebook staff members and celebrity interviews, but is not designed for Facebook users to showcase their own videos. All the content shown on Facebook Live will have some tie-in with Facebook products, features, or how people are using the site. Facebook said this is not an opening to get them into the video distribution space. The first official guest was America Ferrera, the leading actress in the television series *Ugly Betty*. She discussed her new independent film *The Dry Land* that was being promoted almost exclusively through social media channels.

Phone

Facebook user can make a free call through this feature to any of their friends. It is easy to understand and free. The call quality is amazing and clear. You call someone by selecting that person's name in Facebook, tap the "I" button, and then press "Make free call." That person gets a push notification and you can then begin a phone conversation with you entirely for free.

Poke

The poke feature is intended to be a poke gesture to attract the attention of another user. .If you poke someone not in your network and they poke back. You can view their profile even if you're not their friend. A poke is when you allow someone to see your Facebook page for 3 days, so they can know who you are and hopefully add you as a friend.

Like

Clicking **Like** below a post on Facebook is an easy way to let people know that you enjoy it without leaving a comment. Just like a comment, the fact that you liked the post is visible below it.When you like a Facebook Page; you're making a connection to that Page. A story about your like will appear on your Timeline and may also appear in your News Feed. You may be displayed on the Page you're connected to or in ads about that Page. Updates from the Page may also appear in your News Feed.

If you no longer want to be connected to a Page, you can unlike it.

Follow

When user follows someone, he can see their posts in News Feed. User automatically follows people you're friends with. One can also follow the posts of people they are interested in and can also choose to allow people who aren't friends to see the posts in their News Feed. To follow someone, go to their profile and click **Follow**. One will only be able to follow people who are their friends or who allow everybody to follow them.

If one send someone a friend request who allows everybody to follow them, he will automatically follow their posts. Friends follow him automatically, but can also allow people who aren't your friends to follow you. If user allowed everybody to follow him, anyone on Facebook can follow his posts unless you've blocked them. Every time you post, you can choose the audience.

If you've only allowed Friends to follow you, people who aren't your friends won't see the Follow button at the top of your profile and can't follow you.

Messages and Inbox

Since the website's founding, it has allowed users to send messages to each other. A Facebook user can send a message to any number of his/her friends at a time. Deleting a message from one's inbox does not delete it from the inbox of other users, thus disabling a sender to undo a message sent by him or her.

Notifications

Get quick updates about friends' actions that most affect you. To turn on notifications for friends or people and Pages you follow:

1. Go to the person's profile or Page
2. Click Friends or Liked
3. Click to check Get Notifications

When you choose to get notifications, you'll get a notification each time that person or Page posts something shared with you. You can turn off these notifications by unchecking Get Notifications. To turn off notification sounds, go to your notifications settings and uncheck the box next to Play a sound when each new notification is received.

Tagging

When you tag someone, you create a link to their profile. The post you tag the person in may also be added to that person's Timeline. For example, you can tag a photo to show who's in the photo or post a status update and say who you're with. If you tag a friend in your status update, anyone who sees that update can click on your friend's name and go to their profile. Your status update may also show up on that friend's Timeline.

When you tag someone, they'll be notified. Also, if you or a friend tags someone in your post, the post could be visible to the audience you selected plus friends of the tagged person. Learn more about what happens when you create a tag.

Tags in photos and posts from people you aren't friends with may appear in Timeline review where you can decide if you want to allow them on your Timeline. You can also choose to review tags by anyone, including your friends.

Groups

Facebook Groups can be created by individual users. Groups allow members to post content such as links, media, questions, events, editable documents, and comments on these items. Facebook users cannot join more than 6,000 groups.

Groups are used for collaboration and allow discussions, events, and numerous other activities. They are a way of enabling a number of people to come together online to share information and discuss specific subjects. They are increasingly used by clubs, companies and public sector organizations to engage with stakeholders, be they members of the public, employees, members, service users, shareholders or customers. Groups can have three different levels of privacy settings:

1. "Open" means the group, its members and their comments is visible to the public (which includes non-members) but they cannot interact without joining.
2. "Closed" means the group and its members are visible to the public but their comments are not visible until the user has joined the group.
3. "Secret" means that nothing can be viewed by the public unless a member specifically invites another user to join the group.

Event

To create an event:

1. Click Events on the left side of your homepage.
2. Click Create in the centre or on the left side under My Events.
3. Fill in the event name, details, location and time, and then choose your privacy settings. Keep in mind that you must include an event name and time.
4. Click Invite Friends to add friends to the guest list. Check the names of the people you want to invite and then click Save.
5. Click Create.

You'll be taken to your event where you can share posts, upload photos, invite more Guests and edit event details.

List

Facebook list is a useful feature to manage your Facebook feeds and friends. From a Blogger POV, user usually manage list in a way, that one can keep an eye on important updates and at the same time stay connected to the personal friends.

Facebook and Important Privacy settings

Once the user registered in the Facebook site, the profile automatically set in default "recommended" setting until and unless the settings will be changed by the user. In Facebook site users use sharing section where they can choose what they want to share and with whom. Facebook site has four built in security profiles:

1. Everyone
2. Friends off friends
3. Only friends
4. Only me

Default Privacy Setting

The default privacy setting is the first thing users see on their Privacy Settings page. It's also the most important item on the page, since it controls who can and can't see content that you post automatically. Facebook provides three options here: Public, which lets anyone see the new posts; Friends, which limits access to content to Friends; and Custom, which permits user to take a more granular approach to the privacy settings.

Customize Settings

If Facebook user is not satisfied with the current settings then they can use Customize setting, where user can customize their privacy settings. When user select the custom settings, Facebook adds the custom label to the list of sharing profiles displayed on the privacy settings page. One can configure the Custom setting to make posts visible to specific people, to custom lists of people, or to any school/work networks that might be a part of or hide the information from specific people. The customize settings page has 20 different categories of information to choose from. Here, user can select the privacy level in Facebook profile content, posts to the wall, tagging in photos [/URL] and other features.

Blocked List Settings

If user want to block another user. User can give the reason of blocking the particular person which could be useful to alert Facebook to a particular person's behaviour. After blocking the person the Facebook will remove him from the user's friend list. The user can unblock the person by, clicking Unblock by their name on the list provided.

Timeline Setting

Timeline settings, including specifications for who can post on users timeline and who can see those posts. Though the timeline settings are important, the two settings here that will be most useful to users involve Facebook automation. The first controls Facebook's unsettling facial recognition feature, the user can also disable this where user and his friends choose will have to manually tag the face in photos. The second setting lets user review friend's posts that have been tagged in before the posting is approved. If user worried that an embarrassing photo might circulate on Facebook before one can data it, then the user can set Review posts friends tag before they appear on timeline.

Group Privacy Settings

In the Facebook site one can make group or community for similar purpose and there are three group privacy options

1. Public
2. Closed
3. Secret

In public group privacy option anyone can join the group and can see the member's posts and other stories of the group. While in closed group privacy option anyone can ask to join the group or invited by members of the group. Only members of the group can view the posts and other stories of the group. In the secret group privacy option only those can become members who will be invited or added by present members of the group. The group information, member's detail, members post and other stories of the group all can be viewed only by present members.

Ads, Apps and Website Privacy Setting

This privacy setting controls the Facebook profile and personal information; interact with things outside Facebook, including Facebook apps, personalized ads and websites. User can examine carefully to the 'Apps you use' control panel. User can review and remove all of the third-party apps which is not required. Either user can remove each app separately, can elect to delete them all, so the operation may take a while to complete. In the Ads settings, user can turn off social ads and pre-emptively opt out of having your data used in third-party advertising. The Facebook features such as instant personalization and public search will also be turned off.

To Manage Facebook Privacy settings

The users can manage Facebook privacy setting by four methods;

1. **Manage Status Updates**

User can type desired status, name of person if any present with him and update the location He can also decide about the audience for his updates. The status can be visible to the public, friends, or a custom set of people.

2. **Manage Information of profile**

User can edit the profile page by either clicking info tab in the profile, or by clicking edit my profile. He decides which audience can access what information. A drop down menu is there for each of piece information. User can decide which groups of people will see which information by clicking the menu and selecting the desired option.

3. **Manage the Privacy Page**

To choose Privacy Settings one can click on Account. If the user chooses a default privacy setting for the profile then it will be the setting of all posts unless he specified. He can also make the wall and profile completely public or completely private. In comparison to the past Facebook privacy settings this offer more security where one can further customize about the audience.

4. **Viewing Your Profile as Someone Else**

If users are unsure about what their profile looks like to a certain one of their friends, then they can check it out by clicking "View As..." on the right hand side of the profile. User can type the name of the person he wants to view his profile as. He will then be able to view his profile exactly as that person views it. He can also type another name to see how someone else sees his profile.

Important Checklist While Sharing the Information

1. In default setting, the status, photos; posts can be viewed by everyone. So it is recommended to change the settings otherwise all the information's will be completely public which can put the user in trouble. To restrict the audience for any information one should use some of the privacy settings.
2. The users contact information defaults to all friends only that can be harmful. So it is advisable to use the privacy setting and restrict the information to either him or to only few reliable friends instead of all friends.
3. User needs to be careful when they choose Friends of friend's option which aren't in their control. It will be a big challenge for the user to secure the certain content with whom that is stranger for him.
4. User can't take it back once it's out there. Once the posted content is public, anybody could copy and post it elsewhere without users concern. Search engines could cache that content could be cache by search engine and for some period display in its search results. After it has been open to the public then it is not possible to stop the content floating around the internet even if the hide the content later
5. Its the user's responsibility if he is allowing third party to access his information. The users think twice when he is granting to an app or link to Web site, to access the information. Before providing information the user must research the app through reliable sources, and decide it is trustable or not.
6. With the passage of time Facebook also updates or changes its privacy policy. It's the duty of user to keep an eye out for these changes and updates privacy settings accordingly. The important changes that occur in the Facebook should intimate to the user by e-mail

7. Read the Facebook guide for privacy setting carefully before you start.

Advantages of Privacy Settings

1. It helps the user to protect their content.
2. It also protects the user from cybercrime.
3. It avoids the Infamous Photo Tag Mistake.
4. It controls the audience to access the information.
5. A user can set privacy settings according to his requirement.
6. All privacy settings need not to be used at a time.
7. It also helps to avoid embarrassing wall post.
8. It is easy to understand all the settings.

Disadvantages of Privacy Settings

1. Once any post is public it's not possible to stop to float in internet.
2. Another disadvantage of Facebook's privacy settings is that every time an update of the website is implemented, the individual security protocols that a user have in place revert back to the original default setting.
3. Sometimes users don't know how to change the privacy settings.
4. The privacy settings are unable to recognise the fake profiles
5. A user who strictly limits access to their Facebook information will find they restrict
6. Themselves to only the people they already know and missed the opportunity to meet new people.
7. Facebook privacy settings can leave you overly reliant on its privacy settings and encourage you to forget to exercise good judgment.

1.2.4 Advantages of Using Facebook

To connect with family, friends, work and colleges group

It is the latest medium of connecting with your dear ones. You can even customize the settings to be "offline" or "online" for some selected ones and still chat with them easily. Facebook conversation does not even require money which is sometimes a reason for some people for not calling up their pals.

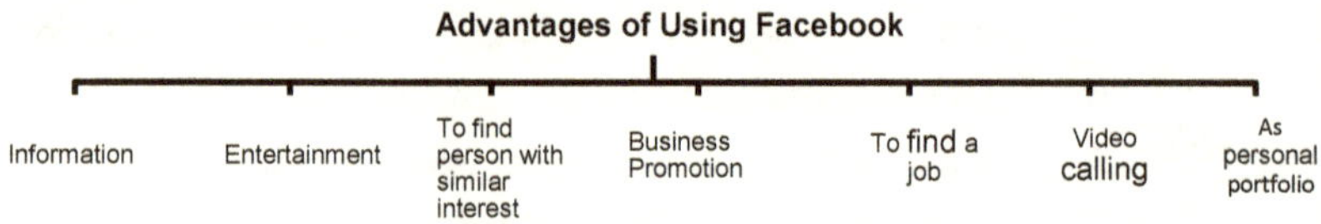

Flow chart 1.2: Advantages of using Facebook

Information

Since you connect globally here, you get the news of the world. There are some pages and communities that are created on Facebook to keep a track of the latest updates in any specific field like sports, educational, political entertainment etc.

Information about the people across the seas as well as the ones near you are also readily available to you. Whatever happens in anybody's life they tend to update it through their "status", or photographs. So, you are there and then informed about any such updates and thus Facebook proves to be very informative.

Entertainment

There are many ways in which Facebook can be used as a source of entertainment. First of all, the gossip that you have with your friends is the biggest way that could never leave you to bore.

Then, there are videos of your interests, lots of interactive games, applications and quizzes for fun. You can even invite your Facebook pals to play games or take the quizzes.

To find person with Similar Interest

User have the freedom to browse the profiles of other people on Facebook until and unless they have not customized and hidden it from the public. User's access to their profiles can help to find people of same interests and can easily send a "friend request" to them OR send a private message.

Image and Video Hosting

You can use Facebook to host your images and videos. You get a direct download link of whatever you upload.

There is unlimited hosting and unlimited bandwidth. Facebook provides this free of cost, whereas other websites offer this service with limited bandwidth, and there are some those have this service a paid one. So, this is for a big benefit for all the bloggers and website owners.

Business Promotion

Facebook is an intelligent place to market your products. The immensely increasing Facebook users can be your future potential customers. Marketers can create a page for their products where they can have the images, videos and detailed descriptions about the products.

The users will visit this page more than the official site of your products to get issues resolved and thus, this is a very good way to reach out to your customers.

Job Opportunity

Through Facebook we can easily contact the manager or create professional contacts with any number of hiring people. Keep updating your status regularly about your job requirements and someone will surely come up to help you.

Video Calling

The tool for video calling of Facebook helps you to have a normal video chat, as the name specifies. Your distant relatives and friends can easily come close to you, as you are in front of each other "live".

Many a times, we can have an interview or meeting with our professional counterparts and thus it helps in establishing relationships.

As Personal Portfolio

If you are an artist, then create a page for yourself and then create a portfolio where you can display your art and maintain the collection.

A portfolio of all the memorable snaps can also be uploaded so that they are there as a backup.

Social Momentum

Facebook is such a powerful weapon that any kind of social issue can gain momentum and can create a wave of enthusiasm amongst the people that any other media cannot, in a short time.

1. Facebook is free and it's one of the best medium for communication. You can send message, start a video call, and upload photos and videos for free.
2. Facebook lets us connect to different people from anywhere in the world, because almost every people these days are familiar with Facebook .This gives us the opportunity to know more about their culture, values, custom and tradition. There is something called "pen pal" where motivated people used to make relationships with other foreign people, by writing regularly to each other via post mail. Time has changed and now people can contact with their "Facebook Pal" instantly, and more frequently. These relationships sometime get serious and might end up in Marriage also.

3. Facebook is the most appropriate tool for finding Old friends. When friends go away to any other place, we often don't get the chance to communicate with them. But now Facebook gives us the opportunity to communicate with our Old friend very easily without any cost. Surely, it is going to make you feel happy to see your old friend sharing some happy photos from another part of the World.
4. We can share our feelings and what's happening around in our daily life through Facebook. We can also get feedback from our friends about their reaction toward our feelings. It is the best medium to share your feelings and thoughts with others. You can share your achievements to get some appreciation, or you can share your sorrows to get support from the generous friends.
5. Facebook has good privacy setting which gives you the option to maintain privacy according to your wish.
6. Facebook Fan pages, groups, events etc. are getting popular day by day. Facebook Fan pages & groups are very handy for promotional activities. This is why almost each and every well-known Brand has a Facebook Fan page and they are investing lot of money to get more exposure to their core Business.
7. You can use Facebook groups to connect all your close friends together. You can also maintain the privacy of the group by making it private. It also has new features like group chatting, notification, file sharing etc. These features would help the members of the group to stay connected.
8. Facebook email is very useful too. Facebook now offers us an email address to receive email outside of Facebook such as, Yahoo, Gmail, outlook and Hotmail. The email address is given based on the user name of your Facebook ID.
9. Facebook plays a very important role in getting latest valuable information. Facebook fan pages and users are constantly sharing many valuable news and information.

10. Facebook advertising and Fan pages are very helpful for a successful marketing campaign to many business organization.
11. You can chat with friends by using Facebook. The Facebook messenger application is very handy for chatting online.
12. Many popular celebrity and organization are using Facebook to give regular updates to their fans. So, through Facebook you stay closer to any famous person or organization.
13. Students can use Facebook for group study by creating a group only for studying. There you can share any information about your projects, homework, assignments, exams, due date etc.
14. Many people are making relationship in Facebook and tying the knot eventually.
15. Facebook online games are really popular and addicting. There are millions of Facebook users enjoying Facebook games and cannot pass a day without playing them.
16. Facebook has thousands of application, quiz, games etc. which keeps the user addicted with the site.
17. We can also use Facebook as social bookmarking site. We can share our article, blogs, photo's etc. to thousands of people.
18. Facebook like button is connecting their user to every other website. With single like button now you can bring everything inside Facebook.
19. If you have a Facebook login ID than you don't need to waste your time for registering other site. Most of the site now allows us to register instantly by integrating our Facebook account.
20. Facebook is well designed There is no fancy colour or design available which distracts people. The simplicity in design and efficiency in the performance made Facebook the best Social site in the World.

1.2.5 Disadvantages of Facebook

Now it's time to talk about some disadvantages of Facebook. There are some Disadvantages of Facebook beside all these advantages. Some of the main disadvantages are:

1. Facebook is Addicting

Using Facebook for your need is actually good for us but when we waste most of our valuable time then it becomes harmful. The biggest disadvantage of Facebook is its addiction which causes many problems, mostly because it kills our precious time.

2. Fake profile and ID

Fake profile is one of the biggest disadvantages of Facebook. Now it is easier to create fake profile with a stolen picture. People often use fake profile to insult or harass someone they don't like. Teen girls are more vulnerable to these activities. There are news found that many girls are mentally depressed or committed suicide after being harassed in Facebook.

3. There are plenty of groups and Fan pages out there which are being created to abuse or violate other religion, personalities, nation etc. This kind of racist disgusting activities is not acceptable in a global site like Facebook. Facebook administrator should take necessary steps against all of these abusing groups & pages.

4. Inability to customize organization of your content

Facebook allow user to customize the profile by editing the code but it is very complicated to understand. The new users don't understand it properly.

5. Privacy settings

It does not seem to be any longer possible to write an app that will periodically download all the messages in a Facebook user's status update feed. Some users post a lot of interesting statuses, but the old ones can't be indexed and Googled the way they could be if they were on another website.

The Facebook is programmed, where one could fix the deficiency by downloading the feeds and posting the statuses to one's site. But it does not seem possible to poll the Facebook API for those feeds without the user's keeping his browser open and logged in to the site that integrates with Facebook. Getting the feed data requires a short-lived access token that has to be frequently renewed. It seems like Facebook wants to tightly control this data. The API does not seem as open as it used to be back in the days of Open Book.

6. Personal status published publicly just to seek attention

It is a human tendency that people take more interest in others' lives rather than their own. The same applies to Facebook too. Maximum of the people post their personal status publicly so that they can seek the attention of others. This misleads people and wastes a lot of time getting involved in such a thing.

7. Writing Worthless Things

Facebook does not stop anyone from writing anything on places like "walls" of their own or their friends, comments, messages etc. This tends to waste a lot of time because many a times these kinds of things uselessly attract the attention of others and they cannot stop themselves from reading it and actually taking part in the conversation.

8. Time Consuming

Facebook is an addiction. Once you join it, you are likely to spend most of your free time doing something or the other on Facebook. And it does not stop here. Some people even start compromising their family get-togethers and professional meetings for this Facebook.

9. Not Using Facebook List Feature:

Many users still don't use Facebook list feature which is very helpful to keep your status updates targeted to specific friend list, like College friends, Office friends and so on. I'm sure you might not like to get fired from your job because of silly status updates against your boss or office.

Flow Chart 1.3: Disadvantages of using Facebook

1.3.0 Background of the Research Problem

As the mode of instruction changed from the traditional classroom lecturing to the online interactive tutoring, educational institutions are currently under pressure to adopt new educational technology within their field. Nowadays, educational technology, such as Web CT and Blackboard, are being used to help students perform better and increase their productivity within the classroom, as well as to encourage them to become more engaged in the learning process. However, the availability of such tools put a tremendous pressure on students to cope with a more complex learning environment and new technologies that they have to become familiar with. On the other hand, the popularity and extensive use of social networking sites, like Facebook, can now be used by teachers and students as an effective communication tool inside and outside the classroom, without requiring that students learn a new technology, since most of them are already using Facebook social networking site... Facebook provides an excellent means of communication between students and teachers during the lifetime of a course.

It was found that students who participated in a web-enhanced class education outperformed those being taught in a traditional lecturing environment. From the perspective of students, using Facebook for learning offers many benefits that may help them perform better and become active learners. In addition, they are used to post assignments, tests, quizzes, links, and extra resources. Through Facebook site, a teacher may take the students' opinion or feedback about certain course content, and can also send and receive messages to an individual or a group of students.

1.4.0 Need and Importance of Research Problem

Rapid development of information and communication technologies has brought changes in various pedagogical and technological applications and processes. Currently, social networks are being adopted rapidly by millions of users most of whom are students with a great number of purposes in mind. Studies showed that social network tools support educational activities by making interaction, collaboration, active participation, information and resource sharing, and critical thinking possible. Students today demand more autonomy, connectivity, interaction and socio-experiential learning opportunities in their learning contexts. Because students complain about lacking opportunities for authentic communication due to non-personalized course content even when alternative delivery methods are employed, providing informal learning contexts by integrating emerging social networks into existing learning practices becomes relationships among students and encompassing students' motivation and engagement ; involving students in achieving the learning tasks and successful transfer of knowledge developing a positive attitude towards learning and improving the quality of learning developing interpersonal intelligence, as well as critical thought developing of communications and interactions on the relationship between students and teacher outside the classes.

Further, Facebook enables teachers to: provide constructive educational outcomes in a variety of fields practice a differential pedagogy, in the best interests of the students integrate diagnostic formative evaluation in the learning process and to calibrate didactic activities accordingly achieve a change in strategy, mentality, attitude and behaviours by using Facebook (e.g. the transfer of significantly important to attain more robust learning and teaching opportunities Facebook has quickly become the social network site of choice by students and an integral part of the "behind the scenes" experience . The proliferation of social technologies has created a culture in which youth participate more in creating and sharing content, profoundly changing the way students communicate, interact, and learn. Previous papers indicated that the adoption rates of Facebook in universities and colleges are remarkable - 85% of college students that have a college network within Facebook have adopted it. Also, in many cases students spend as much (or more) time online in an informal learning environment - interacting with peers and receiving feedback - than they do with their teachers in the traditional classroom. Furthermore, Facebook also has a growing audience in perspective high school and middle school students.

Facebook as a tool can contribute significantly to the quality of education are: fostering positive relationships among students and encompassing students' motivation and engagement involving students in achieving the learning tasks and successful transfer of knowledge developing a positive attitude towards learning and improving the quality of learning developing interpersonal intelligence, as well as critical thought developing of communications and interactions on the relationship between students and teacher outside the classes Further, Facebook enables teachers to: provide constructive educational outcomes in a variety of fields; practice a differential pedagogy, in the best interests of the students integrate diagnostic formative evaluation in the learning process and to calibrate didactic activities accordingly achieve a change in strategy, mentality, attitude and behaviours by using Facebook (e.g. the transfer of knowledge remains one of the functions of teaching, but it is second to organizing and managing learning situations) establish efficient educational relations on a social network accept the student as an interaction partner analyse and compare ways of learning and the knowledge achieved by students develop knowledge and skills in order to perform efficient didactic activities.

1.5.0 Rationale of the Study

There is a general agreement that learning is essential for success in our society. The effective learning improves achievement which is highly valued and important for social and economic advancement.

Most educational theorist agreed that we learn by creating our own knowledge as a result of our own questioning and experience rather than by having it poured into our heads from the outside. We learn at concrete level by building upon a conceptual framework. In a traditional class setting the main instructional tools we use are lectures, small class discussion, problem solving assignments etc. All these methodologies tend to emphasize telling rather than questioning and doing. The use of social networking site i.e. Facebook, is used by teachers and students as an effective communication tool inside and outside the classroom, without requiring that students learn a new technology, since most of them are already using Facebook social networking site. Facebook provides an excellent means of communication between students and teachers during the lifetime of a course. This is the strongest feature that Facebook has to offer and it can be used to assume a major role in the delivery of instruction.

In a normal class the student population is heterogeneous in their abilities, intelligence, characteristics, personality etc. It is impossible to minimize these individual differences by a single teacher. Facebook has a potential to overcome this differences by providing individualized instruction at learners own pace and time to develop individual learners need.

In a traditional class setting, recitation and tutorial sessions has been used to provide a forum in which students can interact directly with an instructor and with each other than large and more formal lecture sessions. With a skilled group leader and a small number of prepared and motivated students, these small classes can work very well. However, the more usual situation in such classes are the inexperienced teaching assistant, face a group of students who came unprepared, will not ask questions and often will never answer. Due to the cultural diversity the student feel fear of "losing face" which resist them to participate actively resulting in a class of passive students who sit there and waiting to be taught but unwilling to make any overt contribution to the process, often preferring to sit in the back rows, hoping not be called by the instructor. Such situation is often reduced to giving mini lectures.

The solution for this problem is in the Facebook e-content which can built around homework style problems which has potential to motivate the learner and transform the class into an active and collaborative learning experience. Facebook e-content have ability to handle more than twice the numbers in conventional mode in class.

To provide such active and motivated learning experiences suitable to Indian scenario. It was decided to explore the area in depth.

Problem solving is an essential part of learning science concepts. The traditional practice of assigning problems, finding solution by very few students and then discussing them in class suffer from several weaknesses. The most serious one is that students one is that students rarely feel comfortable in bringing the individual difficulties they experienced to the attention of the group. So they commonly just write down the solution provided by instructor and learn very little. To overcome this situation Facebook page can be used through which individual learning difficulties can be identified and can be solved patiently in a one on one face situation without involvement of group. The interactive nature of Facebook page has ability to mediate learning by students. A well designed Facebook e-Content can effectively work at this process by knowing what the students already understands, extending it incrementally and always challenging the students to go a step further.

From the review of related literature, it is evident that majority of research studies in the field of use of Facebook site for education purpose were conducted in foreign countries.

The studies conducted in India and other countries are related mainly to web-tools like internet, CAI and e-learning social networking for entertainment purpose etc. study related to Facebook site is still in the mode of infancy in India.

In India the studies are conducted are Dr.Varang Acharya, Mr.Adarsh Patel, Mrs.Sweta Jethava,2013, Raj Kumari Kalra1, Preeti Manani.(2013), Sharda Gangwar, Anita Deshbhratar & Pragya Garg 2013, Shri .Prashant Kale, (2012). Sunitha Kuppuswamy (Anna University Chennai, Chennai, India) and P. B. Shankar Narayan (Pondicherry University, Puducherry, India) (2010), Ateeq Ahmad Department of Computer science & Engineering, Singhania University, Pacheri Bari, Disst. Jhunjhunu (Rajasthan) (2011), Jasimudeen S 1* and Mahesh Rajan M 2**, Srivastava, Preeti. (2012), Neelesh Kumar Jain1, Dr. Ashish Verma2, Dr Rama Shankar Verma3 and Prashant Tiwari (2012) ,Reema Malhotra Bhola, Gopal Chandra Mahakud, P. Sri Jothi*, M. Neelamalar and R. Shakthi Prasad , India.(2011), Peddiboyina Vijaya LAKSHMI, Sri Padmavati Mahila Visvavidyalayam, Pradeep KRISHNATRAY & Sangeeta SHRIVASTAVA (2014), Alka Singh,. (2013), Sunil Tyagi (2012), Anil Kumar, Rajinder Kumar Choudhary Charan Singh (2013), Dr. Harishchandrasingh Rathod1, 2012, Dr. M. Neelamalar & Ms. P. Chitra , Ruchi Sachdev, Manjunatha S., (2013), Mr. Madhur Raj Jain Associate Professor, Ms. Palak Gupta Assistant Professor, Ms. Nitika Anand, (2012), Reema Malhotra Bhola, Gopal Chandra Mahakud.

In India the studies related to see the effect of Social networking sites on teachers perception and blending learning

Dr.Varang Acharya, Mr.Adarsh Patel ,Mrs.Sweta Jethava,2013, Raj Kumari Kalra1, Preeti Manani.(2013), Sharda Gangwar, Anita Deshbhratar & Pragya Garg 2013, Shri .Prashant Kale, (2012)

Sunitha Kuppuswamy (Anna University Chennai, Chennai, India) and P. B. Shankar Narayan (Pondicherry University, Puducherry, India) (2010), Ateeq Ahmad Department of Computer science & Engineering, Singhania University, Pacheri Bari, Disst. Jhunjhunu (Rajasthan) (2011), Jasimudeen S 1* and Mahesh Rajan M 2**, Srivastava, Preeti. (2012), Neelesh Kumar Jain1, Dr. Ashish Verma2, Dr Rama Shankar Verma3 and Prashant Tiwari (2012), Reema Malhotra Bhola, Gopal Chandra Mahakud, Alka Singh,. (2013), Sunil Tyagi (2012)

Anil Kumar Panjab University, Chandigarh (India), Rajinder Kumar Choudhary Charan Singh Haryana Agricultural University, Hisar (India) (2013), Dr. Harishchandrasingh Rathod1,. 2012, Dr. M. Neelamalar & Ms. P. Chitra, Ruchi Sachdev , Manjunatha S. Research Scholar, (2013), Mr. Madhur Raj Jain Associate Professor, Ms. Palak Gupta Assistant Professor, Ms. Nitika Anand, (2012), Reema Malhotra Bhola, Gopal Chandra Mahakud studies are presenting the usage pattern of social networking sites and some social issues.

In foreign countries extensive research work has been done in the field of web-tools technology for achieving educational goals. Out of 70 studies reviewed 39 studies were related with effectiveness of Social networking sites in terms of student's achievement. Majority of studies reported that social networking sites could enhance achievements as compared to conventional classroom instructional alone.

The research studies conducted in this field is divided into following categories for quick and better understandings:-

1. Effectiveness of Facebook for teaching and learning
2. Collaboration and online learning
3. Effect of online tools on cognitive domain

4. Comparative and analytical study of social networking sites
5. Teacher attitude towards Facebook
6. Facebook and student characteristics
7. Usage pattern of social networking sites and Social interaction

1. Effectiveness of Facebook for Teaching and Learning

In foreign countries, the studies conducted on effectiveness of Facebook for teaching and learning in different curricular areas are ALLISON A. ZIMMERMAN (2009), Ashraf Jalal Yousef Zaidieh (2012), Britany Helton written for Dr. Kraemer's Survey Research course, Bernd Skiera/Oliver Hinz/Martin Spann- 2015, Christopher Irwin, Lauren Ball and Ben Desbrow Griffith University Michael Leveritt (2012), Claire Couillard, The Graduate School University of Wisconsin-Stout, Hannah Arendt, Ivan Matic, Lin Zhu, Heng-Li Yang (2003), Hsiu-Ting Hung a & Steve Chi-Yin Yuen (2010) ,Kanda Runapongsa Saikaew1*, Wit Krutkam1, Rina Pattaramanon2, Natthanon, Leelathakul3, Kornchawal Chaipah1, Arnut Chaosakul1, Marina Miloloža, Tajana Ljubin Golub, Melor Md. Yunus1 and Hadi Salehi2*1 (2012), Nikleia Eteokleous Frederick University ,Despo Ktoridou, Iacovos Stavrides and Michalakis Michaelidis (2012),

Pamela Pollara Co-authored with Jie Zhu, (2011), PEI-LIN HSU1, YING-HUNG YEN2, Plamen Miltenoff, P. S. Hegadi G. R. Angadi,Bridge Centre 2015, Reynol Junco *,(2011), Reynol Junco 2011, Reynol Junco - 2014, Saba Mehmood Faculty, Sultanate of Oman. Tarang Taswir Faculty. (2013), Sulaiman Ainin, M. Muzamil Naqshbandi, Sedigheh Moghavvemi, Noor Ismawati Jaafar 31 December 2014 ,Available online 8 January 2015, Suraya Hamid, Shanton Chang and Sherah Kurnia (2009), Thanawan Suthiwartnarueput, Punchalee Wasanasomsithi (2012), Neil Selwyn* (2009).

In India studies conducted are Dr.Varang Acharya, Mr.Adarsh Patel, Mrs.Sweta Jethava,2013, Sharda Gangwar, Anita Deshbhratar

& Pragya Garg 2013. All this studies found to be effective in terms of different areas of study.

Ahsan ul Haq & Sohail Chand 2012, Pattern of Facebook usage and its Impact on Academic Performance of University Students: A Gender Based Comparison -The study reveals that 87.5% of the students have account on the Facebook and no gender differences found. Male and female on the average spend equal time on internet. Though female users spend more time on Facebook than their counterparts but male users have more Facebook friends. Facebook use, in general, adversely affecting the academic performance of students but this adverse effect is observed greater for male students.

Paulsen (2001) noted that receiving a college degree provides numerous social and economic advantages for students, such as students earning more money when entering the workforce.

Cindy Ann Dell Results suggest there were no significant differences between the work submitted by students from the online sections and from the face-to-face students, and that the methods of instruction are more important than the delivery platform.

Yu Liang, Qingya Wang,Wei Chen (2011) Results indicate while most college students use social media and spend many hours checking social media sites, there was a negative aspect to college students' use of social media.

Raj Kumari Kalra1, Preeti Manani (2013) Results revealed that there was no significant difference between academic achievement of users and non-users of Social Networking Sites (SNS)

Shri. Prashant Kale, (2012) the research revealed that a little percentage of students use social media for the educational purpose. Most of the students use it for the purpose of entertainment and to keep in touch with friends.

Sunitha Kuppuswamy (Anna University Chennai, Chennai, India) and P. B. Shankar Narayan (Pondicherry University, Puducherry, India) (2010), the research concludes that social networking websites have both positive as well as negative impact on the education of youth, depending on one€™s interest to use it in a positive manner for his or her education and vice versa.

2. Collaboration and Online Learning

Some foreign researchers conducted their research to see the effect of online learning and collaboration among students when web 2.0 tools are employed for educational purpose are Alan S. Weber, (2010),Muhammad Kamarul Kabilan, Norlida Ahmad, Mohamad Jafre Zainol Abidin (2010) ,Murat Kayri1 and Özlem Çakır, Department of Computer and Instructional Technology, Yuzuncu Yil University, Van, Turkey Department of Computer and Instructional Technology, Ankara University, Ankara,Turkey (2010), Tom Heath, (2008) their studies supported the finding that the online tools are effective and creative a collaborative environment. In India Jasimudeen S 1* and Mahesh Rajan M 2**, Srivastava, Preeti, (2012) researchers conducted their study.

Ateeq Ahmad (2011) The use of collaborative technologies and Social Networking Site leads to instant online community in which people communicate rapidly and conveniently with each other.

Alessandro Cecconi EDD (December 17, 2007)- social networking is bringing distance education to a collaborative learning model which could not "erase" the digital behavior of the learner but draw advantage from a sharing attitude of knowledge that is very precious for learning purposes. In fact, it is quite clear that social networking heavily contributed to mix formal and informal learning; that is because distance education can be even delivered through a personal digital environment

Curtis Clifford Cain 2010 This research is to investigate and develop a collaborative educational environment as a tool to aid teachers in grades K-12 in the STEM, Science, Technology, Engineering and Mathematics, disciplines. This paper seeks to gauge teacher's receptiveness and willingness to utilize an online educational forum to supplement traditional classroom lectures

Irshad Hussain1*, Naushaba Gulrez 2 and Shaheen Ashraf Tahirkheli3 (2012) The study revealed that majority (90%) of the social media users used Facebook. They used social media for developing academic relationships with their contemporaries. It was obvious from the study that social media plays a crucial role in promoting collaboration and linkage to develop Virtual Community across the world. The respondents also faced some problems in using social media. The researchers recommended that proper training may be organized for appropriate use social media.

M.D. Roblyer a, Michelle McDaniel b , 1, Marsena Webb c, 2, James Herman d , 3, James Vince Witty e, (2010), Social Networking Sites (SNSs) such as Facebook are one of the latest example of communications technologies that have been widely-adopted by students and, consequently, have the potential to become a valuable resource to support their educational communications and collaborations with faculty. A comparison of faculty and student responses indicate that students are much more likely than faculty to use Facebook and are significantly more open to the possibility of using Facebook and similar technologies to support classroom work.

3. Effect of Online Tools on Cognitive Domain

Cognitivist places a greater importance on learner's cognitive styles, thinking etc. The studies conducted in the area are Julie Willems, Debra Bateman, 2011,Nataša Petrović, Dalibor Petrović, Veljko Jeremić,Nemanja Milenković, and Marko Ćirović (2012), Sana Rouis, (2012), Neelesh Kumar Jain1, Dr. Ashish Verma2, Dr Rama Shankar Verma3 and Prashant Tiwari (2012), Reema Malhotra Bhola, Gopal Chandra Mahakud.

4. Comparative and Analytical Study of Social Networking Sites

Some foreign researchers conducted their research to compare and analyses the various social networking sites in different areas are

Alan E. Mislove (2009), Danah M. Boyd, Kaitlyn Flad (2010), Kevin P. Brady, Lori B. Holcomb, and Bethany V. Smith (2010), Silvio Lattanzi (2010) and in India P. Sri Jothi*, M. Neelamalar and R. Shakthi Prasad. (2011), Peddiboyina Vijaya LAKSHMI, Sri Padmavati Mahila Visvavidyalayam (Pradeep KRISHNATRAY & Sangeeta SHRIVASTAVA (2014)

Alay Rameshbhai Patel, (2011) This thesis will serve as a single point of data access for the aspiring networking site developers to learn about technical architectures, corresponding supporting customized services, data models and all other required technical details of the two existing most popular networking sites.

Manar I. Hosny, Shameem Fatima (2012) The study tries to give an insight into how Facebook and similar social networking sites can be used as a medium of communication to help students, teachers as well as the institution's library. In this paper, we try to derive conclusions about best recommendations and practices that academics can follow to improve teaching and learning through using Facebook and other similar social networking sites.

Ngonidzashe Zanamwe, Taurai Rupere and Owen Kufandirimbwa (2013) This study explored social networking technologies being used in higher education, their uses, extent of use, benefits and skills learners acquire from use of these technologies. An analysis of the results seems to suggest that the majority of learners were mainly using Facebook and Myspace. It was also established that social networking technologies improved learners' technology proficiency, enhanced learners' social skills and help learners to communicate in new ways with new people.

S. Griffith University of Western Sydney,L. Liyanage,University of Western Sydney(2008) –The study reviews Social Networking Sites (SNS) that have become available via the Internet in the light of usability for teaching and learning. Thus, the negative and positive aspects of SNS are reviewed in detail. This knowledge will form the basis to assist with regulating SNS for teaching and learning.

Waqas Tariq1, Madiha Mehboob2, M. Asfandyar Khan1 and FaseeUllah3 (2012) This paper presents impact of social networks on education, students and impact on life of teenagers, further it describes how social networking websites are auditory and dangerous for youth and teenagers.Were variable with only 51% of students stating that it was effective. Despite this, the majority of students 76.4% recommended using Facebook in future course.

Whitney Sue Thoene (2012) - This research study examines the effect of social media, particularly Facebook and Twitter, on the purchasing habits of college students by testing for correlations between recommendations on social media and consumption patterns.

5. Teacher Attitude Towards Facebook

Teacher's attitude towards Facebook is another area in which researchers have studied the effect of Facebook and SNS how teachers use the Facebook for instructional work and towards subject etc.

Caroline Lego Muñoz (2009) - The purpose of this research is to propose the idea of using the social network site, Facebook, for teacher education. In addition, it provides specific instructions on how to use Facebook and a discussion of "best practice" policies that can be ethically implemented within the classroom. Specific attention is given to suggestions for creating a professional Facebook presence in which future teachers can emulate

Filiz Tiryakioglu, Funda Erzurum, (2011) the present study investigated the views and attitudes of instructors in the Faculty of Communication Sciences at Anadolu University in Turkey, which is a country where the total number of Facebook users ranks fourth in the world.

Huseyin Bicen, Huseyin Uzunboylu (2012) - The purpose of this research is to find out how Facebook and Web 2.0 tools create a positive effect when used in education and to investigate teachers' opinions about the Online learning environment.

Joseph P. Mazera*, Richard E. Murphyb and Cheri J. Simondsc (2009) this experimental study examined the effects of computer-mediated teacher self-disclosure on perceptions of teacher credibility. Implications for classroom pedagogy, technology use, and areas for future research are discussed. Joseph P.Mazer,Richard E.Murphy&Cheri J.Simonds (2007), study also supported the result.

Alka Singh, (2013) -As the present paper is focused on teacher education, the curricular areas of initial teacher education is recommended in NCTE (2009) is to develop habits and the capacity for self-directed learning, have time to think, reflect, assimilate and articulate new ideas; be self-critical and to work collaboratively in groups (p.24). Use in classroom settings.

Sunil Tyagi (2012) the results indicate that the faculty attitude and their perceived behavioural control are strong predictors to their intention to use Web 2.0. This article reports on study that attempted to find out the usage of Web 2.0 tools (wiki's, blogs, RSS feed, collaborative writing, video sharing, social networks, etc.) by Indian faculties to support teaching and learning in higher education at NCR of India.

Most of the studies indicate that pre service teachers confidence in using web 2.0 tools gives them more confidence in incorporating these technologies in their future teaching practice, and Facebook can contribute to more engage and in depth student and it was also clearly mentioned, Facebook can be very useful and adaptable learning and that can promote student centred learning.

6. Facebook and Student Characteristics

Learner achievement is always influenced by learner characteristics such as intelligence, aptitude, personality etc. some researcher also have conducted their studies in the directions to see the effect of Facebook with different students characteristics some of them are cited here.

The finding of these researches put some conclusions that are:-

1. Facebook is mainly used to keep in touch with other people, but not in a conventional way as users tend to 'spy' on other users' profiles. This phenomenon leads to a growing exhibitionism, which is in turn related to individuals' personality traits. Use of Facebook is also influenced by peers and experience with the website.
2. Facebook users employ a number of features including notes (blog), games, chat, joining fan pages, starting groups, posting statuses, and writing on other's walls. Through these experiences, users develop their self-concept and affiliate identities to create their image, and to produce their own spotlight through a micro celebrity experience on Facebook.
3. The majority of respondents disclosed that they share news to stay connected with family and friends. The respondents report that they depend on their network of friend to guide them to news articles, as they are a good representation for their own interest.
4. Facebook has become a daily part of respondent's lives. Participants reported using Facebook has made their relationships mildly stronger.
5. The factors enable users to overcome the negative characteristics associated with social networking sites. If used successfully, social networking sites can offer lecturers and students a useful tool with which to develop their relationship and contribute to their learning experience.
6. It is found out that purpose statements related to social and daily activities had a higher score than educational and school related purposes.

7. In 2008, half of the students were completely unfamiliar with Facebook, while in 2009 all our respondents were aware of it and 59% of them were also using it on a regular basis.

The studies are Ivan Di Capua 2012, Jerry L. Allen, (2007), Jessica Lee Pugh (2010), Jilin Chen, Joseph Konstan and John Riedl, (2011), Jonna Howe (December 2011), Kelli Elise Kapp (2011), Kesaraporn Wanajak 2011, .L Schlenkrich1, DA Sewry2 (2012), Müge Akyıldız Anadolu University Metin Argan Anadolu University, Nicola Cavalli, Elisabetta Ida Costa, Paolo Ferri, Andrea Mangiatordi, Marina Micheli, Andrea Pozzali, Francesca Scenini and Fabio Serenelli.

7. Social Interaction and Usage Pattern of Social Networking Sites

Some researchers conducted their research on Usage pattern and Social interaction are Marc Stumpel (2010), Michael Beye1,Arjan Jeckmans2, ZekeriyaErkin1, PieterHartel2, Reginald Lagendijk1 and QiangTang2, Anil Kumar, Rajinder Kumar Choudhary Charan Singh (2013) Dr. M. Neelamalar & Ms. P. Chitra , Reema Malhotra Bhola, Gopal Chandra Mahakud.

Dr. Harishchandrasingh Rathod1, Prof. Digvijay Barot11 Associate Professor, 2012The results show that the three top-used social media tools are Facebook, Yahoo Group and Orkut; the top four reasons for using social media tools are for social engagement, direction communication, instant messaging, and relationship building. Even though students aware about cybercrime but most of them do not understand the meaning of phishing, vishing and cyber-squatting.

Manjunatha S. (2013)the findings of the study acknowledge the rampant usage of SNS among young college students in India. Their usage pattern of SNS, hours spending per week, gender differentiation in its usage, purpose of membership, their level of intimate relationships with online friends and much more interesting aspects have been dealt scientifically in this paper

Mr. Madhur Raj Jain Ms. Palak Gupta, India, Ms. Nitika Anand, Student- (2012) Research is conducted on youths between age group of 18-30 years with a view to know the level of awareness on the social issues and how far social networking sites awakened the today's youth in expressing their views on current and burning issues like corruption, human rights, girl education etc.

Ruchi Sachdev The research focused on the fact that how SNS are implementing and used in an effective manner that is also beneficial for Indian society and what are the role of Indian youth. In this paper researcher focused on the positive as well as negative impact of these social networking sites on the Indian youth and what are the ethical responsibilities of the users of these sites.

From the above review of various studies it is concluded that most of the studies are stressing the significance and attitude towards web tools among the students.

Less research studies related with social networking (Facebook) in India is reported so far thus the present study was selected to explore the area in depth and to advance the previous studies that are conducted in this area to reach the generalization, to bring the consistency in result and to fill the gap in researchers.

1.6.0 Present study

The present study entitled "Effectiveness of social networking Facebook for teaching science"-A study in the area of educational technology. The main aim of the study was to develop Facebook page and study its feasibility, accessibility and effectiveness in classroom. In the developed Facebook page certain features like pages, post, photos and upload video option were there which convenient for the user to use and to achieve the multidimensional objective of education.

Facebook page was developed for fifteen chapters of science of class IX for CBSE syllabus 2006 developed by National Council of Educational Research and Training, New Delhi. Facebook page was developed for the fifteen chapters of science of class IX for CBSE syllabus. It is an attempt to find out the effectiveness of Facebook in terms achievement and as well as the reaction of the learner. The effectiveness of developed Facebook page is determined on the basis of comparison between the achievement score of students studying with only conventional method of teaching with those studying through Facebook with regular classroom teaching by taking intelligence and study habit as co-variate. The comparison between overall achievement of male and female students studying through Facebook along with conventional method was also done.

1.6.1 Statement of the Problem

"Effectiveness of social networking Facebook for teaching science"-A study

1.6.2 Objectives of the Study

Objectives of the present study are set out as follows

1. To develop learning material using Facebook pages for teaching science to students of class IX CBSE and study its effectiveness in terms of:
    a) Achievement of students
    b) Reaction of students towards developed Facebook page
2. To compare the mean overall achievement score of the students studying through Facebook along with conventional teaching method, with those studying through conventional method by taking intelligence as co-variate.
3. To compare the mean overall achievement score of the students studying through Facebook with those studying through conventional method by taking study habit as co-variate.
4. To compare the overall achievement of male student with female student studying through Facebook.

1.6.3 Hypothesis

1. There will be no significant difference between the pre and post-test mean overall achievement score of students studying through Facebook.
2. There will be no significant difference between the adjusted mean overall achievement score of students studying through Facebook with those studying through conventional method by taking intelligent as co-variate.
3. There will be no significant difference between the adjusted mean overall achievement score of students studying through Facebook with those studying through conventional method by taking habit as co-variate
4. There will be no significant difference between the overall achievement score of male & female studying through Facebook.

1.6.4 Operational Definition of Key Terms

Effectiveness

The degrees to which objectives are achieved and the extent to which targeted problems are solved.

Social networking

Social network sites are website to connect with people who share personal or professional interest, place of origin, education at a particular school etc.

Facebook

Facebook is a popular free social networking website that allows registered users to create profiles, upload photos and video, send messages and keep in touch with friends, family and colleagues.

Intelligence

Intelligence is the ability to learn about, learn from, understand and interact with one`s environment.

Study Habits

As buying out a dedicated scheduled and uninterrupted time to apply one`s self to the task of learning. Without it one does not grow and becomes self-limiting in life.

Achievement

A thing done successfully, typically by effort, courage or skill or fact of achieving something.

1.6.5 Scope and Delimitation of the Study

1. The study will be limited to students of CBSE class IX only.
2. This study will evaluate the impact of only those students who are studying through English medium.
3. This study is limited to Nagpur area of Maharashtra state only.
4. This study is limited for teaching science subject only.
5. Central Board of Secondary Education syllabus will be taken for development of Facebook.

Chapter – II
REVIEW OF RELATED LITERATURE

2.0.0 Introduction

The present study entitled "Effectiveness of social networking Facebook for teaching science"-A study it is an attempt to develop a web-based Facebook for teaching Science to class IX students. Teaching through Facebook was followed by online test, discussion and problem solving session, apart from this Facebook page was developed for the fifteen chapters of science of class IX for C.B.S.E syllabus. It is an attempt to find out the effectiveness of Facebook in terms of achievement and as well as the reaction of the learner.

Thus an attempt has been made in this study to utilize the Facebook site as an educational tool and compare the academic achievement, study habit, intelligence of students studying through Facebook along with conventional method with those students studying through Conventional method. It also compares the overall achievement of male students with female students studying through Facebook. The present study has also attempted to develop learning material using Facebook page for teaching students and study its effectiveness in terms of reaction of students towards developed Facebook page.

2.1.0. Studies Conducted Abroad

The study of Facebook is common in abroad. Majority of research work in the above field has been done in abroad. A new study from two researchers at the Ohio State University found that when people are in a good mood, they're drawn to the profiles of their successful and attractive friends. However, when they're feeling down, they lurk around the profiles of people who have had more difficulties in their lives. The findings will be published in the

December issue of the journal Computers in Human Behaviour. These results imply that emotions themselves might ripple through social networks to generate large-scale synchrony that gives rise to clusters of happy and unhappy individuals,

In a recent study conducted by University of Minnesota's Christine Greenhow, a learning technologies researcher from the College of Education and Human Development, students using social networking Web sites are practicing the 21st century skills needed to be successful in today's society.

Students are improving their communication through social networks, such as Facebook, a skill the study found is essential for a successful career. The study involved teenagers aged 16 to 18, of many different economic backgrounds and from urban high schools in the Midwest.

The study found even the students in the lower class used such social networks as Facebook and Myspace to build connections and form relationships with people all over the world. Professionals throughout the country use Facebook to keep their clients, customers, or users informed on a variety of topics, and it can be used in the exact same manner for educators. "Social media is not only a great way to communicate with stakeholders, but is an awesome way to make connections for learning," said Stacy Behmer, Coordinator of Digital Learning at Grant Wood AEA. With Facebook, teachers are following groups and pages that offer free resources. RSS (Really Simple Syndication) Feeds, like Google Reader, offer teachers a way to find articles, blogs, and news about education to enhance how they teach. More importantly, these tools can help students learn and help meet them where they are already at with technology.

2.2.1 Research studies related with Facebook in Education

Various researches have been conducted on Facebook site. Researchers have done extensive work on Facebook and its impact on the students. The studies are conducted on academic performance, maintaining communication, advantages, disadvantages of Facebook and its effect on cognitive behavioural and social aspects of children with reference to their gender, environment and other variable.

The research studies conducted in this field is divided into following categories for quick and better understandings:-

1. Effectiveness of Facebook for teaching and learning
2. Collaboration and online learning
3. Effect of online tools on cognitive domain
4. Comparative and analytical study of social networking sites
5. Teacher attitude towards Facebook
6. Facebook and student characteristics
7. Usage pattern of social networking sites and Social interaction

2.2.2 Effectiveness of Facebook for Teaching and Learning

Technology has had a significant effect on the educational system for many years. It is hard to talk about schools today without talking about technology. Enthusiasts celebrate the wonders of tablets, virtual schools and blended learning.

In the past, learning and education simply meant face-to face lectures, reading books or printed hand-outs, taking notes and completing assignments generally in the form of answering questions or writing essays. In short education, learning and teaching were considered impossible without a teacher, books, and chalkboards. Today education and training have taken on a completely new meaning. Computers are an essential part of every classroom and teachers are using DVDs, CD-ROMs and videos to show students how things work and operate. Students can interact with the subject matters using such web based tools and CD-ROMs. Moreover, each student can progress at his/her own pace.

The role of technology in the field of education is four fold. It is included as a part of the curriculum, as an instructional delivery system as a means of aiding instructions and as a tool to enhance the entire learning process. Through technology education has gone from passive and reactive to interactive and aggressive.

Educational technology improves student learning outcomes. Evidence suggests that educational technologies can improve student achievement, so long as such tools are integrated thoughtfully into teaching and learning. When digital capabilities like online environments incorporated meaningfully into instruction, students have new opportunities to learn and achieve. Researchers have found that intelligent computer assisted tutoring systems are about 90% as effective as in person tutors are-

Haq Ahsan ul & Chand Sohail in 2012 explored the popularity and usage pattern of the Facebook among the University students. A self-administered questionnaire is used for collecting data from a sample of 384 students. The study reveals that 87.5% of the students have account on the Facebook and no gender differences found. Male and female on the average spend equal time on internet. Though female users spend more time on Facebook than their counterparts but male users have more Facebook friends. Facebook use, in general, adversely affecting the academic performance of students but this adverse effect is observed greater for male students. The social interaction with the existing friends is found the most common use of the Facebook among students.

Allison A. Zimmerman in 2009 researched on the various factors that contribute to retention of students in colleges and universities. There are many factors that contribute to retention, and no single factor can address retention problems at a college or university.

Rather, it is finding the right combination of practices and using them in conjunction with one another to experience successful retention. It is the responsibility of each institution to determine what retention practices will produce maximum results. Universities and colleges are continually seeking new ways to keep retention rates up, and in the world of college retention, building and maintaining a relationship with current students is vital. Effective implementation of public relations (PR) and communication tactics can be key players in the formation of these relationships. Higher education institutions use PR and communication in the recruitment of students and, according to Parnell and Parmley (2009), these same tactics can also be used to retain students. Educational institutions are a business and must create a relationship that is mutually beneficial for the students and the institutions and this relationship must be fostered through effective communication. A common theme observed in the retention process is connectivity. Creating a community where students feel connected to their institution contributes to successful retention. Social networking sites have created a new form of communication and an avenue through which public relations can be carried out. These sites have become increasingly popular in today's society, particularly among young adults. According to Pempek, Yermolayeva and Calvert, ―Social networking sites are designed to foster social interaction in a virtual environment‖ (Pempel, 2008 p.228). Specifically, the social networkining site Facebook has more than 500 million active users and has made online communication more interactive and a common practice among college students (Facebook, 2010). While using Facebook alone will not guarantee and increase in retention, as previously mentioned, using Facebook in Unisom with other retention practices may help increase retention rates. Increased student retention results in more student dollars being invested into the college or university. According to Parnell and Parmley (2009), ―As university costs rise, so has the competition for student dollars. The PR offices in higher education play a major role in boosting enrolment, ranking, and publicity—so it is vital for them to understand and use best practices and social media to accomplish their communication goals‖ (p.16). Wandel (2008) maintained that colleges and universities must necessarily adapt, or they will fall behind in the realm of the –wired generation.‖ Failing to connect with students where they are, via social media, may be one factor contributing to lower retention rates, resulting in a detrimental impact to educational institutions. Universities and colleges place heavy emphasis on recruitment of potential students, but what happens once they have acquired those students? Are the higher education institutions placing sufficient emphasis on building lasting relationships to retain students? Not only does student retention benefit colleges and universities, but also it benefits the students as well. According to Ackerman and Schibrowsky (2007), getting a college degree is the American dream of a better way of life. Completion of a degree allows students a better chance of success in the work field after college. Paulsen (2001) noted that receiving a college degree provides numerous social and economic advantages for students, such as students earning more money when entering the workforce.

Zaidieh Ashraf Jalal Yousef in 2012 and found thatsocial Networking has become very popular during the past few years, and it plays an important role in our life nowadays. It helps us in the every fields of life such as political field, economic field and educational field. This paper will summarize some of challenges and opportunities to use social networking as educational tool.

Bernd Skiera/Oliver Hinz/Martin Spann in 2015 analysed how Facebook use and students' social network positions within it relate to their academic performance. We use a unique data set obtained from a survey of students' perceptions, actual Facebook connections to measure social network positions, and objective grades provided by the university registrar to measure academic performance. We find that Facebook activities during class relate negatively to academic performance, that students located in densely connected sub networks earn better grades and that in contrast to female students, male students benefit from a general use of Facebook, particularly if they are highly connected.

Britany Helton written for Dr. Kraemer's Survey Research course studied that Facebook is a social networking site that has become so popular among college students that it is not too farfetched to believe that social networking of this magnitude might have some negative effects on college life. There have been many studies about using Facebook as a learning tool. One study showed that "most students joined Facebook because Facebook was associated with university-level education" (Madge et. al., 2009). This same study also found that Facebook is mainly used to keep up with social aspects of college life and it is a part of most students' daily routine (Madge, et. al., 2009). However, students also did not seem to agree that Facebook helped their academic life (Madge et. al., 2009). Other studies have found that when students are asked why they did not put more effort into schoolwork that Facebook distraction was a regular explanation (Yazedijan et al., 2008). Facebook offers many different options for social networking and entertainment. As far as communication goes, Facebook offers a chat option in which people can send messages instantly to one another. You can also talk to several people at the same time. Another way of communication is using a private message option to write messages to another person. Facebook also offers the option to write on another person's profile where other people may view the message. However, these are not the only things Facebook does. Many applications and games can also be found on this site. There are ways to post items in other people's profiles. A person can play interactive games that involve playing with other people on the site. The things that this website provides continue to grow and in turn it continues to keep people intrigued and keeps them coming back. Therefore, it is obvious that Facebook has become a very important feature of college life. However, what are the effects of so much Facebook use on academic success? Academic success is usually measured by grade point average (GPA). The following study examines whether or not a student's Facebook habits are at all related to the student's GPA and if so how exactly they are related. Opinions on the different uses of Facebook might also be related to just exactly how a person uses Facebook. It might even be possible that certain uses of Facebook cause more distraction than others. This study examines all of these questions.

Christopher Irwin, Lauren Ball and Ben Desbrow in 2012 researched that Facebook is a popular platform that may facilitate learning activities at university. In this study students perception of using Facebook pages with in individual university subject offerings were evaluated. Individual Facebook pages were developed for four university courses and used to provide information relevant to the courses and allow opportunities for student's interaction. An initial questionnaire administered in the first lecture of semester indicated that nearly all students (n-161, 93.1%) possessed an active Facebook account. Most students (n-135, 78.0%) anticipated that a Facebook page facilitates their learning by increased interaction between students and teachers. A second questionnaire was completed in final lecture of semester indicating that 81.9% of students engaged with the course Facebook page at some stage. However perception of effectiveness of the page as a learning tool.

Cindy Ann Dell, Jeanine F. Wilkerboth conducted a research project to analyse student achievement using submitted assignments for two sections of a graduate course in human development and learning, taught both online and face-to-face, as well as three sections of undergraduate educational psychology, two of which were taught face-to-face, and one taught online. Results suggest there were no significant differences between the works submitted by students from the online sections and from the face-to-face students, and that the methods of instruction are more important than the delivery platform.

Claire Couillard researched that the Information and Communication Technology is the field of study that involves all technical means of processing and communicating information. ICT is based on the convergence of Information Technology and Telecommunication Systems. Within ICT, there are many different ways to disseminate information. Multiple types of technology pave the way for communication in the 21st century. Because of the rapid pace of technology, there are bound to be gaps in many sectors of business and education. For the purpose of this research, the author is going to focus on ICT in education. All across the world, education faces major challenges. In the United States and throughout Europe, schools are faced with three major problems in the system: truancy, dropouts and apathy. According to the Alliance for Excellent Education, over a million students in America who enter their freshman year of high school do not graduate with their peers four years later. There are countless reasons why students drop out of school, including difficult transitions to high school, deficient basic skills and a lack of engagement. Many schools today are stuck in the 1950"s. No cell phones allowed in classrooms, limited computer access, restricted web-page browsing, all these restrictions are hurting students and the educational system. The fear of the unfamiliar, equal access and loss of control are the three main reasons why technology has been restricted. (Farr, 2009) After looking at this information, one thing is clear; students are suffering. Because of this, the nation and the world will suffer as well. It is our job to educate children now because they are the future. In this paper, the author will explore the Social Media Technology, Facebook.

By looking at this growing technology, delving into the pros and cons associated with using Facebook in education, the author will make recommendations for the use of Facebook in education with the hope that it will bring teachers and students together and bring back student" desire to learn.

Hannah Arendt, Ivan Matic,Lin Zhu found that an academic group and discussion forum were established on Facebook for a cohort of postgraduate students studying the concepts and principles of e-learning. The Forum had a constructivist, student centric ethos, in which students initiated topics for discussion, while the course leader and administrator facilitated. Previous research was conducted content analysis of the topics and academic discourse, but the present study focuses on social aspects, investigating social- and study related pursuits and determining whether synergy can exist between them. A literature study shows how social networking by students, initially social, began to overlap with academia, leading to establishment of groups for academic purposes and forums for subject-related discussions. In the present study, data was triangulated and two methods of data analysis were used. Qualitative analysis was undertaken of free-text data from students' reflective essays to extract socially-related themes. Heuristic evaluation was conducted by expert evaluators, who investigated forum contributions and discourse in line with contemporary learning theory and considered the social culture of participation. Findings of the qualitative analysis of students' perceptions and results of the heuristic evaluation of forum participation confirmed each other, indicating a warm social climate and a conducive, well-facilitated environment that supported individual styles of participation. It fostered interpersonal relationships between distance learners, as well as study-related benefits enhanced by peer teaching and insights acquired in a culture of social negotiation. The environment was effectively moderated, while supporting student-initiative. The mixed-methods approach of evaluating essays and discussions showed a virtual community where most participants experienced a sound balance of social- and study-related benefits, but with a stronger focus on academic matters.

Heng-Li Yang in 2003 investigated the effects of social networks on students' performance in online education which uses networking as an adjunct mode for enhancing traditional face-to-face education or distance education. Using data from a 40-student course on Advanced Management Information Systems (AMIS), we empirically tested how social networks (friendly, advising, and adversarial) related to students' performance. First, advising network variables are positively related to student performance both in the class and on the forum. Adversarial variables are negatively correlated with almost all students' performance. Second, advising and adversarial network variables are good determinants for overall academic performance; however, adversarial network variables are not influential on students' performance on the forum. Friendship network variables are not determinants of students' performance. Implications for the results are also discussed.

Hsiu-Ting Hung a & Steve Chi-Yin Yuen in 2010 explored how social networking technology can be used to supplement face-to-face courses as a means of enhancing students 'sense of community and, thus, to promote classroom communities of practice in the context of higher education .Data were collected from 67 students who enrolled in four face-to-face courses at two public universities in Taiwan. Findings indicated that the majority of participants developed strong feelings of social connectedness and expressed favourable feelings regarding their learning experiences in the classes where social networking sites were used as a supplementary tool. Learner difficulties and concerns of instructors about the educational use of social media are addressed with recommendations for future research and practice.

Kanda Runapongsa Saikaew1*, Wit Krutkam1, Rina Pattaramanon2, Natthanon, Leelathakul3, Kornchawal Chaipah1, Arnut Chaosakul1 studied that the Facebook is a social media web application, is a part of million student lives. Students use Facebook for communicating with friends and playing games. Since they use Facebook frequently and comfortably, we may exploit this entertainment-oriented site as an edutainment tool. Although there are many tools available for eLearning, Facebook seems to be one of the most effective tools because students generally respond to discussions quickly and are comfortable enough in their "space" to share their information and opinions. By using Facebook in learning, the role of students can therefore shift from only receiving knowledge to both searching and sharing their knowledge. Moreover, interactions with teachers can become more instant since teachers and students can respond quickly via Facebook It is worthy to realize, however, that teachers cannot use Facebook as a single teaching and learning tool. Facebook still lacks features such as file submission and file sharing to support the complete learning process. This paper presents the approach and the experience in using Facebook for both undergraduate and graduate courses as well as for both informal and formal learning. In the formal courses, Facebook is used for discussion, Moodle is used for assignment submission, and Google Docs is used for sharing documents. In the informal courses, Facebook is used for discussion, sharing video and document links. We found that students actively and quickly participated in both asking and answering a teacher's questions. In addition, students also shared their new knowledge even after the classes have ended and grades were assigned. As a result, Facebook has an excellent potential to serve as a lifelong learning channel for teachers and students.

Marina Miloloža, Tajana Ljubin Golub compared Facebook users and non-users on self-esteem and academic achievement variables and to investigate the factors related to perceived positive and/or negative impact of Facebook on academic performance. A total of 277 Croatian undergraduates participated in the study, 99 (35.7%) of which were male and 178 (64.3%) female. Facebook users were younger in comparison to non-users, but did not differ in any variable of academic achievement (GPA, hours per week spent studying, academic performance proficiency) or in self-esteem. Self-esteem was correlated positively with frequency of using Facebook for communication with friends. There was no significant positive relation between self-esteem and GPA, but self-esteem was positively correlated with academic performance proficiency. As predicted, students' perceived positive impact of Facebook on their academic performance was found to be positively related to their Facebook intensity and to frequency of Facebook based communication for academic purposes, even after controlling for Facebook intensity. As predicted, students' perceived negative impact of Facebook on their academic performance was positively related to Facebook intensity. Active multitasking, i.e. interrupting studying or homework with Facebook activities was predictive even after intensity of using Facebook and recreational purpose was controlled for. The study demonstrated the important role of multitasking in the relationship between Facebook and impaired academic performance.

Melor Md. Yunus1 and Hadi Salehi2*1 in 2012 attempted to investigate the students' perceptions on the effectiveness of Facebook (FB) groups for teaching and improving writing. The authors see a need to carry out this study as it provides a platform to discover pedagogical implications that would benefit the Y-generation in terms of improving their writing skills in a Malaysian ESL context. The respondents of this research comprise 43 third year students completing their bachelor's degree in TESL, in the Faculty of

Education, University Kebangsaan Malaysia (UKM). The students' perceptions were measured through a questionnaire comprising 10 close-ended items and 3 open-ended ones. Respondents were required to participate in a Facebook group created by the researchers. The Facebook group, called 'Write Out Loud' was hosted by Facebook. The findings showed that 'Facebook groups' is an effective tool in improving the students' writing skills, especially in the brainstorming of ideas before the actual writing. The results of this study may be beneficial to ESL educators in incorporating ICT into their teaching repertoire.

Neil Selwyn* in 2009 researched that the social networking sites such as Facebook and Myspace have been subject to much recent debate within the educational community. Whilst growing numbers of educators celebrate the potential of social networking to (re)engage learners with their studies, others fear that such applications compromise and disrupt young people's engagement with 'traditional' education provision. With these on-going debates in mind, the current paper presents an in-depth qualitative analysis of the Facebook 'wall' activity of 909 undergraduate students in a UK university. Analysis of these data shows how much of students' education-related use of this social networking application was based around either the post-hoc critiquing of learning experiences and events, the exchange of logistical or factual information about teaching and assessment requirements, instances of supplication and moral support with regards to assessment or learning, or the promotion of oneself as academically incompetent and/or disengaged. With these themes in mind, the paper concludes that rather than necessarily enhancing or eroding students' 'frontstage' engagement with their formal studies, Facebook use must be seen as being situated within the 'identity politics' of being a student. In particular, Facebook appears to provide a ready space where the 'role conflict' that students often experience in their relationships with university work, teaching staff, academic conventions and expectations can be worked through in a relatively closed 'backstage' area.

Nikleia Eteokleous Frederick University, Despo Ktoridou, Iacovos Stavrides and Michalakis Michaelidis in 2012, examined and evaluated the role, usefulness and value of social networking as perceived by higher education students. It also attempted to examine the educational role of social networking by developing Special Interest Groups within a social networking site (in this case Facebook). Specifically, it describes and presents an evaluation of the use of three Facebook Interest Groups: MIS – Management Information Systems, Science, and Engineering, by the faculty and students of five Universities in Cyprus. The preliminary analysis of the results highlights the promising and important role and value of such groups in both social and academic life. Finally, the paper discusses "best practice" policies for Facebook integration for educational purposes.

Pamela Pollara Co-authored with Jie Zhu, Louisiana in 2011 researched on the acceptance of Facebook by school-aged users is evident, but the potential of using social networking sites for educational purposes is still being debated. This paper explores the use of Facebook within a high school science-mentoring program. Results indicate that the use of Facebook positively affected the relationships between mentors and mentees. In addition, students believed that they learned more by using Facebook and would like to use Facebook for other educational purposes.

Hegadi P. S. G. R. found that social networking is a tool being explored by many institutions as a means of connecting to and communicating with students. Researcher has felt in the present mega information age in India all young generation are very much acquainted with smart phone operation, mobile phones, internet connected computer gadgets in the college and educational environment. At this time number of research works have been taking place in the western countries like USA, European countries using various internet based social media sites as instructional method formally and informally naming My space, Facebook, twitter etc. utilized at different levels right from nursery to till higher educational institutions by the teachers whereas most negligible number of studies conducted on social media sites. The administrative bodies like UGC brought norms encouraging research and innovative works at university and college level to incorporate various instructional practices and methodology. Thus, a lead to individual growth and development of teacher and professional efficiency is also going to be heightening. The social media site mainly Facebook is very popular among Indian students community motivates the students to share their photos, videos and post the text, notes etc. Another vital feature of Facebook is links of educational and social sites which accessed very easily which are available using web 2.0 technologies. These content related interactive materials which are available on various links posted on Facebook wall could be used through classroom instruction. Thus, researcher made an effort of Facebook method of teaching formally with videos, power point presentations, tutorials and notes, scanned materials on Growth and Development of individual which are posted on it as a unique and innovative technique. This study explored Facebook as an Instructional Tool in Fostering Academic Achievement, Social Interaction Skills and Attitude towards Use of Facebook. The purpose of this study is to describe how social media networks impact student-teachers when utilized as an instructional tool. The problem this study seeks to address is exploring the roles that social media play in the lives of student-teachers and the experiences they encounter by utilizing these networks academically and socially. The theoretical framework driving this study is motivational theory. Participants in this study completed experimentation and interviews and participated in a series of classroom observations. Findings revealed that Facebook method helped in increasing achievement in Educational Psychology subject than the traditional method of teaching. It helped student-teachers to enhance their various elements of social interaction skills and the number of elements of 11 attitudes towards use of Facebook. The study clearly shows that Facebook is an effective teaching strategy which is not only helps in academic gains but also in developing the aspects of the learner, which at present, is the need of the hour. Implementing Facebook method and assessing needs a lot of patience and time and is not an easy task. Only with the joint efforts of school authorities, teachers, students and parents, can these goals of Facebook method be achieved. The present study is a step made in this regard. The findings of this study can help teachers, parents, students and others involved in the educational field to cope with the present problems and issues being faced while implementing Facebook formally and informally.

Pei-Lin Hsu1, Ying-Hung Yen2 and Sihchuan Rd. explored the relationship between Facebook Group participation and the academic achievement of college students in Taiwan. The ten-week educational discussions among fifty Taiwanese college students on two Facebook discussion pages were recorded and analysed. The online participation frequency of each student was then subsequently compared with his Grade Point Average. The result indicates that there is a significant positive correlation between a student's online participation frequency and his GPA. Furthermore, it was found that evaluation criteria and teacher facilitation can have an effect on the direction of online discussions. According to the results, we can conclude that educational discussions on Facebook may enhance student learning, and hence Facebook may serve as a promising teaching tool to be used by educators.

Plamen Miltenoff, discussed on the advantages and disadvantages of employing social networking sites, in particular Facebook for educational purposes was organized by four faculty members from three different educational institutions in two countries, the USA and Bulgaria. The faculty organized an extensive bibliographic overview of published research from around the world regarding the application of social networking sites (SNS) in education. The findings were organized into topics and issues regarding the application of social networking in education. The bibliographic review of publications reveals strong interest by all stakeholders: administrators, instructors, students, and librarians in determining if SNS, Facebook in particular, can improve recruitment and retention for education and the learning process for both K-12 and higher education. Parallels with Course Management Systems such as Blackboard, Moodle, Sakai and with other Web 2.0 tools are involved in the discussion. Suggestions for future research, based on the conclusions are shared. Other noticeable findings, such as difficulty of finding similar research on other languages, then English, are reflected in the article.

Reynol Junco in 2011 found that Educators and others are interested in the effects of social media on college students, with a specific focus on the most popular social media website Facebook. Two previous studies have examined the relationship between Facebook use and student engagement, a construct related to positive college outcomes. However, these studies were limited by their evaluation of Facebook usage and how they measured engagement. This paper fills a gap in the literature by using a large sample (N ¼ 2368) of college students to examine the relationship between frequency of Facebook use, participation in Facebook activities, and student engagement. Student engagement was measured in three ways: a 19 item scale based on the National Survey of Student Engagement, time spent preparing for class, and time spent in co-curricular activities. Results indicate that Facebook use was significantly negatively predictive of engagement scale score and positively predictive of time spent in co-curricular activities. Additionally, some Facebook activities were positively predictive of the dependent variables, while others were negatively predictive.

Reynol Junco in 2011 researched how Facebook use is related to academic performance. A small number of prior studies have examined the relationship between Facebook use and college grade point average (GPA); however, these studies have been limited by their measures, sampling designs and failure to include prior academic ability as a control variable. For instance, previous studies used non-continuous measures of time spent on Facebook and self-reported GPA. This paper fills a gap in the literature by using a large sample (N = 1839) of college students to examine the relationship among multiple measures of frequency of Facebook use, participation in Facebook activities, and time spent preparing for class and actual overall GPA. Hierarchical (blocked) linear regression analyses revealed that time spent on Facebook was strongly and significantly negatively related to overall GPA, while only weakly related to time spent preparing for class. Furthermore, using Facebook for collecting and sharing information was positively predictive of the outcome variables while using Facebook for socializing was negatively predictive

Reynol Junco in 2014 examined the time students at different class ranks spent on Facebook, the time they spent multitasking with Facebook, as well as the activities they engaged in on the site (N = 1649). The results showed that seniors spent significantly less time on Facebook and spent significantly less time multitasking with Facebook than students at other class ranks. Time spent on Facebook was significantly negatively predictive of GPA for freshmen but not for other students. Multitasking with Facebook was significantly negatively predictive of GPA for freshmen, sophomores, and juniors but not for seniors. The results are discussed in relation to freshmen transition tasks and ideas for future research are provided.

Mehmood Saba Faculty,. Taswir Tarang in 2013 investigated pedagogical impacts of social networking sites on undergraduate students at the College of Applied Sciences (CAS), Nizwa, Oman. Blogs, wikis, tweets, RSS feeds, discussion boards, podcasts are educational nodes in a huge network. The study tabulates the usage of these web2.0 applications and their impact on linguistic and social behaviours of young learners. The demographic segmentation constructs a framework to evaluate social tools and e-learning technologies popular amongst learners. The results of empirical evidence explore classroom and social software as paradigms that build young knowledgeable societies. It studies variables that examine the effectiveness of these social tools in knowledge sharing and general awareness of student communities.

Sulaiman Ainin, M. Muzamil Naqshbandi, Sedigheh Moghavvemi, Noor Ismawati Jaafar research was accepted in 31 December 2014 and available online in 8 January 2015 examined the impact of Facebook usage on students' academic performance. In addition, it also analyse whether Socialization influences Facebook usage. Empirical data was collected from 1165 Malaysian university students using a questionnaire survey. It was found that the construct Socially Accepted influences Facebook usage while Acculturation does not have any significant relationship with usage. The results also illustrated that there is a positive relationship between students' Academic Performance and Facebook usage i.e. the higher the usage the better they perceived they perform.

Suraya Hamid, Shanton Chang and Sherah Kurnia `- Online social networking (OSN) is a range of activities enabled by social technologies and operationalized by a group of people. More recently, web 2.0 social technologies have been widely used to facilitate OSN. OSN is currently popular mostly for non-educational purposes among young generations categorised as Digital Natives. It can be appropriated and repurposed to support teaching and learning delivery. Despite the availability of implementation cases, studies on the effectiveness of the deployment are still lacking. Therefore, based on a critical literature review, this study investigates which OSN activities are relevant in the education context and what social technologies can support these activities. Specifically, four OSN activities that have been identified and relevant in the education context are content generating, sharing, interacting and collaboratively socialising. The study finding provides a general guide for academics who want to use OSN in improving their teaching and learning.

Thanawan Suthiwartnarueput, Punchalee Wasanasomsithi in 2012 explored the effects of using Facebook as a medium for grammar and writing discussions of low-intermediate EFL students. The data were collected from the students' utterances asking for explanations about English grammar and writing that were posted on Facebook, their gain scores in the pre-test and post-test, and interview responses.

This study attempts to investigate the students' perceptions on the effectiveness of Facebook (FB) groups for teaching and improving writing. The authors see a need to carry out this study as it provides a platform to discover pedagogical implications that would benefit the Y-generation in terms of improving their writing skills in a Malaysian ESL context. The respondents of this research comprise 43 third year students completing their bachelor's degree in TESL, in the Faculty of Education, University Kebangsaan Malaysia (UKM). The students' perceptions were measured through a questionnaire comprising 10 close-ended items and 3 open-ended ones. Respondents were required to participate in a Facebook group created by the researchers. The Facebook group, called 'Write Out Loud' was hosted by Facebook here: http://www.facebook.com/home.php?sk=group_193133474042344&ap=1. The findings showed that 'Facebook groups' is an effective tool in improving the students' writing skills, especially in the brainstorming of ideas before the actual writing. The results of this study may be beneficial to ESL educators in incorporating ICT into their teaching repertoire. It is suggested that future research should focus on the challenges of integrating Facebook groups for teaching and improving writing, and look into the perceptions of the teachers as well. In addition, experimental research could also be done to see how FB and FB groups help in improving writing skills.

Yu Liang, Qingya Wang,Wei Chen in 2011 conducted a descriptive, exploratory research study drew a random sample (N=48) of males (n=26) and females (n=22) who were administered a student perception questionnaire on how social media affects college students. Thirty-five percent of the participants were undergraduates and 65% were graduate students, studying at Johnson & Wales University. Thirty-one percent of participants have full-time jobs, 30% have part-time jobs and 39% do not have jobs. The results of the survey questionnaire indicate that 45% of the sample admitted that they spent 6-8 hours per day checking social media sites, while 23% spent more than 8 hours; 20% spent 2-4 hours and only 12% spent less than 2 hours on this task. Results indicate while most college students use social media and spend many hours checking social media sites, there was a negative aspect to college students' use of social media.

2.2.2. Collaboration and Online Learning

Nine studies were found related to collaboration and online learning are as follows –

Alan S. Weber, (2010) – studied that the social Networking Sites (SNSs) such as Facebook, Google+, Myspace, LinkedIn and Twitter have now become commonplace in international virtual space. Approximately 75% of all online adults maintain at least one social network profile. As SNSs are becoming more ubiquitous, they are also becoming more sophisticated and many operate on a free service model based on advertising revenues. Free services are obviously attractive to educational institutions in the developing world with small education budgets. With the exception of sites such as Edmodo, SNSs, however, are generally commercially driven and educational goals and purposes were not part of their original design: educational uses have generally been the result of the creative adaptation of SNSs by educators and application builders. Therefore some serious issues of data privacy, trust, and security have arisen since both the educational, medical, and medical education realms operate in the U.S. under strict data protection laws such as HITECH, HIPAA, FERPA, and COPPA. Potential educational advantages of SNSs are similar to general eLearning benefits such as: anytime / anywhere instruction, lower cost for institutions, knowledge crowdsourcing, interconnectivity and facilitation of online collaborative work, peer-to-peer instruction, and the provision of virtual training scenarios (role-playing) not available or practical in the non-virtual world. However, the business models of many SNSs as essentially advertising platforms and as a means of tracking online behaviours which can be monetized (with non-transparent policies of data collection and retention) raise some key concerns for educators

Alessandro Cecconi (December 17, 2007) – studied that the social networking is bringing distance education to a collaborative learning model which could not "erase" the digital behaviour of the learner but draw advantage from a sharing attitude of knowledge that is very precious for learning purposes. In fact, it is quite clear that social networking heavily contributed to mix formal and informal learning; that is because distance education can be even delivered through a personal digital environment (such as Elgg). Distance education, therefore, does not have to "connect" learners each other, but it is absolutely necessary to find out how the pre-existing digital networks are structured in order to let the learners interact and transform their educational performances in social performance.

Anneke Emerson (2008) investigated that the social networking in the school setting has the potential to motivate student participation and deepen cultural understanding. Social networks emphasize collaboration and interaction within a learning community. There is tremendous potential for this software to support the human interaction between teachers and students. Face-to-face and online activities can be blended, creating multi-layered communities, which may add new resources and stimuli to the in-classroom community. Controlled, private networks can connect students within a school, connect students within school districts, or connect students across the world. And these safe networks are the perfect "sandbox" to educate students to make informed choices in their "online" lives. This simple, but often overlooked, life skill may be as essential as any other subject taught in 21st century schools today.

Curtis Clifford Cain 2010investigated and develops a collaborative educational environment as a tool to aid teachers in grades K-12 in the STEM, Science, Technology, Engineering and Mathematics, disciplines. The resulting model will be used as a component of a larger learning environment that will remove the social networking taboo stigma currently associated with social networking sites. The model will extend beyond that of traditional social networking by supplementing class lectures in a fun, engaging and thought provoking manner instead of the typical classroom lectures. The final product will be a web-based collaborative educational tool for online interactive tool development. Surveys were used to analyse the perceived effectiveness and receptiveness to the proposed educational tool as determined by K-12 teachers. This paper seeks to gauge teacher's receptiveness and willingness to utilize an online educational forum to supplement traditional classroom lectures.

Irshad Hussain1*, Naushaba Gulrez 2 and Shaheen Ashraf Tahirkheli3 (2012) researchers conducted present study with the objectives to a). Examine the academic use of social media by university students, b). Evaluate the opinion of university students about social media in promoting educational opportunities, and c). Identify the problems of university students in using social media. This study was delimited to the Faculty of Education of the Islamic University of Bahawalpur, Pakistan. The population of the study consisted on all students of the faculty of education. The sample size comprised of 600 students taken through convenient sampling technique. A questionnaire was developed for data collection. The research tool was finalized after its pilot testing. The researchers administered finalized research tool and collected data. The study revealed that majority (90%) of the social media users used Facebook. They used social media for developing academic relationships with their contemporaries. They used such media for sharing their learning experiences with their colleagues and international community. It was obvious from the study that social media plays a crucial role in promoting collaboration and linkage to develop Virtual Community across the world. The respondents also faced some problems in using social media. They faced problems of bandwidth and speed of internet and electricity break down/ load shedding. The researchers recommended that proper training may be organized for appropriate use social media.

M.D. Roblyer a, Michelle McDaniel b , 1, Marsena Webb c, 2, James Herman d , 3, James Vince Witty e, (2010) determined how likely higher education faculty are to use Facebook for either personal or educational purposes, higher education faculty(n=62)and students (n=120) at a mid-sized southern university were surveyed on their use of Facebook and email technologies .A comparison of faculty and student responses indicate that students are much more likely than faculty to use Facebook and are significantly more open to the possibility of using Facebook and similar technologies to support classroom work. Faculty members are more likely to use more "traditional" technologies such as email.

Muhammad Kamarul Kabilan, Norlida Ahmad, Mohamad Jafre Zainol Abidin (2010) researched that the Facebook (FB) is currently considered as the most popular platform for online social networking among university students. The purpose of this study is to investigate if university students consider FB as a useful and meaningful learning environment that could support, enhance and/or strengthen their learning of the English language. A survey was carried out with 300 undergraduate students at University Sains Malaysia (USM), Penang. It was found that the students believed FB could be utilized as an online environment to facilitate the learning of English. Nevertheless, teachers or language instructors have to integrate FB as an educational project with predetermined learning objectives and outcomes for the learning experience to be meaningful. It is suggested that future research should focus on the meaningfulness of FB to students' language learning experiences

Murat Kayri1 and Özlem Çakır2 1, (2010) examined educational use of Facebook. The Computer Networks and Communication lesson was taken as the sample and the attitudes of the students included in the study group towards Facebook were measured in a semi-experimental setup. The students on Facebook platform were examined for about three months and they continued their education interactively in that virtual environment. After the-three-month-education period, observations for the students were reported and the attitudes of the students towards Facebook were measured by three different measurement tools. As a result, the attitudes of the students towards educational use of Facebook and their views were heterogeneous. When the average values of the group were examined, it was reported that the attitudes towards educational use of Facebook was above a moderate level. Therefore, it might be suggested that social networks in virtual environments provide continuity in lifelong learning.

Tom Heath, (2008) investigated how synergies between the Web and social networks can enhance the process of obtaining relevant and trustworthy information. A review of literature on personalised search, social search, recommender systems, social networks and trust propagation reveals limitations of existing technology in areas such as relevance, collaboration, task-adaptively and trust. In response to these limitations I present a Web-based approach to information-seeking using social networks. This approach takes a source-centric perspective on the information-seeking process, aiming to identify trustworthy sources of relevant information from within the user's social network. An empirical study of source-selection decisions in information- and recommendation seeking identified five factors that influence the choice of source, and its perceived trustworthiness. The priority given to each of these factors was found to vary according to the criticality and subjectivity of the task. A series of algorithms have been developed that operationalize three of these factors (expertise, experience, affinity) and generate from various data sources a number of trust metrics for use in social network-based information seeking. The most significant of these data sources is Revyu.com, a reviewing and rating Web site implemented as part of this research, that takes input from regular users and makes it available on the Semantic Web for easy re-use by the implemented algorithms. Output of the algorithms is used in Hoonoh.com, a Semantic Web-based system that has been developed to support users in identifying relevant and trustworthy information sources within their social networks. Evaluation of this system's ability to predict source selections showed more promising results for the experience factor than for expertise or affinity. This may be attributed to the greater demands these two factors place in terms of input data. Limitations of the work and opportunities for future research are discussed.

2.2.3. Effect of Online Tools on Cognitive Domain

Three studies were found related to effect of online tools on cognitive domain

Julie Willems, Debra Bateman, 2011, studied that the popular social networking sites such as Facebook demonstrate an emerging opportunity for students and educators within formal higher education contexts to share ideas, celebrate creativity and participate in an environment which offers immediate feedback from others who belong within a specific network. As this is an emerging use of the technology, an auto ethnographic approach has helped capture the potentials and pitfalls of incorporating social networking within higher education. The findings highlight implications for the key stakeholders in higher education.

Nataša Petrović, Dalibor Petrović, Veljko Jeremić,Nemanja Milenković, and Marko Ćirović (2012), considered the Facebook as one of the most popular platforms for online social networking among youth, and - as many researches show – university students. Also, the impact of Web 2.0 and social networking tools on education has been much elaborated on. Educators need to consider how to meet the needs of their students by utilizing Web 2.0 and other social networking tools. Social networking sites such as Facebook (and Myspace) have been subject to much recent debate within the educational community. Facebook has quickly become the social network site of choice by college students and an integral part of the "behind the scenes" college experience (Selwyn, 2007). Thus, it is essential to integrate social networking tools with the education. The key aspect of this paper will be focused on research of achievement levels of higher environmental education by educational use of Facebook among students of the Faculty of Organizational Science, University of Belgrade, Serbia. An analysis of the results was carried out using the SPSS software package.

Sana Rouis, (2012), investigated that the largest online social network in the world, Facebook continues to prompt debate about users' behaviours. The effects of online activities on themselves and their interactions with others have been discussed extensively. In particular, students are a main class of Facebook users who spend long hours on the social network, which has worried parents and educational authorities about their academic performance. The students themselves argue that their presence on Facebook, as a leisure activity, does not hinder their academic efforts, though some evidence suggests that their grades decline after they join Facebook. To address these questions, I have designed five separate, complementary studies, supported by a conceptual research model derived from flow theory, capacity theory, and the "very rich" model of information system usage. These studies measure actual and perceived impacts and compare them, both in a single cultural context and across widely divergent cultures. Specifically, the first study assessed actual impacts in Tunisia; the second measured the perceived impacts in Sweden. In a third study, I analysed differences between perceived and actual impacts among undergraduate students from the United States. Finally, I performed two comparative studies to investigate the role of culture in moderating perceptions of the effect of time spent and cognitive immersion on Facebook (Sweden and the United States) and then regulating the actual effect of such usage (Tunisia and the United States), in consideration of the level of conscientiousness and extroversion of students from each country.

2.2.4. Comparative and Analytical Study of Social Networking Sites

Twelve studies were found related to comparative and analytical study of social networking sites are -

Alan E. Mislove (2009) exploded. That the numerous sites are dedicated to finding and maintaining contacts and to locating and sharing different types of content. Online social networks represent a new kind of information network that differs significantly from existing networks like the Web. For example, in the Web, hyperlinks between content forma graphs that are used to organize, navigate, and rank information. The properties of the Web graph have been studied extensively, and have led to useful algorithms such as PageRank. In contrast, few links exist between content in online social networks and instead, the links exist between content and users, and between users themselves. However, little is known in the research community about the properties of online social network graphs at scale, the factors that shape their structure, or the ways they can be leveraged in information systems. In this thesis, we use novel measurement techniques to study online social networks at scale, and use the resulting insights to design innovative new information systems. First, we examine the structure and growth patterns of online social net- works, focusing on how users are connecting to one another. We conduct the first large-scale measurement study of multiple online social networks at scale, capturing information about over 50 million users and 400 million links. Our analysis identifies a common structure across multiple networks, characterizes the underlying processes that are shaping the network structure, and exposes the rich community structure. Second, we leverage our understanding of the properties of online social networks to design new information systems. Specifically, we build two distinct applications that leverage different properties of online social networks. We present and evaluate, Ostra, a novel system for preventing unwanted communication that leverages the difficulty in establishing and maintaining relationships in social networks. We also present, deploy, and evaluate Peer Spective, a system for enhancing Web search using the natural community structure in social networks. Each of these systems has been evaluated on data from real online social networks or in a deployment with real users.

Patel Alay Rameshbhai, (2011) analysed that the social networking sites have become an integral part in the modern world today. This thesis focuses on comparing and analysing in detail the technical architectures of the two topmost leading networking sites--Facebook and LinkedIn. Detailed research on the communication services and network update services is presented. Scaling techniques: Functional partitioning, class partitioning along with data archiving and load balancing schemes have been explored in depth, and improvements have been proposed. The technical workflow between MySQL, Memcache, Alternative PHPcache, custom partitioning data, graph based data access libraries, leaf servers, aggregators, chat loggers, channel clusters, Network resolvers, Network collectors, Network digesters and supporting programming languages have been explored and documented. An extensive support to the open source platform with the customized developed frameworks has been well studied. Business aspects, strategies keeping the target audience in context, have been researched and then underlying opportunities in e-commerce world have been explored. An official survey was conducted with the approval from the Institutional Review Board among the target audience to learn about the users issues: following this appropriate solutions have been proposed. This thesis will serve as a single point of data access for the aspiring networking site developers to learn about technical architectures, corresponding supporting customized services, data models and all other required technical details of the two existing most popular networking sites.

Danah M. Boyd, Berkeley Nicole B. Ellison investigated that the social network sites (SNSs) are increasingly attracting the attention of academic and industry researchers intrigued by their affordances and reach. This special theme section of the Journal of Computer-Mediated Communication brings together scholarship on these emergent phenomena. In this introductory article, we describe features of SNSs and propose a comprehensive definition. We then present one perspective on the history of such sites, discussing key changes and developments. After briefly summarizing existing scholarship concerning SNSs, we discuss the articles in this special section and conclude with considerations for future research.

Kaitlyn Flad (2010), researched that the participation with technology for social purposes has become the mainstream communication method for many people in the past several years. In particular, adolescents in high school have adopted these forms of communication as the paramount way to keep in touch with family and friends. Social Networking websites, such as Facebook and Myspace are the most popular places for these students to spend their time, and are the primary focus of this study. The researcher examined the impact of social networking participation among a sample of high school students to determine how this involvement affects academic performance, future plans, and overall attitude towards school. Differences between male and female students regarding academic achievement, performance, and social networking use will also be identified and discussed. Recommendations for school counsellors and further studies will be offered.

Kevin P. Brady, Lori B. Holcomb, and Bethany V. Smith (2010) studied that the distance education as a primary means of instruction is expanding significantly at the college and university level. Simultaneously, the growth of social networking sites (SNS) including Facebook, LinkedIn, and Myspace is also raising among today's college students. An increasing number of higher education instructors are beginning to combine distance education delivery with SNSs. However, there is currently little research detailing the educational benefits associated with the use of SNSs. Non-commercial, education-based SNSs, such as Ning in Education, have been recently shown to build communities of practice and facilitate social presence for students enrolled in distance education courses. In order to evaluate the largely unexplored educational benefits of SNSs, we surveyed graduate students enrolled in distance education courses using Ning in Education, an education-based SNS, based on their attitudes toward SNSs as productive online tools for teaching and learning. The results of our study suggest that education-based SNSs can be used most effectively in distance education courses as a technological tool for improved online communications among students in higher distance education courses.

MA, JUN (2009) - witnessed a substantial emergence of social networking sites (SNSs) which some even refer as an arising phenomenon. Besides the main function of communication of SNSs, the applications integrated within the SNSs are of great popularity and thus help gain more users. Currently, there is no standard for social application development. In this context, the thesis proposes a methodology based on the traditional system development life cycle, with a view to help the developers in implementation of the applications. The thesis is identified as a theoretical creative research. The study is conducted based on the qualitative approach. To be more specific, a series of experimental actions in developing a new social application are taken in order to examine the operation in practice. The methodology offers a collection of models, tools, procedures to assist the experiment. The empirical part consists of a whole development life cycle of the proposed methodology and illustrative actions. The six stages include feasibility study, end-user investigation, developing specification, application analysis and design, application implementation, application publication, review and maintenance. With its own plans, timelines, controls and monitoring procedures, the activities of each stage are defined as their associated end products, which facilitate the use of project management techniques. In conclusion, evaluation of the created methodology is given. The thesis thoroughly evaluates in terms of philosophy, model, techniques and tools, scope, outputs, practice and product, based on which the future possible development is introduced.

Manar I. Hosny, Shameem Fatima (2012) tried to give an insight into how Facebook and similar social networking sites can be used as a medium of communication to help students, teachers as well as the institution's library. The aim is to encourage the use of Facebook to complement and enhance classroom teaching. We investigate the benefits of using such medium from the perspectives of the student, the teacher and the librarian. We then review some case studies where Facebook was used to promote the learning experience. In this paper, we try to derive conclusions about best recommendations and practices that academics can follow to improve teaching and learning through using Facebook and other similar social networking sites.

Ngonidzashe Zanamwe, Taurai Rupere and Owen Kufandirimbwa (2013) researched that the advent of social networking technologies has been met with mixed reactions in academic circles in developing countries like Zimbabwe as is the case in developed countries. Few studies have considered the use of social networking technologies in spite of their widespread use by students in higher education. There is therefore a need to explore the usage of social networking technologies in higher education by focusing on the learner. This study explored social networking technologies being used in higher education, their uses, extent of use, benefits and skills learners acquire from use of these technologies. The study followed a descriptive research design wherein a questionnaire was used as the main research tool. Data was gathered from 124 university students from five institutions of higher learning in Zimbabwe. The collected data was analysed using SPSS. An analysis of the results seems to suggest that the majority of learners were mainly using Facebook and Myspace. Furthermore, it also emerged out that learners used social networking technologies for academic purposes and more specifically to conduct group work. It was also established that social networking technologies improved learners' technology proficiency, enhanced learners' social skills and help learners to communicate in new ways with new people.

S. Griffith, L. Liyanage, (2008) reviewed that the Social Networking Sites (SNS) that have become available via the Internet in the light of usability for teaching and learning. Membership rules relating to entries for some popular sites, such as "Facebook" and "Myspace" are reviewed. Characteristics of these sites are reviewed and then compared to evaluate the trust and privacy issues of shared information available to any given social group. Trust and privacy plays a critical role when SNS are used for the purpose of teaching and learning. Thus, the negative and positive aspects of SNS are reviewed in detail. This knowledge will form the basis to assist with regulating SNS for teaching and learning.

Silvio Lattanzi (2010) investigated that the coming-together of the Internet and large scale social networks (i.e. Flickr, Facebook, MSN, Bebo, Twitter etc.) is having a deep and fruitful impact on the study of social networks. Thanks to the new amount of data available nowadays is now possible to observe social phenomena with greater precision and to study their evolution at a relatively fine temporal scale. These opportunities, together with the increasing economic importance of the internet economy create new interest on studying networks as unifying theme of research between computer science, economy, sociology and biological science. In this context, to fully characterize the statistical properties and to find suitable stochastic model for these kinds of graphs is now a central problem in theoretical and experimental computer science. Within this umbrella, our research focus is to develop mathematical models of behavioural social networks and to study the performances of algorithms on real world graph both from a theoretical that from practical point of view. More specifically we first give a new model that explains the evolving properties of social networks and we analyse its algorithmic implications. Then we consider the diffusion of information in real networks and we give an explanation to the rumour spreading based on a statistical property of social network, i.e. the conductance. Finally, we study the compressibility of the Worldwide Web and of its models, and we use our findings to design an algorithm to compress other social networks.

Waqas Tariq1, Madiha Mehboob2, M. Asfandyar Khan1 and FaseeUllah3 1 (2012) researched the impact of social websites can be good on students but if we have a closer look on the real impact of social networks. Today it is ruining the future and carrier of students. The social networking websites like https://www.linkedin.com, http://,www.facebook.com/, https://twitter.com/ and https://www.orkut.com/ etc. are continuously distracting students from their studies. The main focus of student should be education but unfortunately today's student are emphasizing on such sites which can be a complete wastage of time. Social Networks was only an electronic connection between users but unfortunately it has become an addiction for students, teenagers and even adults. This paper presents impact of social networks on education, students and impact on life of teenagers, further it describes how social networking websites are auditory and dangerous for youth and teenagers. Were variable with only 51% of students stating that it was effective. Despite this, the majority of students 76.4% recommended using Facebook in future course.

Whitney Sue Thoene (2012) examined the effect of social media, particularly Facebook and Twitter, on the purchasing habits of college students by testing for correlations between recommendations on social media and consumption patterns. Moreover, the research also examines the role of gender and social media usage frequency on consumption patterns

2.2.5. Teacher Attitude Towards Facebook

Much of the researcher that examine the effect of Facebook and other social networking sites on students learning outcome also investigated its effect upon teachers attitude. This line of inquiry has brought most of the researchers to the conclusion that the use of Facebook leads to more positive teachers attitudes than the of conventional instruction. The studies conducted were-

Caroline Lego Muñoz Fairleigh, Terri L .Towner (2009) proposed the idea of using the social network site, Facebook, for teacher education. Specifically, this research explores the advantages of this new Web 2.0 medium, and illustrates the different levels of course integration at an instructor's disposal. In addition, it provides specific instructions on how to use Facebook and a discussion of "best practice" policies that can be ethically implemented within the classroom. Specific attention is given to suggestions for creating a professional Facebook presence in which future teachers can emulate.

Filiz Tiryakioglu, Funda Erzurum, (2011) – defined Facebook as a unique online service, platform, or area where social communication and/or social relations can be established and individuals intensely share information. This definition implies that communication specialists should have more expertise and interest in social media than any other group of experts. Based on this assumption, the present study investigated the views and attitudes of instructors in the Faculty of Communication Sciences at Anadolu University in Turkey, which is a country where the total number of Facebook users ranks fourth in the world. The sample of the study consisted of 67 professors with various levels of academic titles. Data were gathered through a specially-designed survey form including 52 items in four subcategories. Results suggest that three fourth of instructors have a Facebook account and they spend less than half an hour per day on Facebook. There is no gender related difference among the faculty in terms of attitudes toward Facebook. Instructors who are younger than 45 years old login Facebook on daily basis, while senior faculty login several times a week. Two in every three instructors use Facebook mainly as a tool of communication with friends. Finally, two thirds of the faculty think that Facebook can provide important contributions to social interactions among students as well as to communications between instructors and students.

Findings - Findings revealed that both Facebook and Twitter are being used to obtain sales information and promotions. Furthermore, gender has an impact on both social networking sites. Additionally, this study found the higher the frequency of social media usage the more likely customers are to shop at the businesses they have befriended.

Findings -The findings showed a statistically significant difference between the mean scores of the pre-test and the post-test ($t = 6.65$, $p = 0.00$). Most common topics of discussion involved sentence structures, followed by word meanings, parts of speech and then relative clauses.

Finding-The results show that students' presence on and cognitive absorption in Facebook do not immediately threaten their academic performance. Their cultural background affects perceptions and thus behaviours. Personality characteristics, such as personality traits, trust in people, self-regulation, and multitasking skills, also significantly moderate the effects. A student's interest in school and his performance goal orientation represent strong determinants of academic achievement. Finally, satisfaction with life is a key difference between cultures; it reflects various aspects of a person's life. Thus, it was perceived differently between Swedes and U.S. students; it emerges as a key concept to consider in analysing the effects of a leisure activity, such as Facebook, on individuals and their performance.

Huseyin Bicen, Huseyin Uzunboylu (2012) researched to find out how Facebook and Web 2.0 tools create a positive effect when used in education and to investigate teachers' opinions about the Online learning environment. This experimental study was carried out in primary and secondary schools with teachers who use Facebook. The study took six weeks and 30 hours. The teachers attended lessons and accessed materials online and offline, in face-to-face learning environment. Moreover, they were able to co-operate and share information with their colleagues via Facebook. The study sample consisted of 35 teachers from primary and secondary school who constituted a blended learning group and 36 teachers from primary and high school who formed an online learning group that enrolled in the material development for Facebook course. These teachers were chosen randomly. The participation was anonymous and the study was carried out amongst volunteered teachers. Data was collected using a 5-point Likert scale questionnaire created by the authors and entitled "Teachers' Opinions about Facebook in Education". The questionnaire consisted of 39 positive statements about Facebook. It was completed by teachers at the beginning (pre-experience test) and the end of the study (post-experience test). Results show that, if used for educational purposes, Facebook could bring about a positive change in teachers' opinions. Results also indicate that Facebook virtual environment helps teachers to do many activities with online classes, which is not possible to do in schools. Teachers are convinced that this environment helps students not only to improve their team work, but also to improve their learning skills. Based on the findings, recommendations are made about using Facebook in education.

Joseph P. Mazera*, Richard E. Murphyb and Cheri J. Simondsc (2009) suggested that teachers who personalize their teaching through the use of humour, stories, enthusiasm, and self-disclosure are perceived by their students to be effective in explaining course content. This experimental study examined the effects of computer-mediated teacher self-disclosure on perceptions of teacher credibility. Participants who accessed the Facebook website of a teacher high in self-disclosure reported higher levels of teacher credibility than participants who viewed a low self-disclosure Facebook website. Implications for classroom pedagogy, technology use, and areas for future research are discussed.

Joseph P.Mazer,Richard E.Murphy&Cheri J.Simonds (2007) examined the effects of teacher self-disclosure via Facebook on anticipated college student motivation, affective learning, and classroom climate. Participants who accessed the Facebook website of a teacher high in self-disclosure anticipated higher levels of motivation and affective learning and a more positive classroom climate. In their responses to open-ended items, participants emphasized possible negative associations between teacher use of Facebook and teacher credibility. Participants offered recommendations for teachers regarding the use of Facebook and other weblog services.

2.2.6. Facebook And Student Characteristics

Learner achievement is always influenced by learner characteristics such as intelligence, aptitude, personality etc. Some researchers also have conducted their studies in these directions to see the effect of blogs with different student's characteristics some of them are cited here-

Ivan Di Capua 2012 represented a review of more than one hundred studies on the social networking website Facebook. An initial selection has been made and has led to the identification of eight main research themes: effects on the users, friendship, construction of impressions, privacy, use, Facebook and politics, self-expression and construal, social capital, and the merging of social spheres. This paper focuses on Facebook use, which is currently the most researched theme. How do individuals use Facebook and why? Six different categories are identified: initiating and maintaining relationships, learning about others, recognition, personality and willingness to communicate, social influence, and experience. The major studies for each category are presented, with an emphasis on the most influential ones in the field. The focus of this literary review is on the commonalities and differences that arise from the results. Hypotheses are presented when possible, and a few theoretical explanations are provided. As a result, one could notice that Facebook is mainly used to keep in touch with other people, but not in a conventional way as users tend to 'spy' on other users' profiles. This phenomenon leads to a growing exhibitionism, which is in turn related to individuals' personality traits. Use of Facebook is also influenced by peers and experience with the website. A few limitations are discussed, and gender is found to be a possible factor influencing Facebook use. Suggestions for further study are provided.

Jerry L. Allen, University of New Haven ,Kathleen M. Long, Joan O'Mara, Ben B. Judd,(2007) examined the impact of communication on instructors' affinity with students (Frymier & Wanzer, 2006), compliance-gaining strategies (Paulsel & Chory-Assad, 2004; Plax & Kearney, 1992), communication style and clarity (Andersen, Norton, Nussbaum; Chesebro, 2002), interpersonal attractiveness and caring (Teven & McCroskey, 1997), nonverbal immediacy (Andersen, 1979; O'Mara, Allen, Long, & Judd, 1996; Richmond, Gorman, & McCroskey, 1987; Richmond, Lane, & McCroskey, 2006). Researchers have reported on the relationship of instructors' communication and students' motivation to learn (Christensen & Menzel, 1998; Christophel, 1990; Richmond, 1990), and a myriad of related variables related to student and teacher interactions at all educational levels—elementary, secondary, undergraduate, graduate, adult, and applied (Mottet, Richmond, & McCroskey, 2006). Most of this research is concerned with either the teacher's communication behaviour or his/her perception of students' communication behaviours. A few attempts, largely concerned with communication apprehension, have been made to examine the contributions that students' communication competencies, skills, and behaviours make to the learning equation, but the effects of student communication behaviours on the learning process have not been saliently studied (McCroskey, Richmond, & McCroskey, 2006).

Jessica Lee Pugh (2010) – studied what better place to be your absolute funniest, most attractive, interesting and appealing self than a Facebook profile? Social networking websites (SNWs) have opened the doors of communication, allowing people from around the world to engage in identity creations and relationship development. As the leading SNW, Facebook boasts over 400 million active users, engaging in the Website on a daily basis to facilitate an on-going dialogue of their identity and generating influence amongst their networks. Facebook users employ a number of features including notes (blog), games, chat, joining fan pages, starting groups, posting statuses, and writing on other's walls. Through these experiences, users develop their self-concept and affiliate identities to create their image, and to produce their own spotlight through a micro celebrity experience on Facebook. This study extends prior research of computer-mediated environments (personal Websites) to develop theory of how people contemporarily define themselves in their social online space. The Facebook user celebrity experience is brought about through connected networks/fan base, a highly regarded image, and associations that are developed throughout this analysis.

Jilin Chen, Joseph Konstan and John Riedl, advisors (2011) researched that the Social network sites have experienced an explosion in both the number of users and the amount of user-contributed content in recent years. Today, millions of people visit Facebook, Twitter and the like to keep up with friends, to engage in random chatter, and to share and consume photos, news, useful tips and fun stories. Many active users of social network sites are, however, constantly troubled by information overload – there are too many other people to interact with and too much content to read. As a result, the difficulty in finding the right people and content to focus on has been identified as a key challenge for social network sites. In this thesis we seek to meet the challenge by designing three personalized recommender systems. The first system is a people recommender, which helps users find potential friends to connect with on social network sites; the second system is an information recommender, which helps users find interesting pieces of information from their online social network; the third system is a conversation recommender, which helps users find interesting conversations happening around their online social network. In designing the recommender systems, we adapt algorithms from related domains and create new algorithms. We refine these algorithms through offline data analysis. We then design and improve user interfaces of the recommender systems through participatory design. With the full recommender systems designed and implemented, we deploy these systems to real users of social network sites, and evaluate a variety of recommender algorithms online through user studies. Through these user studies we not only provide qualitative and quantitative comparisons of recommender algorithms, but also provide broader insights for designing recommender systems on social network sites.

Jonna Howe (December 2011) provided insights on how the popularity of blogs, social media, and other user-generated content venues have impacted the way in which news is consumed and reported. However, little research has been done specifically related to whether or not individuals believe they are better informed as a result of social media. The study explored how the popularity of social media and other user generated content venues have impacted the way in which news is consumed and distributed. The study examined the way in which individuals use social media to share and consume news stories and if they feel more informed as a result. The study was conducted using an online survey. The majority of respondents disclosed that they share news to stay connected with family and friends. The respondents report that they depend on their network of friend to guide them to news articles, as they are a good representation for their own interest. The study found that individuals under the age of 35 rely heavily on their social networks for tips and alerts to news stories. The majority of all respondents are exposed to news stories that they may have otherwise missed or overlooked as a result of Facebook and Twitter.

Kelli Elise Kapp (2011) - Researched that the date on Facebook users has not included part of Generation Y, those born from 1976 through 1989. This study examined the use of Facebook to maintain relationships to extend previous work by Steinfield and Lampe (2009), Pennington (2009), and Bryant and Marmo (2009) whose work served as a lens for comparison. A survey questionnaire (N=215) was administered to Facebook users to determine their uses for the site, frequency of use, and perceived closeness of Facebook friends. Results suggested Facebook has become a daily part of respondent's lives. Questions regarding Facebook use indicated the number one motivator for using Facebook is to keep in touch with friends and family. Participants reported using Facebook has made their relationships mildly stronger. These findings indicated participants use Facebook in similar ways as reported in previous research.

Kesaraporn Wanajak 2011 contributed to the international literature on IA by generating a consensus definition and diagnostic criteria of IA, testing this definition and criteria in a sample of Thai secondary school students to identify a cohort of students fitting the criteria of IA, as well as identifying intervention strategies recommended by the Delphi panel and students that may help minimise harm caused by IA.

L Schlenkrich1, DA Sewry2 (2012),Factors for Successful Use of Social Networking Sites in Higher Education studied that the social networking sites are extremely popular online destinations that offer users easy ways to build and maintain relationships with each other, and to disseminate information in an activity referred to as social networking. Students, lecturers, teachers, parents and businesses, in increasing numbers, use tools available on social networking sites to communicate with each other in a fast and cost-effective manner. The use of social networking sites to support educational initiatives has received much attention. However, the full potential of social network sites has yet to be achieved as users continue to strive for optimal ways of using these sites, as well as battle to overcome the negative characteristics (for example, privacy, security, governance, user behaviour, information quality) of these sites. This paper proposes factors for successful use of social networking sites in higher educational institutions. These success factors need to be adopted by users in order to develop the positive aspects of social networking, while at the same time mitigating the negative characteristics. An initial set of factors for successful use of social networking sites, as well as measures to test successful use of social networking sites were derived from the literature. These factors were tested by means of an online survey of students at a university, the results of which informed the final factors for successful use of social networking sites. The factors enable users to overcome the negative characteristics associated with social networking sites. If used successfully, social networking sites can offer lecturers and students a useful tool with which to develop their relationship and contribute to their learning experience.

Müge Akyıldız Anadolu University Metin Argan focused on examining how much, why and how students use Facebook, one of the most popular social networking site, and understanding its impact on The aim of this study is to examine the purposes of Facebook use in an undergraduate sample and explore time investment of the students to Facebook Social, daily and educational purposes while using Facebook were measured via a questionnaire administered to 1300 undergraduate students. The results indicated that only 6.2% students have no Facebook account. Facebook members participated reported that they had been on Facebook for 2 years or more, log in to Facebook several times in a day and spend approximately 15 min or half an hour on Facebook daily and they have 101-300 friends on Facebook. According to results, it is found out that purpose statements related to social and daily activities had a higher score than educational and school related purposes.

Nicola Cavalli, Elisabetta Ida Costa, Paolo Ferri, Andrea Mangiatordi, Marina Micheli, Andrea Pozzali, Francesca Scenini and Fabio Serenelli* investigated that the Facebook has significantly transformed the online habits of young Italians. Our research assesses this change through a two-year survey conducted among undergraduate students. The data we collected in 2008 (N=1088) and 2009 (N=1123) allowed us to define profiles of media use based on indicators such as time spent online, consumption or creation of content, and familiarity with digital technologies as compared to analog media. Results have also shown the quick adoption of Facebook: in 2008, half of the students were completely unfamiliar with Facebook, while in 2009 all our respondents were aware of it and 59% of them were also using it on a regular basis. To grasp the magnitude of this change, we conducted a qualitative research study based on 30 semi-structured interviews with randomly selected university students (aged 19-24). Our research questions whether the massive adoption of Facebook, both in terms of frequency and time spent online, is really producing a change in how Italian students are using the Internet, or whether it is merely reproducing old forms of media consumption. To explore this issue, we will focus on how students are appropriating Facebook - in terms of uses and meanings they attach to it - and on the transformation of the relationship between more traditional forms of media consumption (like television) and digital media.

2.2.7. Usage Pattern of Social Networking Sites and Social Interaction

Marc Stumpel (2010) examined the governance of contemporary social media and the potential of resistance. In particular, it sheds light on several cases in which Facebook has met with resistance in its attempt to exercise control. This social networking site has raised concerns over privacy, the constraints of its software, and the exploitation of user-generated content. By critically analysing the confrontations over these issues, this thesis aims to provide a framework for thinking about an emerging political field. This thesis argues that discursive processes and (counter) protocological implementations should be regarded as essential political factors in governing the user activities and conditions on large social networking sites. A discourse analysis unveils how Facebook enacts a recurrent pattern of discursive framing and agenda-setting to support the immediate changes it makes to the platform. It shows how contestation leads to the reconfiguration and retraction of certain software implementations. Furthermore, a software study analyses how the users are affected by Facebook‘s reconfiguration of protocological assemblages. Several tactical media projects are examined in order to demonstrate the mutability of platform‘s software.

Michael Beye1,Arjan Jeckmans2, ZekeriyaErkin1, PieterHartel2, Reginald Lagendijk1 and QiangTang2 studied that in recent years, Online Social Networks (OSNs) have become an important part of daily life for many. Users build explicit networks to represent their social relationships, either existing or new. Users also often upload and share aple thora a of information related to their personal lives. The potential privacy risks of such behaviour are often underestimated or ignored. For example, users often disclose personal information to a larger audience than intended. Users may even post information about others without their consent. A lack of experience and awareness in users, as well as proper tools and design of the OSNs, perpetuate the situation. This paper aims to provide insight into such privacy issues and looks at OSNs their associated privacy risks, and existing research into solutions. The final goal is to help identify the research directions for the Kindred Spirits project.

2.3.0. Studies Conducted In India

The study of Facebook is at an evolving stage. As per a latest 'GenY Survey' done by Tata Consultancy Services (TCS) across 14 Indian cities, Ahmedabad's school-going teenagers emerged as 'hyper-connected', as they topped the charts in using Facebook to stay connected with their friends and relatives.

The survey concluded that Facebook usage in Ahmedabad city by teenagers is among the highest in the country. More than 94 percent teenagers out of 1,100-odd respondents in the age group of 12-18 in Ahmedabad claimed that they have a Facebook account.

The Associated Chambers of Commerce and Industry (Assocham) says workers use Orkut, Facebook, Myspace and Linkedin for "romancing" and other purposes. Office employees questioned in the survey spent on average an hour a day on sites like Facebook, leading to a loss in productivity of nearly 12.5%. The findings were based on responses from nearly 4,000 corporate employees.

The findings, a part of Tata Consultancy Services (TCS) Gen-Y survey 2012-13, reveal that today's youth are collaborating through social networking tools and building virtual communities aided by affordable bandwidth and smart devices. The exhaustive study by India's largest software services exporter covered nearly 17,500 high-school students across 14 Indian cities and claimed to have conducted the first such survey in India

1. Effectiveness of Facebook for teaching and learning
2. Collaboration and online learning
3. Effect of online tools on cognitive domain
4. Comparative and analytical study of social networking sites
5. Teacher attitude towards Facebook
6. Usage pattern of social networking sites and Social interaction

2.3.1 Effectiveness of Facebook for Teaching and Learning

Acharya Dr.Varang, Patel Mr. Adarsh, Jethava Mrs. Sweta, in 2013 researched that social networking is becoming more and more powerful tool for the young generation for communication and sharing of information. People have started using the social networking sites for different purposes. The common reason behind use of the social networking is to stay in touch with friends, share each and every event with friends and that's too free of cost. But if we think about learning on social networking platform then it becomes very easy to learn while having fun with the friends. This paper shows features that are already available for the students and professors for learning and teaching, while some of them are required to incorporate to enhance the learning process over the social networking website "Facebook".

Kalra1Raj Kumari, Manani Preeti. In 2013 investigated the effect of use of Social Networking sites on academic achievement among Introverts and Extroverts. The sample of the study was comprised of 150 students of class XI of C.B.S.E. English medium schools of Agra City. Selection of the sample was done by using 'Simple Random Sampling Method'. The age range of the students was 16-18 years. The Introversion-Extroversion Inventory (2009) developed by Aziz & Gupta was used to identify the type of personality in terms of introversion and extroversion. Grades obtained in the previous class served as the indicator of academic achievement of the students.

Results revealed that there was no significant difference between academic achievement of users and non-users of Social Networking Sites (SNS). It was also found that even with personality differences among the students there was no significant difference found among extroverts and introvert students using and not using SNS with reference to their academic achievement.

Gangwar Sharda, Deshbhratar Anita & Garg Pragya in 2013 studied that the social media generally refer to media used to enable social interaction. For our purposes, the term social media technology (SMT) refers to web-based and mobile applications that allow individuals and organizations to create, engage, and share new user generated or existing content, in digital environments through multi-way communication. The use of social media approaches enhanced the learning experiences of undergraduate business students. Their use caused both the instructor and students to realize their roles in the course and behaviour in the classroom had to change significantly. Although some may feel that incorporating social media approaches takes time away from important course topics, they should see these as alternative ways to cover topics and even as a means for introducing additional topics.

Kale Prashant, in 2012 found that social networking sites are very effective media to get in touch with our family, friends and current important social events. No doubt it is a faster media than the newspapers. Besides communication with friends, family members and entertainment social media can be effectively used for the educational purpose also. College students can form groups and can share their views, material discuss about various things. This study was undertaken in keeping a view that how many students use social networking sites for the educational purpose. For this study 200 students studying in B.Ed. colleges were studies with survey method. The research revealed that a little percentage of students use social media for the educational purpose. Most of the students use it for the purpose of entertainment and to keep in touch with friends.

Kuppuswamy Sunitha and Narayan P. B. Shankar in 2010, - investigated that Social networking websites like Orkut, Facebook, Myspace and Youtube are becoming more and more popular and has become part of daily life for an increasing number of people. Because of their features, young people are attracted to social networking sites. In this paper, the authors explore the impact of social networking sites on the education of youth. The study argues that these social networking websites distract students from their studies, but these websites can be useful for education based on sound pedagogical principles and proper supervision by the teachers. Moreover, the research concludes that social networking websites have both positive as well as negative impact on the education of youth, depending on one€™s interest to use it in a positive manner for his or her education and vice versa.

2.3.2 Collaboration and Online Learning

Ahmad Ateeq (2011) studied that the use of collaborative technologies and Social Networking Site leads to instant online community in which people communicate rapidly and conveniently with each other. The basic aim of this research paper is to find out the kinds of social network are commonly using by the people.

Jasimudeen S 1* and Rajan Maghesh M 2 explained the advantages of academic networks and the issue of access to journal articles via e-journal consortium's in India. Proposal for an educational social network on the National Knowledge Network (NKN) platform is put forth. Digitization of indigenous academic resources and its dissemination through networks for better access is also emphasized.

Shrivastav, Preeti., (2012) investigated that teachers and students have a vast array of social-networking sites and tools—from Ning to Voice Thread and Second Life—to draw on for such serious uses as professional development and project collaboration. Educators who support using social networking for education say it has become so ubiquitous for students—who start using sites like Webkinz and Club Penguin when they are in elementary school—that it just makes sense to engage them this way. Though teachers and students are now pushing learning beyond the borders of the classroom through social networking, which move also comes with hurdles, including the fact that many schools still block access to such sites within their walls. School officials must also confront the uncertainties and questions surrounding privacy issues, proper management, and cyber security when they open their doors to social-networking sites. On the other hand, educators can help students realize even more benefits from their social network site use by working to deepen students' still emerging ideas about what it means to be a good digital citizen and leader online. However it's a world that some educators are realizing students feel at home in and is unlikely to disappear. A study by the Washington-based Pew Research Centre's Internet & American Life Project released early this year found that 73 percent of Americans ages 12 to 17 now use social-networking websites, up from 55 percent in 2006.

2.3.3 Effect of Online Tools on Cognitive Domain

Jain1 Neelesh Kumar, Verma2 Dr. Ashish, Verma3 Dr Rama Shankar and Tiwari Prashant (2012) studied that the growth and the popularity of the Social networks has a high impact on the development of the students in the field of Personality, Attitudes, Knowledge and on its whole academic performance in classroom and society. This paper envisage on the impact of Social Network on Education and Training of the students.

Bhola Reema Malhotra, Mahakud Gopal Chandra investigated that the social networking sites (SNSs) are emerging trends that deeply influence the societal interactions and psychological well-being. Qualitative themes of social acceptance, physical maladjustment and tool for career growth were found to be the most common experiences around social networking.

2.3.4 Comparative and Analytical Study of Social Networking Sites

Jothi P.*, Neelamalar M. and Shakthi Prasad R. (2011) – investigated that the internet is the emerging information technology with the credibility of immediacy and fastness, thus, it brings globalization in every aspects of communication. Communication through internet is more specified, with effective interactive strategy among its users. In recent days, internet advertising has taken new forms which have more advantages over the traditional mediums like print media, television and radio. Marketing communication is becoming precise, personal, interesting, interactive and social. Different strategies of communication are followed in various social networking sites like Face book, Twitter and Orkut. They not only create impact over the audience but also make them interact with the marketing statistics created. People get attached to brand communication in social networking sites than usual banner and pop up ads. These networking sites bring more interactive communication with advertising. Social networking sites will become the primary arena for highly targeted marketing and advertising. Therefore, it is necessary to study the effectiveness of brand communication strategy followed in social networking sites which are mainly accessed by Indian users. This research attempts to find the effectiveness of brand communication strategy in promoting and advertising their brand in social networking sites. The effectiveness is determined with the help of survey from people who use these sites, and the content of three social networking sites is analysed.

Peddiboyina Vijaya Lakshmi, Pradeep Krishnatray, & Shrivastava Sangeeta. (2014) researched that the social networking sites have a primary purpose of promoting communication and interactions amongst users. Such sites like Facebook, Orkut, and Twitter have become popular and a vital part of social life in India, especially among teenagers. However, available literature indicates lack of in-depth study to evaluate how and why Indian teenagers engage with social networking sites. This study hopes to fill this gap as it uses Focus Group Discussion to explore the experiences of Indian teenagers with social networking sites. Information from the groups was analysed in terms of their use of social networking sites, online versus offline friendships, and extending friendships beyond cyberspace. Our findings indicate that both boys and girls use other forms of communication channels to strengthen existing friendships more with the same gender than with the opposite. However, the boys enjoy more freedom when compared with the girls and they admitted talking to online friends and meeting them outside cyberspace without any hesitation. The girls, on their part, were hesitant to extend online friendships beyond virtual space because of security issues and resistance from family members.

2.3.5 Teacher Attitude Towards Facebook

Singh Alka. (2013) focused on teacher education, the curricular areas of initial teacher education is recommended in NCTE (2009) is to develop habits and the capacity for self-directed learning, have time to think, reflect, assimilate and articulate new ideas; be self-critical and to work collaboratively in groups (p.24).Use in classroom settings. The study consist 70 student teachers and 30 teacher educators from B.Ed. institutions located in Delhi who responded to a questionnaire developed by the researcher. The result reveals that student teachers and teacher educators both are positivity agreed with the statements related to the potential of Facebook in teacher education. Student teachers responded that Facebook can be used to easily share campus events, news, classroom updates, presentations, photos and other information, and can promote effective teacher-student relationship. On the other hand, teacher educators found that Facebook can be used to facilitate study in academic groups and it can be used as to share classroom updates, presentations, photos.

Tyagi Sunil (2012) -conducted study in six (6) Indian Universities at NCR (National Capital Region) of India to explore the usage analysis of Web 2.0 technologies in learning environment by faculty members. The investigator conducted a survey with the help of structured questionnaire on 300 respondents. A total of 300 self-administered questionnaires (out of total population 693) were distributed among Professors, Associate Professors, and Assistant Professors of different streams and departments (Agriculture, Arts, Education, Engineering, Management and Science) by adopting stratified random sampling, 147 valid samples were collected and analysed. Web 2.0 is especially useful and creative when knowledge is digitized, modular and allowed to be used and distributed in a flexible way. The application of the Web 2.0 tools in Indian higher education is still marginal and will have to overcome a lot of obstacles in order to hold its ground as in higher education of developed countries. The adoption of Web 2.0 tools at universities is associated with important challenges (potential risks, institutional fears) and an effective strategy to deal with implementation problems may therefore include learning from (others') experience, as well as open access to content and reliance on open platforms for knowledge sharing and creation. The majority of the faculty members have been using Web 2.0 tools for the three major purposes; for Web based teaching & research; for interactive learning features; and to keep themselves up to date on related topic of interest. The results indicate that the faculty attitude and their perceived behavioural control are strong predictors to their intention to use Web 2.0. This article reports on study that attempted to find out the usage of Web 2.0 tools (wiki's, blogs, RSS feed, collaborative writing, video sharing, social networks, etc.) by Indian faculties to support teaching and learning in higher education at NCR of India.

2.3.6 Usage Pattern of Social Networking Sites and Social Interaction

Anil Kumar, Rajinder Kumar (2013) - made an attempt to study the activities and reasons for using Social Networking Sites by the Post Graduate students and research scholars of Maharishi Dayanand University, Rohtak, India. A self-structured questionnaire was distributed among the target population and primary data gathered through questionnaire were analysed and discussed in accordance with the objectives of the study. It was found that majority of the respondents to be aware and making use of such applications in their research work. The study also reveals that Facebook is the most popular SNSs among the all categories of students and research scholars.

Rathod1 Dr. Harishchandrasingh, 2012, shared a research study that was conducted in rise of 2012 in north Gujarat region. The study investigated student's use of different social media tools, their usage rate, and their preference of social networking groups. The study also investigated the awareness level of students towards cybercrime. The results show that the three top-used social media tools are Facebook, Yahoo Group and Orkut; the top four reasons for using social media tools are for social engagement, direction communication, instant messaging, and relationship building. Even though students aware about cybercrime but most of them do not understand the meaning of phishing, vishing and cyber-squatting. Based on their response, the research evoked some educational implications of some of these tools as valuable resource for teaching and learning.

Neelamalar Dr. M. & Chitra Ms. P. investigated the primary objective of the research undertaken has been to shed light on the evolution of the dominance of social networking sites among the Internet users and its eventual outcome in the social behaviour patterns of youth (17 22 yrs.). Previous research in spheres of social networking sites and its impact on youth in different global and demographic context provided an extensive secondary source base for the study. As with many technologies, adoption of the Internet especially for its social uses has seen its highest levels of usage among younger users. The majority of current college students have had access to the Internet and computers for a large percentage of their lives. These digital natives see these technologies as a logical extension of traditional communication methods, and perceive social networking sites as often a much quicker and more convenient way to interact. That they are aware of the danger and risk involved in these sites is a positive indicator that Indian youth are not only techno-savvy and socially active through social networking sites but they also possess social consciousness.

Manjunatha S. (2013) study is placed in the context, aimed at presenting usage pattern of SNS by the Indian college students. For the said purpose a survey has been conducted among 500 students in various colleges and universities throughout India. The findings of the study acknowledge the rampant usage of SNS among young college students in India. Their usage pattern of SNS, hours spending per week, gender differentiation in its usage, purpose of membership, their level of intimate relationships with online friends and much more interesting aspects have been dealt scientifically in this paper.

Jain Mr. Madhur Raj, Gupta Ms. Palak, Anand Ms. Nitika, (2012) considered the fact, there are so many burning issues around us which we need to think upon and act, it's an alarm for us to be aware about the society and its issues. Current issues like violation of human rights, girl's education, adverse effects of global warming, wrong deeds of political leaders, crime against women, corruption etc. need to be discussed openly with the society in an effort to do something about it and bring a revolution. Social Networking sites provide a platform for discussion on such issues as it is this media which majority mass rely on and extend warm support. One such burning issue that has been overlooked in today's scenario is the impact of social networking sites in the changing mind-set of the youth. Our research is conducted on youths between age group of 18-30 years with a view to know the level of awareness on the social issues and how far social networking sites awakened the today's youth in expressing their views on current and burning issues like corruption, human rights, girl education etc. Study was conducted on 100 people mostly through email or sending link of questionnaire on various social sites.

Ruchi Sachdev focused to find out the answer whether the social networking sites are boon or bane for today's society. No doubt these SNS provides employment, marketing, personal growth, sharing of information but the most prevalent danger through often involves online predators or individuals. These SNS has great impact on youth of India. One can easily see the entry gate of these social networking sites but it is unable to find exit for these SNS. One side these sites provide to communicate with our dear ones on the other side it creates platform for many cybercrimes. The SNS is a "child of" computing "by computing" but" for the society". So we focused on the fact that how SNS are implementing and used in an effective manner that is also beneficial for Indian society and what are the role of Indian youth .In this paper we focused on the positive as well as negative impact of these social networking sites on the Indian youth and what are the ethical responsibilities of the users of these sites.

2.4.0. Conclusion

Social media are really a sub-category of computer technology, but their development deserves a section of its own in the history of educational technology. Social media cover a wide range of different technologies, including blogs, wikis, You Tube videos, mobile devices such as phones and tablets, Twitter, Skype and Facebook. Social media are strongly associated with young people and 'millennials' – in other words, many of the students in post-secondary education. In India the awareness of using Facebook in education is still at preliminary stage. Facebook is one of the popular social networking site which can be used anytime and from anywhere. From reviewing the above cited literature, the research done by the researchers and their efforts to increase awareness of Facebook are to be applauded.

The majority of current students access to the Internet and computers for a large percentage of their lives and also investigated the awareness level of students towards cybercrime. Majority of the research found social networking sites like Facebook useful in the academic and can be used to facilitate study in academic groups and also share classroom updates, presentations, photos. It was also found from the research that there is both positive as well as negative effect of all the social networking websites on the Indian young people

On the basis of the reviews of the related literature researcher has found that there is a relationship between Facebook and academic achievement of the students. It is also observed that various researcher have worked on various aspects on the use of Facebook for educational purpose.

Researcher also found social networking websites like Facebook, Myspace, word press, twitter and one tube are been growing fast among people, and playing a key role in our daily lives, majority of them are youth. They love to be online and increase networking members and not only this, it`s help them for gaining knowledge, information gathering and for educational purpose.

It has been seen the majority of the studies reported so far in our country is related with CAI, Education TV, Programmed learning material, linear programme, Branching programme, Hybrid programme development of multimedia programme package etc. Only few research studies related with social networking (Facebook) is reported; so far hence an attempt has been made the effectiveness of social networking (Facebook) for teaching science. Hence this study is taken to increase the knowledge and understanding the use of Facebook as educational tool among teachers, parents, students and society to improve the academic, behavioural and social functioning of students. Some general teaching strategies and videos are described that can help the students to achieve success in science.

From the review of related literature, it is evident that majority of research studies in the field of use of Facebook site for education purpose were conducted in foreign countries.

The studies conducted in India and other countries are related mainly to web-tools like internet, CAI and e-learning social networking for entertainment purpose etc. study related to Facebook site is still in the mode of infancy in India.

In India the studies are conducted are Dr.Varang Acharya, Mr.Adarsh Patel, Mrs.Sweta Jethava,2013, Raj Kumari Kalra1, Preeti Manani.(2013), Sharda Gangwar, Anita Deshbhratar & Pragya Garg 2013, Shri .Prashant Kale, (2012). Sunitha Kuppuswamy (Anna University Chennai, Chennai, India) and P. B. Shankar Narayan (Pondicherry University, Puducherry, India) (2010), Ateeq Ahmad Department of Computer science & Engineering, Singhania University, Pacheri Bari, Disst. Jhunjhunu (Rajasthan) (2011), Jasimudeen S 1* and Mahesh Rajan M 2**, Srivastava, Preeti. (2012), Neelesh Kumar Jain1, Dr. Ashish Verma2, Dr Rama Shankar Verma3 and Prashant Tiwari (2012) ,Reema Malhotra Bhola, Gopal Chandra Mahakud, P. Sri Jothi*, M. Neelamalar and R. Shakthi Prasad , India.(2011), Peddiboyina Vijaya LAKSHMI, Sri Padmavati Mahila Visvavidyalayam, Pradeep KRISHNATRAY & Sangeeta SHRIVASTAVA (2014), Alka Singh,. (2013), Sunil Tyagi (2012), Anil Kumar, Rajinder Kumar Choudhary Charan Singh (2013), Dr. Harishchandrasingh Rathod1, 2012, Dr. M. Neelamalar & Ms. P. Chitra , Ruchi Sachdev, Manjunatha S., (2013), Mr. Madhur Raj Jain Associate Professor, Ms. Palak Gupta Assistant Professor, Ms. Nitika Anand, (2012), Reema Malhotra Bhola, Gopal Chandra Mahakud.

In India the studies related to see the effect of Social networking sites on teachers perception and blending learning Dr.Varang Acharya, Mr.Adarsh Patel ,Mrs.Sweta Jethava,2013, Raj Kumari Kalra1, Preeti Manani.(2013), Sharda Gangwar, Anita Deshbhratar & Pragya Garg 2013, Shri .Prashant Kale, (2012)

Sunitha Kuppuswamy (Anna University Chennai, Chennai, India) and P. B. Shankar Narayan (Pondicherry University, Puducherry, India) (2010), Ateeq Ahmad Department of Computer science & Engineering, Singhania University, Pacheri Bari, Disst. Jhunjhunu (Rajasthan) (2011), Jasimudeen S 1* and Mahesh Rajan M 2**, Srivastava, Preeti. (2012), Neelesh Kumar Jain1, Dr. Ashish Verma2, Dr Rama Shankar Verma3 and Prashant Tiwari (2012), Reema Malhotra Bhola, Gopal Chandra Mahakud, Alka Singh,. (2013), Sunil Tyagi (2012)

Anil Kumar Panjab University, Chandigarh (India), Rajinder Kumar Choudhary Charan Singh Haryana Agricultural University, Hisar (India) (2013), Dr. Harishchandrasingh Rathod1,. 2012, Dr. M. Neelamalar & Ms. P. Chitra, Ruchi Sachdev , Manjunatha S. Research Scholar, (2013), Mr. Madhur Raj Jain Associate Professor, Ms. Palak Gupta Assistant Professor, Ms. Nitika Anand, (2012), Reema Malhotra Bhola, Gopal Chandra Mahakud studies are presenting the usage pattern of social networking sites and some social issues.

In foreign countries extensive research work has been done in the field of web-tools technology for achieving educational goals. Out of 70 studies reviewed 39 studies were related with effectiveness of Social networking sites in terms of student's achievement. Majority of studies reported that social networking sites could enhance achievements as compared to conventional classroom instructional alone.

CHAPTER- III

DEVELOPMENT OF FACEBOOK PAGE FOR TEACHING AND LEARNING

3.0.0 Introduction

The present experimental study is related to the teaching of science, using social networking site i.e. Facebook page. For this, an online web based Facebook page was design. The steps followed for developing an online web-based Facebook page, textual contents are explained under various headings like selection of topic, Entering behaviour, Terminal behaviour, content analysis, initial try out, final try out etc.

The developed Facebook page consisted of e-contents, discussion and problem solving sessions and current link up videos and photos that are well related to the contents so as to make easy for the learners to understand the lesson in better way.

Facebook an Online Website

For the present study, Facebook page was developed on the 15 chapters of science of class IX CBSE syllabus, developed by NCERT in 2006.It covers the whole syllabus of IX class Science prescribed by CBSE.

3.1.0. Setting up A Facebook Page

The researcher used a free Facebook website the process of creating a Facebook page is a fairly simple, below are given in detail the whole process how the account have been created for teaching science for class IX CBSE students. Till completion of the research the created Facebook page was a closed group of 100 students studying in Nagpur. Later it has been open for all.

The researcher has made only a text page. All the learning modules were arranged logically based on psychological principles of learning, i.e. proceeding from easy to difficult, simple to complex and from the known to the unknown.

Once the Facebook page is created, the researcher added as many post and page of content. All the post and pages are listed chronologically in the Facebook page. Readers/students can freely view the contents of the page and post comments. The owner /researcher of the Facebook page visited the comments left on Facebook postings and the communication continues. This way an asynchronous interaction can take place.

The website address of Facebook page is given below
https://www.facebook.com/Dr-Rajshree-vaishnav-and-Vandanas-page-for-class-9-CBSE-Science-220327441442111/

The investigator developed the Facebook page for the following topics of science class IX CBSE students. The topics are:

- **Chapter-I** Matter In Our Surroundings
- **Chapter- II** Is Matter Around Us Pure
- **Chapter-III** Atoms And Molecules
- **Chapter- IV** Structure Of The Atom
- **Chapter- V** The Fundamental Unit Of Life
- **Chapter- VI** Tissues
- **Chapter- VII** Diversity In Living Organisms
- **Chapter- VIII** Motion
- **Chapter- IX** Force And Laws Of Motion
- **Chapter- - X** Gravitation
- **Chapter- XI** Work And Energy
- **Chapter- XII** Sound
- **Chapter- XIII** Why Do We Fall Ill
- **Chapter- XIV** Natural Resources
- **Chapter- XV** Improvement In Food Resources

3.2.0. Steps For Developing Facebook Page Are As Follow:-
Create a valid email account

One should need; A computer with an internet facility

Step 1: Open the internet browser and check the websites home page.

Step 2: Click on the icon "Create Account" for this one as to follow the procedure:-

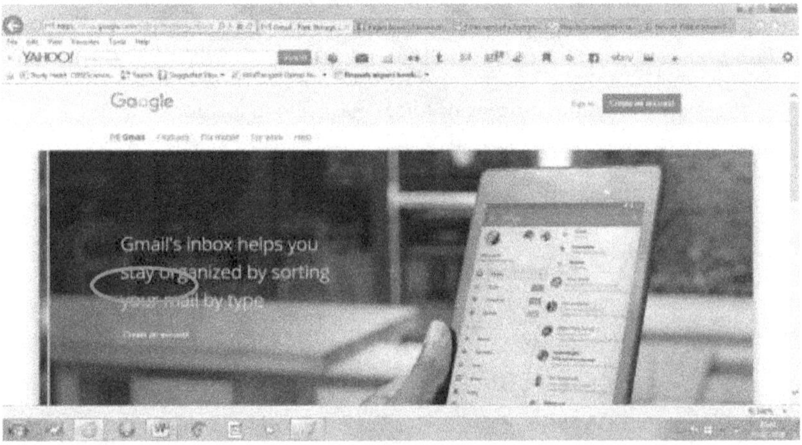

Step 3: The sign –up form will appear. Follow the directions and enter the required information, such as your name, birth date and gender etc. .Once you create an account, you will be able to start adding contracts and adjusting your mail settings.

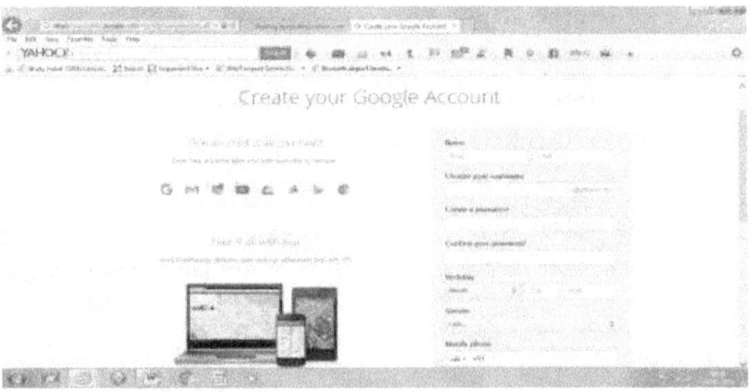

Finally review Terms of Service and privacy policy of website, click the check box, and then click to the next step.

After all the procedure followed, in the end your account will be created, and the website welcome page will appear.

Note: It`s very necessary to have own valid e-mail ID before making an account on Facebook website because whenever one forgot the password they can gain it through their ID.

This page is about how to sign up and to register for your Facebook. Some steps are to be followed to create your own account.

Step 1:

Go to www.facebook.com a sign up page will appear, click on to the sign up icon you will get the next page which is to be fill up all the details mentioned in that page.

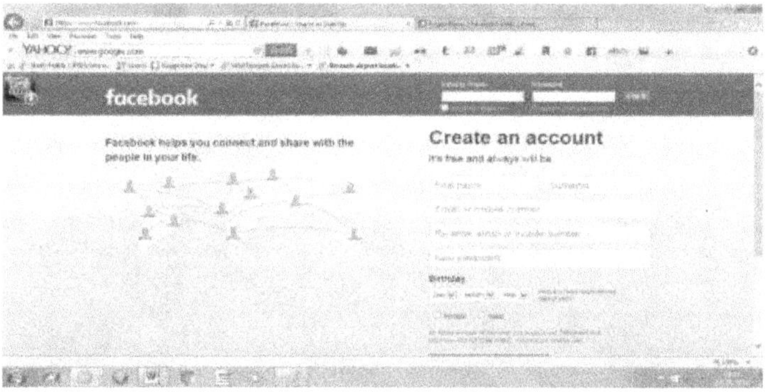

Step 2:

Enter your details like username, password, domain title etc. and then click to start button.

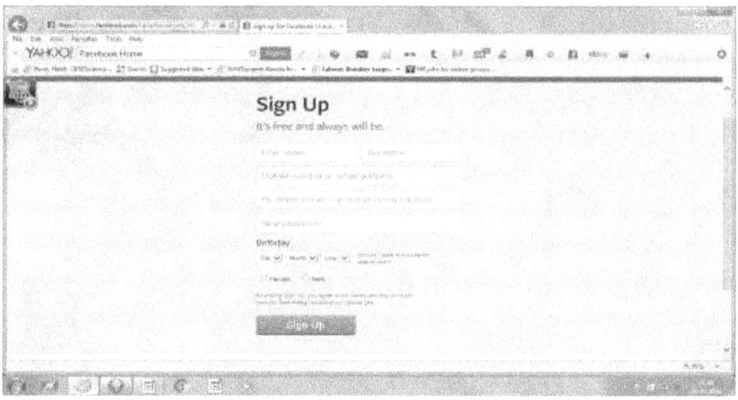

Step 3:

On the next page your login details are displayed.
Make sure to write down your password if our e-mail option is not use we won`t be able to reset it again.

Step 4:

After creating a Facebook account on www.facebook.com

- Go to the home page of the Facebook.
- Click on the login icon, a drop – down box will appear, Login to your Facebook account by using your own username and password.

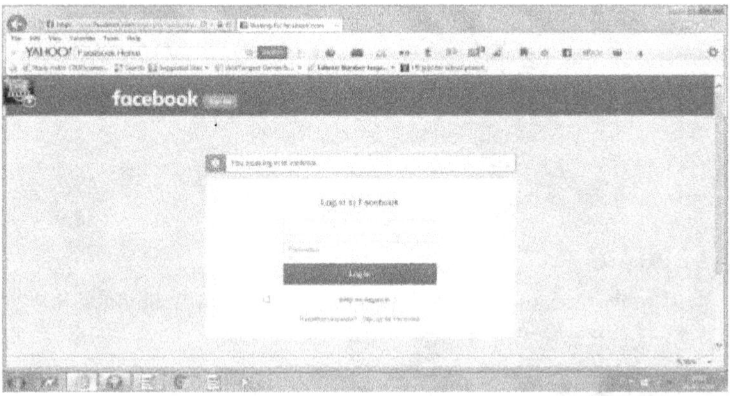

Step 5

After successful login one can click on Create a page

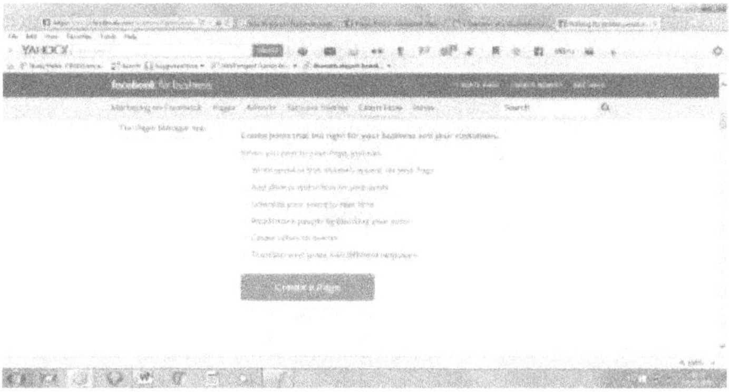

Step 6

Introduction to pages

Pages on Facebook is normally used for information that we want to share with the readers but don't expect to update frequently.

Page Title-tells the reader what the page is about.

Page content – information we want to share on this page. Posts are where we normally publish the latest update or new article on a page. They are commonly displayed in reverse chronological order with the most recent post at the top of the page. Most of the content published on a page is normally written as posts.

Comments- Pages support comments at the bottom of the page. This allows our readers to add a comment to our page.

Step 7

Log out

We have to click on the right side of our Facebook. A drop down menu will appear and then click to logout.

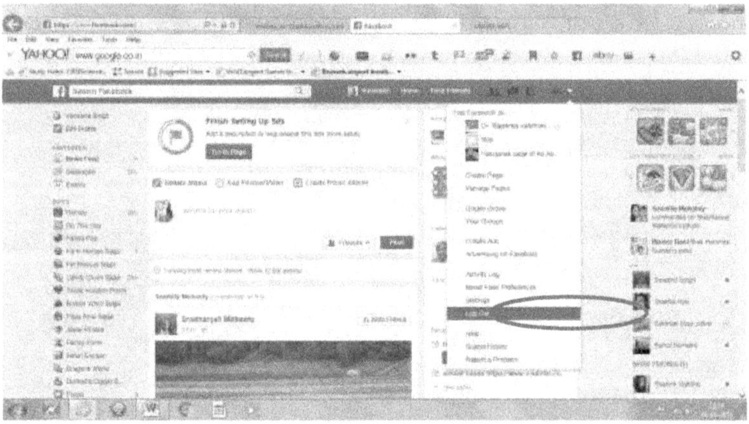

The Basic structure of a Facebook page

Facebook page is normally made up of the following main elements:

Page Roles

There are five different roles for people who help manage Pages. When you create a Page, you automatically become the Page's admin, which means only you can change how the Page looks and publish as the Page.

You can then assign roles to other people to help you manage your Page. Each person will log into their own personal account and work on the Page from there. You don't need to share any passwords to have multiple people help manage your Page

Page Insight

Insights provide information about the Page's performance and are available after at least 30 people like the Page. Find demographic data about audience, and see how people are discovering and responding to the posts

Access the New Insights

Access the new Insights from within your admin panel.

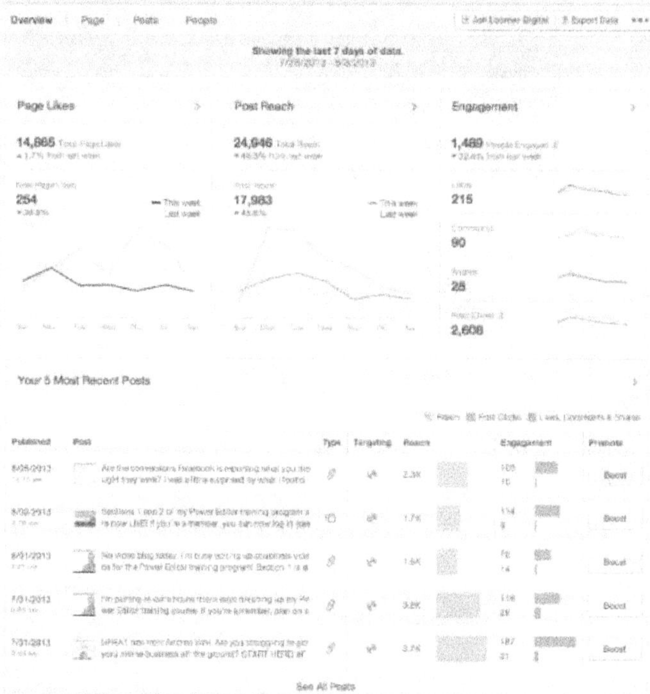

The Overview tab of Facebook Insights summarizes what's going on with your page.

Activity Log

The Page's activity log helps to manage the Page's Timeline. It shows a complete list of posts and comments by your Page, including posts you've hidden. Only people who help manage your Page can see the activity log.

From the *Edit Page* dropdown the Admin Panel: Click *Edit Page>Use Activity Log*:

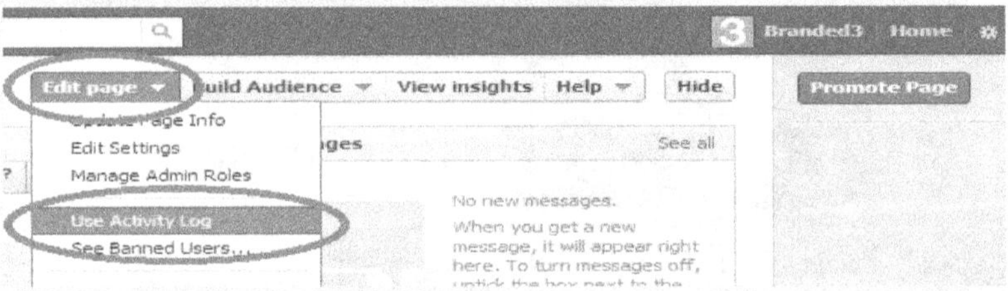

Header

The header is the area at the top of a page where the title, graphics and possibly navigational links appear. Using your own custom image header, we can obtain a much more customized look and feel adding our own personal touch to our Facebook page.

Uploading your own custom header image is as simple as

1. Go to more option > page info> Change page name
2. Click on the default image we want to use for our header image. Below is the screenshot of suggested header.
3. Your new header image should appear in your page preview window.
4. Click save and publish on the new header on your Facebook page.

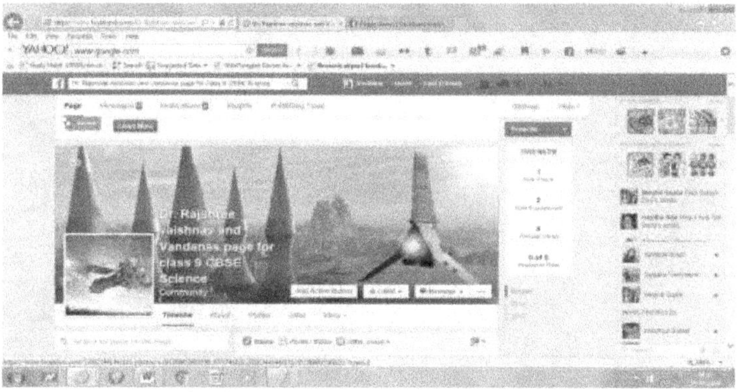

Tabs and apps

Tabs and apps can be found below your Page's cover photo.

Tabs come with your Page when you create it. They help people see specific parts of your Page, like photos and events.

Apps are made by third-party developers. You can add apps to your Page build your own or work with one of Facebook's Facebook Marketing Partners to create a unique app experience on your Page

Post Scheduling

Now this isn't a new feature by any means, but I thought I'd throw it in because it makes managing a Facebook Page and its content strategy really easy. It's great.

And Facebook has recently updated it, which makes its inclusion here even more legitimate: we no longer have to go through the rigmarole of picking the day, month and year from separate dropdowns – it now throws up a simple calendar. because that was a bit of a mission.

One thing to note, you can't edit the copy or photo/video attachment once you've scheduled your post. If you need to make any changes, you'll need to delete it and start from scratch, which is a bit annoying. Apart from that though, it's a really great feature.

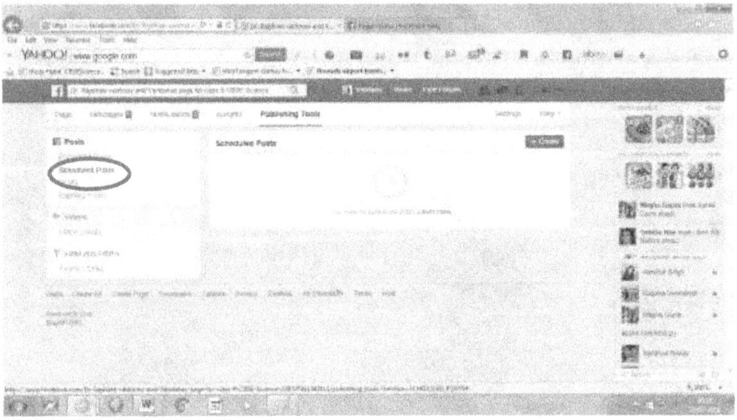

Posts in Page

Type your post into the box at the top of the Page's Timeline. Click in the top right of the box and select whether to post as yourself or one of the Pages you manage. You can tag friends or add a location. Depending on the Page's settings, you may be able to add a photo or video.

Table No. 3.1: Chronology investigator/teacher and students activities carried out during the teaching process through Facebook page

Date	Step of the planning	Teacher/Investigator activities/Action	Students activities Through Reflection/Comments
April 2014	Login process on Facebook website	Facebook site is an online website; an account was created and registration form was prepared by the investigator.	
April 2014	Draft design of Facebook	Firstly, sign –up process including username mail, password, Facebook page, Facebook page title, Link to pages, appearance, menu images and videos was properly set-up	

Date	Step of the planning	Teacher/Investigator activities/Action	Students activities Through Reflection/Comments
May 2014	Procedure for collection of material related to the chapters	All the material related to 15 chapters of science like videos, photo, ppt etc. was jot down to upload it on the Facebook page by the investigator.	
May 2014	Uploading process	The investigator uploads the chapter one by one of subject science, videos, ppts etc. on the Facebook page.	
June 2014	Collection of registration form	Registration form (including name, sex, school name, phone No., email) was given to the 200 students from two schools of Nagpur city.	Students duly filled up the form and return back to the investigator at the same time.
June 2014	Sort out procedure carried out by the investigator	200 students of both the school of Nagpur city were divided into two groups i.e. control and experimental group	
June 2014	Testing of previous knowledge of the subject	The investigator instructed the students how to login for online test. And to check the previous knowledge a pre-test on the 15 chapters of science was taken on the control and experimental group by the investigator.	The experimental group students given the test online i.e. www.cbsesciencelear ning.in And the control group students had gone through paper pencil test
July 2014	Question on previous knowledge about Facebook	The investigator asked questions base on the previous knowledge about social media, whether they were aware of SNS and Facebook.	The students paid attention to the question asked and replied , they were aware of SNS and its types ONLY 10% OF STUDENTS HAD HEARD OF FACEBOOK
July 2014	Introduction of Facebook page to the students	The investigator along with the computer teacher orally gave a detail description and full explanation about Facebook.	The class was quite all the students were enthusiastic and motivated in this new and interesting project. Students

Date	Step of the planning	Teacher/Investigator activities/Action	Students activities Through Reflection/Comments
			asked about all queries during the introductive class session and their query was solved.
August 2014	Beginning of the session through Facebook	During the beginning period, computer teacher and investigator took the students to the computer lab to go through the Facebook.	Students showed their abilities in management of computer tool, enjoyed viewing contents and asked difficulties during the session.
September 2014	Reading the content of the Facebook page	The teacher /investigator helped the students throughout the learning	The students gone through the Facebook page contents as per their time and suitability along with their regular classroom teaching.
October 2014	Comments on the Facebook page by the students	The students published their comments and opinion on Facebook page.	The students participated in teaching learning process via Facebook through comments.
November 2014	For the Post-test on the chapters	Online test was uploaded by the investigator	The students actively performed the online test onwww.cbsesciencelearning.in for all the chapters of science of class IX CBSE
December 2014 to January 2015	Communication process	Face to face decision session was held with the students as well as contacted through website, email and phone by me the investigator.	
February 2015	Data collected	Analysis & tabulation of the data was done by the investigator.	

Instruction to follow to attempt pre-test for the subject science

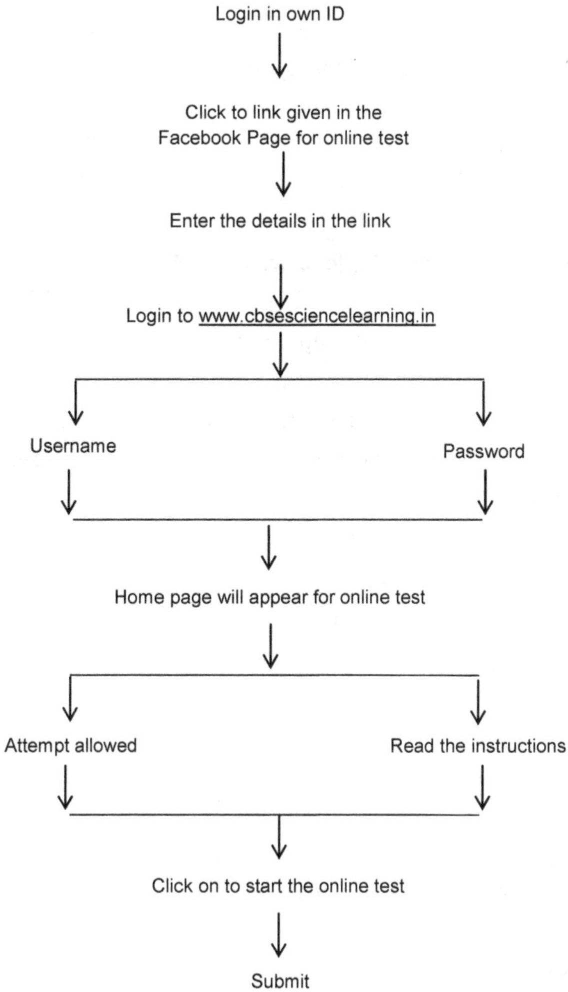

Flow chart 3.1: Instruction to be follow to attempt pre-test for the subject science

3.3.0 Steps for Developing Facebook e-content

The steps involved in developing Facebook were as follows

1. Selection of topic/unit and subunit
2. Writing assumptions about learner
3. Criterion test
4. Content analysis

3.3.1 Selection of the Topic/Unit and Sub-Unit

The most important step for developing Facebook page is the selection of topic. For the present study class IX syllabus of science force schools was selected for convenience the 15 chapter was divided into small sub-units. These topics are highly conceptual in nature instruction were provided through text as well as through pictures and videos. The whole syllabus of class IX science was selected because the investigator is well versed with the subject being a graduate in science. To make presentation more effective and interesting, expert programmer help and suggestion were also taken and the Facebook page was been developed by the investigator.

3.3.2. Assumptions About Learner

The investigator has set the norms for developing an online Facebook page. The pre –requisite to be possessed by the learner for learning different units has been presented as entering behaviour. The specification of objectives to be achieved through Facebook has been stated in behavioural terms under terminal behaviour.

- ➢ The present Facebook page is meant for the students of IX class CBSE affiliated schools of India.
- ➢ It is suitable for the age group between 13 and above.
- ➢ It is suitable for English medium students only.

- Students should read and write English as well as Hindi.
- Students should have working knowledge of computer and internet operation use.

3.3.3. Entering Behaviour

Entering behaviour shows the present status of the students' knowledge. Learning can take place better when the previous knowledge is related to the new knowledge. Hence it is important to know the pre-requisite of the students called entering behaviour before providing them new knowledge. Keeping this in mind, entering behaviour has been written.

In CBSE syllabus up to VIII standard, science as a subject is included in the curriculum. The entering behaviour of the students for teaching science subject is stated as below

1. Students can define matter.
2. Student's s can tell the meaning of volume & mass.
3. Students can familiar that there are three states-solid, liquid& gas.
4. Students can tell the measurable quantities and their units.
5. Students can familiar that the Matter is made up of small particles.
6. Students can state the properties of three states— solid, liquid and gas.
7. Students can explain that the states of matter are inter-convertible. The state of matter can be changed by changing temperature or pressure.
8. Students can tell that the Sublimation is the change of gaseous state directly to solid state without going through liquid state, and vice versa.
9. Students can explain that the boiling is a bulk phenomenon. Particles from the bulk (whole) of the liquid change into vapour state.

10. Students can explain that the Evaporation is a surface phenomenon. Particles from the surface gain enough energy to overcome the forces of attraction present in the liquid and change into the vapour state.
11. Students can tell the mixture contains more than one substance (element and/or compound) mixed in any proportion.
12. Students can aware that the element is a form of matter that cannot be broken down by chemical reactions into simpler substances.
13. Students can familiar with the compound is a substance composed of two or more different types of elements, chemically combined in a fixed proportion.
14. Students can explain that the Properties of a compound are different from its constituent elements.
15. Students can aware that the during a chemical reaction, the sum of the masses of the reactants and products remains unchanged. This is known as the Law of Conservation of Mass.
16. Students can explain an atom is the smallest particle of the element that can exist independently and retain all its chemical properties.
17. Students can know that a molecule is the smallest particle of an element or a compound capable of independent existence under ordinary conditions. It shows all the properties of the substance.
18. Students can state a chemical formula of a compound shows its constituent elements and the number of atoms of each combining element.
19. Students can state the difference between living & nonliving.
20. Students can familiar with living things are made up of cell.
21. Students can aware that the cells are varying in shape & size.
22. Students can know the Cell is the structural and functional unit of life

23. Students can tell Tissue is a group of cell.
24. Students can give the comparison of plant cell & animal cell.
25. Students can give the comparison of prokaryotic and eukaryotic cell.
26. Students can describe the characteristics that define all living things (e.g. are made up of one or more cells, require energy for life processes, respond to stimuli in their environment, and have the ability to reproduce).
27. Students can describe the concept of living and nonliving things.
28. Students can know that there is diversity in living organisms.
29. Students can define the meaning of motion.
30. Students can tell the difference between rest and motion.
31. Students can state the types of motion.
32. Students can familiar with the vector and scalar quantity.
33. Students can define the acceleration.
34. Students can tell the difference between speed and velocity.
35. Students can familiar with the distance and displacement.
36. Students can aware about the rest and motion of the body.
37. Students can explain that the force is the cause of motion.
38. Students can state that force is needed to change the speed or direction of motion of an object.
39. Students can tell that an object dropped from a height falls towards the earth.
40. Students can tell that all the planets go around the sun.
41. Students can tell the ways of describing the motion of objects.
42. Students can explain the cause of motion and gravitation.
43. Students can describe the weight of a body is the force with which the earth attracts it.
44. Students can state Conservation of energy which states that energy can neither be created nor destroyed.
45. Students can tell different form of energy.
46. Students can state that the sound is a form of energy.

47. Students can aware that the cells are basic unit of life.

48. Students can state that the cells are made of a variety of chemical substances.

49. Students can explain that the cells move from place to place. Even though cells that do not move, there is repair going on.

50. Students can describe that the food is a necessity for cells and tissues function.

51. Students can explain that the life on earth is dependent on many factors.

52. Students can state that most life forms need an ambient temperature, water and food.

53. Students can know the resources available on the Earth and the energy from the sun is necessary to meet the basic requirements of life forms on the Earth.

54. Students can identify that all living organisms need food.

55. Students can familiar with the food supplies protein, carbohydrates fats, vitamins and minerals, all of which we require for body development, growth and health.

56. Students can tell both plants and animals are major sources of food for human being.

57. Students can understand that the human being obtained most of this food from agriculture and animal husbandry.

3.3.4. Terminal Behaviour

After knowing about the potentiality of the learner, setting of norms and writing of entering behaviour, the investigator has decided the terminal behaviour for the uploading the contents on Facebook page. Terminal behaviour is the learning outcome which students should attain after getting instruction. The terminal behaviour represents the future status of the students in terms of acquisition of certain new behaviour. They are the specific instructional objectives which students should attain after completion of the segment of instruction. The objective is presented here in behavioural terms. They termed as anticipated outcome or anticipated change in learner's behaviour. The following terminal behaviour have been specified and presented chapter wise for each topic and its sub-topic as follows.

Matter in Our Surroundings

Students will be able to understand that:-

1. The forces of attraction between the particles are maximum in solids, intermediate in liquids and minimum in gases.
2. The spaces in between the constituent particles and kinetic energy of the particles are minimum in the case of solids, intermediate in liquids and maximum in gases.
3. The arrangement of particles is most ordered in the case of solids, in the case of Liquids layers of particles can slip and slide over each other while for gases, there is no order, particles just move about randomly.
4. Boiling is a bulk phenomenon. Particles from the bulk (whole) of the liquid change into vapour state.
5. Evaporation is a surface phenomenon. Particles from the surface gain enough Energy to overcome the forces of attraction present in the liquid and change into the Vapour state.
6. The rate of evaporation depends upon the surface area exposed to the atmosphere, the temperature, the humidity and the wind speed.
7. Evaporation causes cooling.
8. Latent heat of vaporisation is the heat energy required to change 1 kg of a liquid to gas at atmospheric pressure at its boiling point.
9. Latent heat of fusion is the amount of heat energy required to change 1 kg of solid into liquid at its melting point.

Is Matter around Us Pure

Students will be able to:-

1. Understand that mixture contains more than one substance (element and/or compound) mixed in any proportion.
2. Realize that the Mixtures can be separated into pure substances using appropriate separation techniques.
3. Learn that the solution is a homogeneous mixture of two or more substances. The major component of a solution is called the solvent, and the minor, the solute.
4. Learn that the concentration of a solution is the amount of solute present per unit volume or per unit mass of the solution/solvent.
5. Identified the Materials that are insoluble in a solvent and have particles that are visible to naked eyes, form a suspension. A suspension is a heterogeneous mixture.
6. Understand that the Colloids are heterogeneous mixtures in which the particle size is too small to be seen with the naked eye, but is big enough to scatter light. Colloids are useful in industry and daily life. The particles are called the dispersed phase and the medium in which they are distributed is called the dispersion medium.
7. Realize that the pure substances can be elements or compounds. An element is a form of matter that cannot be broken down by chemical reactions into simpler substances. A compound is a substance composed of two or more different types of elements, chemically combined in a fixed proportion.
8. Understand that the Properties of a compound are different from its constituent elements, whereas a mixture shows the properties of its constituting elements or compounds.

Atoms and Molecules

Students will be able to understand that

1. During a chemical reaction, the sum of the masses of the reactants and products remains unchanged. This is known as the Law of Conservation of Mass.
2. In a pure chemical compound, elements are always present in a definite proportion by mass. This is known as the Law of Definite Proportions.
3. An atom is the smallest particle of the element that can exist independently and retain all its chemical properties.
4. A molecule is the smallest particle of an element or a compound capable of independent existence under ordinary conditions. It shows all the properties of the substance.
5. A chemical formula of a compound shows its constituent elements and the number of atoms of each combining element.
6. Clusters of atoms that act as an ion are called polyatomic ions. They carry a fixed charge on them. The chemical formula of a molecular compound is determined by the valency of each element.
7. In ionic compounds, the charge on each ion is used to determine the chemical formula of the compound.
8. Scientists use the relative atomic mass scale to compare the masses of different atoms of elements. Atoms of carbon-12 isotopes are assigned a relative atomic mass of 12 and the relative masses of all other atoms are obtained by comparison with the mass of a carbon-12 atom.
9. The Avogadro constant 6.022×1023 is defined as the number of atoms in exactly 12 g of carbon-12.
10. The mole is the amount of substance that contains the same number of particles (atoms/ ions/ molecules/ formula units etc.) as there are atoms in exactly 12 g of carbon-12.
11. Mass of 1 mole of a substance is called its molar mass.

Structure of the Atom

Students will be able to understand that

1. Credit for the discovery of electron and proton goes to J.J. Thomson and E.Goldstein, respectively.
2. J.J. Thomson proposed that electrons are embedded in a positive sphere.
3. Rutherford's alpha-particle scattering experiment led to the discovery of the atomic nucleus.
4. Rutherford's model of the atom proposed that a very tiny nucleus is present inside the atom and electrons revolve around this nucleus. The stability of the atom could not be explained by this model.
5. Neils Bohr's model of the atom was more successful. He proposed that electrons are distributed in different shells with.
6. Discrete energy around the nucleus. If the atomic shells are complete, then the atom will be stable and less reactive.
7. J. Chadwick discovered presence of neutrons in the nucleus of an atom. So, the three sub-atomic particles of an atom are: (i) Electrons, (ii) protons and (iii) neutrons. Electrons are negatively charged, protons are positively charged and neutrons have no charges. The mass of an electron is about 12000 times the mass of a hydrogen atom. The mass of a proton and a neutron is taken as one unit each.
8. Shells of an atom are designated as K, L, M, N,
9. Valency is the combining capacity of an atom.
10. The atomic number of an element is the same as the number of protons in the nucleus of its atom.
11. The mass number of an atom is equal to the number of nucleons in its nucleus.
12. Isotopes are atoms of the same element, which have different mass numbers.

13. Isobars are atoms having the same mass number but different atomic numbers.
14. Elements are defined by the number of protons they possess.

The Fundamental Unit of Life

Students will be able to:-

1. Understand that the fundamental organisational unit of life is the cell.
2. Realised that Cells are enclosed by a plasma membrane composed of lipids and proteins.
3. Learn that the cell membrane is an active part of the cell. It regulates the movement of materials between the ordered interior of the cell and the outer environment.
4. Understand that in plant cells, a cell wall composed mainly of cellulose is located outside the cell membrane.
5. Identified that the presence of the cell wall enables the cells of plants, fungi and bacteria to exist in hypotonic media without bursting.
6. Recognise that the nucleus in eukaryotes is separated from the cytoplasm by double-layered membrane and it directs the life processes of the cell.
7. Learn that the ER functions both as a passageway for intracellular transport and as a manufacturing surface.
8. Understand that the Golgi apparatus consists of stacks of membrane-bound.
9. Vesicles that function in the storage, modification and packaging of substances manufactured in the cell.
10. Learn that most plant cells have large membranous organelles called plastids, which are of two types – chromoplasts and leucoplasts.
11. Identified that Chromoplasts that contain chlorophyll are called chloroplasts and they perform photosynthesis.

12. Learn that the primary function of leucoplasts is storage.
13. Recognise that most mature plant cells have a large central vacuole that helps to maintain the turgidity of the cell and stores important substances including wastes.
14. Understand that Prokaryotic cells have no membrane-bound organelles, their chromosomes are composed of only nucleic acid, and they have only very small ribosomes as organelles.

Tissues

Students will be able to understand that-

1. Tissue is a group of cells similar in structure and function.
2. Plant tissues are of two main types – meristematic and permanent.
3. Meristematic tissue is the dividing tissue present in the growing regions of the plant.
4. Permanent tissues are derived from meristematic tissue once they lose the ability to divide. They are classified as simple and complex tissues.
5. Parenchyma, collenchyma and sclerenchyma are three types of simple tissues. Xylem and phloem are types of complex tissues.
6. Animal tissues can be epithelial, connective, muscular and nervous tissue.
7. Depending on shape and function, epithelial tissue is classified as squamous, cuboidal, columnar, ciliated and glandular.
8. The different types of connective tissues in our body include areolar tissue, adipose tissue, bone, tendon, ligament, cartilage and blood.
9. Striated, unstriated and cardiac are three types of muscle tissues.
10. Nervous tissue is made of neurons that receive and conduct impulses.

Diversity in Living Organisms

Students will be able to understand that

1. Classification helps us in exploring the diversity of life forms.
2. The major characteristics considered for classifying all organisms into five major kingdoms are:
   (a) whether they are made of prokaryotic or eukaryotic cells.
   (b) whether the cells are living singly or organised into multicellular and thus complex organisms.
   (c) Whether the cells have a cell-wall and whether they prepare their own food.
3. All living organisms are divided on the above bases into five kingdoms, namely Monera, Protista, Fungi, Plantae and Animalia.
4. The classification of life forms is related to their evolution.
5. Plantae and Animalia are further divided into subdivisions on the basis of increasing complexity of body organisation.
6. Plants are divided into five groups: Thallophytes, Bryophytes, Pteridophytes, Gymnosperms and Angiosperms.
7. Animals are divided into ten groups: Porifera, Coelenterata, Platyhelminthes,
8. Nematoda, Annelida, Arthropoda, Mollusca, Echinodermata, Protochordata and Vertebrata.
9. The binomial nomenclature makes for a uniform way of identification of the vast diversity of life around us.
10. The binomial nomenclature is made up of two words – a generic name and a specific name.

Motion

Students will be able to: understand the

1. Motion is a change of position; it can be described in terms of the distance moved or the displacement.

2. The motion of an object could be uniform or non-uniform depending on whether its velocity is constant or changing.
3. The speed of an object is the distance covered per unit time, and velocity is the displacement per unit time.
4. The acceleration of an object is the change in velocity per unit time.
5. Uniform and non-uniform motions of objects can be shown through graphs.
6. The motion of an object moving at uniform acceleration can be described with the help of three equations, namely

   $v = u + at$

   $s = ut + ½ at2$

   $2as = v2 – u2$

   Where u is initial velocity of the object, which moves with uniform acceleration a for time t, v is its final velocity and s is the distance it travelled in time t.
7. If an object moves in a circular path with uniform speed, its motion is called uniform circular motion.

Force and Laws of Motion

Students will be able to understand the

1. First law of motion: An object continues to be in a state of rest or of uniform motion along a straight line unless acted upon by an unbalanced force.
2. The natural tendency of objects to resist a change in their state of rest or of uniform motion is called inertia.
3. The mass of an object is a measure of its inertia. Its SI unit is kilogram (kg).
4. Force of friction always opposes motion of objects.
5. Second law of motion: The rate of change of momentum of an object is proportional to the applied unbalanced force in the direction of the force.

6. The SI unit of force is kg m s–2. This is also known as newton and represented by the symbol N. A force of one newton produces an acceleration of 1 m s–2 on an object of mass 1 kg.
7. The momentum of an object is the product of its mass and velocity and has the same SI unit is direction as that of the velocity. Its kg m s–1.
8. Third law of motion: To every action, there is an equal and opposite reaction and they act on two different bodies.
9. In an isolated system (where there is no external force), the total momentum remains conserved.

Gravitation

Students will be able to understand the

1. The law of gravitation states that the force of attraction between any two objects is proportional to the product of their masses and inversely proportional to the square of the distance between them. The law applies to objects anywhere in the universe. Such a law is said to be universal.
2. Gravitation is a weak force unless large masses are involved.
3. Force of gravitation due to the earth is called gravity.
4. The force of gravity decreases with altitude. It also varies on the surface of the earth, decreasing from poles to the equator.
5. The weight of a body is the force with which the earth attracts it.
6. The weight is equal to the product of mass and acceleration due to gravity.
7. The weight may vary from place to place but the mass stays constant.
8. All objects experience a force of buoyancy when they are immersed in a fluid.
9. Objects having density less than that of the liquid in which they are immersed, float on the surface of the liquid. If the

density of the object is more than the density of the liquid in which it is immersed then it sinks in the liquid.

Work and Energy

Students will be able to understand the

1. An object having capability to do work is said to possess energy. Energy has the same unit as that of work.
2. An object in motion possesses what is known as the kinetic energy of the object. An object of mass, m moving with velocity v has a kinetic energy of 2mv1 2.
3. The energy possessed by a body due to its change in position or shape is called the potential energy. The gravitational potential energy of an object of mass, m raised through a height, h from the earth's surface is given by m g h.
4. According to the law of conservation of energy, energy can only be transformed from one form to another; it can neither be created nor destroyed. The total energy before and after the transformation always remains constant.

Sound

Students will be able to understand the

1. Sound is produced due to vibration of different objects.
2. Sound travels as a longitudinal wave through a material medium.
3. Sound travels as successive compressions and rarefactions in the medium.
4. In sound propagation, it is the energy of the sound that travels and not the particles of the medium.
5. Sound cannot travel in vacuum.

6. The change in density from one maximum value to the minimum value and again to the maximum value makes one complete oscillation.
7. The distance between two consecutive compressions or two consecutive rarefactions is called the wavelength, λ.
8. The time taken by the wave for one complete oscillation of the density or pressure of the medium is called the time period, T.
9. The number of complete oscillations per unit time is called the frequency (ν), 1T.
10. The speed v, frequency ν, and wavelength λ, of sound are related by the equation, $v = \lambda\nu$.
11. The speed of sound depends primarily on the nature and the temperature of the transmitting medium.
12. The law of reflection of sound states that the directions in which the sound is incident and reflected make equal angles with the normal to the reflecting surface at the point of incidence and the three lie in the same plane.
13. For hearing a distinct sound, the time interval between the original sound and the reflected one must be at least 0.1 s.
14. The persistence of sound in an auditorium is the result of repeated reflections of sound and is called reverberation.
15. Sound properties such as pitch, loudness and quality are determined by the corresponding wave properties.
16. Loudness is a physiological response of the ear to the intensity of sound.
17. The amount of sound energy passing each second through unit area is called the intensity of sound.
18. The audible range of hearing for average human beings is in the frequency range of 20 Hz – 20 kHz.

Why Do We Fall Ill

Students will be able to:

1. Understand how diseases are caused and spread
2. Realise that for every disease that is communicable, there is a factor that causes and a factor that spreads the disease.
3. Identify the vectors responsible for spreading diseases like malaria, rabies and dengue.
4. Differentiate between chronic and acute diseases.

Natural Resources

Students will be able to understand the

1. Life on Earth depends on resources like soil, water and air, and energy from the Sun.
2. Uneven heating of air over land and water-bodies causes winds.
3. Evaporation of water from water-bodies and subsequent condensation give us rain.
4. Rainfall patterns depend on the prevailing wind patterns in an area.
5. Various nutrients are used again and again in a cyclic fashion. This leads to a certain balance between the various components of the biosphere.
6. Pollution of air, water and soil affect the quality of life and harm the biodiversity.
7. We need to conserve our natural resources and use them in a sustainable manner.

Improvement in Food Resources

The students will be able to understand

1. There are thirteen nutrients essential for crops. Of these, six are required in large quantities and are known as macronutrients whereas seven nutrients are required in small quantities and are known as micro-nutrients.
2. Manure and fertilizers are the main sources of nutrient supply to crop Organic farming
3. It is a farming system with minimal or no use of chemicals as fertilizers, herbicides, pesticides etc.
4. And with a maximum input of organic manures, recycled farm wastes, and bio-agents, with healthy cropping systems.
5. Mixed farming is a system of farming on a particular farm which includes crop production, raising of livestock etc.
6. Mixed cropping is growing of two or more crops simultaneously on the same piece of land.
7. Growing two or more crops in definite row patterns is known as inter-cropping.
8. The growing of different crops on a piece of land in pre-planned succession is called crop rotation.
9. Varietal improvement is required for higher yield, good quality, biotic and abiotic resistance, shortening the maturity duration, wider adaptability and desirable agronomic characteristics.
10. Farm animals require proper care and management such as shelter, feeding, breeding and disease control. This is called animal husbandry.
11. Poultry farming is done to raise domestic fowls. Poultry production includes egg production and broiler production for poultry meat.
12. To enhance poultry production, cross breeding is done between Indian and exotic breeds for variety improvement.

13. Fish may be obtained from marine resources as well as inland resources.
14. To increase production of fish, they can be cultured in marine and inland ecosystems.
15. Marine fish capture is done by fishing nets guided by echo sounders and satellites.
16. Composite fish culture system is commonly used for fish farming.
17. Bee-keeping is done to get honey and wax.

3.3.5 Criterion Reference Test:

The criterion reference tests are designed to ascertain the effectiveness of a Facebook page by measuring the learner's performance on clearly defined educational tasks. For the present study, fifteen criterion tests were developed by the investigator on fifteen chapters of science. The criterion tests are effective as:

1. It helps to evaluate the instructional process
2. It provides feedback to the instructor so that modifications can be done.

The developed criterion tests consisted of objective type question. Objective types of questions are there, which include multiple choices type of items. Some reasoning and thinking based questions are included in the test. The 15 criterion tests are given in appendix. Some examples of each type of questions are presented below.

1) Multiple Choice items

Q. Which of the following is not an important factor for growth of plants?

A.Nutrient content of soil Distance of water body from the soil
Amount of humus present in the soil Depth of soil

Q. The husk of the isabgol seed with water produces relief from________.

A. Malaria B. Jaundice C.Flu Diarrhoea

2) Thinking Based type

Q. The weight of an object of mass 15 kg at the centre of the earth is _____.

A. 147 N B. 147 kg C. Zero D. 150 N

Q. If the distance between two bodies is doubled, the force of attraction F between them will be

A. 1/4 F B. 2 F C. 1/2 F D. F

3) Application Types:

Q. Ciliated epithelium is found in ______________.

A.tongue B.oesophagus C. trachea D. uterus

Q. Solute concentration is higher in the external solution -

A. Hypotonic B. Isotonic C. Hypertonic D. None of the above

3.3.6 Content Analysis:

The Facebook page was developed for IX class science subject. For the development of Facebook page, the content related to science of class IX syllabus followed by C.B.S.E New Delhi was analysed. The Content analysis of each chapter is given here under different caption.

Chapter-I -Matter in Our Surroundings

1. Matter :-definition, general concept, meaning
2. Classification Of Matter
    a. On the basis of the physical state matter.
    b. On the basis of chemical composition matter
3. Physical Nature Of Matter
4. Characteristics Of Particles Of Matter
    a. Particles Of Matter Have Space Between Them
5. States Of Matter-Properties of all three matter

a. Solid

b. Liquid

c. Gas

6. Matter Can Change Its State

7. Study the effect Of Change Of Temperature on matter

   a. Melting (Fusion)

   b. Boiling

8. Study the effect Of Change Of Pressure on matter

9. Evaporation- General concept and explain the factors affecting it, study how the Evaporation Causes Cooling

Chapter- II - IS MATTER AROUND US PURE

1. Classification of matter- On the basis of chemical composition,

   a. Pure substance- definition. Meaning.

   b. Mixture- definition, meaning

   c. Differences between pure substances and mixtures

2. Types Of Mixtures-

   a. homogeneous mixture- Study true solution and its properties

   b. Heterogeneous mixture- Study about suspension and colloidal solution and its properties. Understand the concept of Tyndall effect.

3. Solution

   a. Saturated

   b. Unsaturated

   c. Concentration of the solution

4. Separating the components of a mixture- Study the special techniques

   a. Evaporation

   b. Centrifugation

   c. Decantation (Using separating funnel)

   d. Sublimation

   e. Centrifugation

f. Chromatography

g. Distillation and fractional distillation

h. Separation of components of air

i. Purification of solids by crystallization

5. Types of pure substances

   a. Element- Definition , types and their properties

      I. Metal

      II. Non Metal

      III. metalloids

   b. Compound

   c. Difference between mixtures and compounds

Chapter-III ATOMS AND MOLECULES

1. Laws of chemical combination- Explain with the help of activity

   a. Law of conservation of mass

   b. Law of constant proportion or Law of definite proportion

2. Dalton's atomic theory—Study the theory and its limitations

3. Atom- Meaning and concept

4. Symbols of atoms of different elements- Study the rules for assigning symbols for atoms of various elements, Given examples of atomic masses of some elements

5. Atomic mass unit

6. Relative atomic mass

7. Molecule- Study the Molecules Of Elements

8. Classification of matter

   a. Monoatomic molecules

   b. Diatomic molecules

   c. Triatomic molecules

   d. Tetra atomic molecules

9. Molecules Of Compounds- Study about ions and valency

   a. Chemical Formulae

   b. Molecular mass / Formula unit mass

10. Mole-Definition and explain with example

Chapter- IV - STRUCTURE OF THE ATOM.

1. Introduction Study -the existence of different kinds of matter is due to different atoms
2. Charged particles in matter- three types of sub atomic particles
    a. Electrons
    b. Protons
    c. Neutrons
3. Discovery of sub atomic particles
4. Structure of an atom
    a. Thomson's model of an atom
    b. Rutherford's model of an atom- Explain the activity, Model, observations, conclusion and defects of model
    c. Bohr's model of an atom- Study the postulates about the model of an atom
5. Neutrons
6. Distribution of electrons in different shells
7. Valency
8. Atomic number and Mass number :
9. Difference between Isotopes and Isobar

Chapter- V - CELL: THE FUNDAMENTAL UNIT OF LIFE

1. Cell- Definition, meaning, characteristics, history of discovery of cells and cell theory
2. Structure Of Cell
3. Shape and Size of Cells
4. Detailed structure and function of
    a. Cell wall
    b. Plasma membrane
    c. Nucleus
    d. Cell organelles, their nature, structure and function
        I. Mitochondria
        II. Endoplasmic Reticulum
        III. Golgi Complex

   IV. Lysosome
   V. Ribosome
   VI. Plastids
   VII. Vacuoles
5. Difference between animal and plant cell

Chapter- VI TISSUES

1. Tissues- Definition, general concept, meaning
2. Types of tissue
   a. Plant tissue
   b. Animal tissue
3. Plant tissue- Types of plant tissue
   a. Meristematic tissue –Nature, occurrence , character features and its types
      I. Apical
      II. Lateral
      III. Intercalary
   b. Permanent tissues- general concept , Structure , functions and its type
      I. Simple permanent tissues
         - Parenchyma
         - Collenchyma
         - Sclerenchyma
      II. Complex permanent tissues
         - Xylem
         - Phloem
      III. Protective tissue
         - Epidermis
         - Cork
4. Structure and functions of stomata
5. Difference between xylem and phloem
6. Study of Animal tissue- Nature, occurrence, structure and functions. And its type

a. Epithelial tissues-Study the structure, occurrence and functions

   I. Types of epithelial tissues

      - Squamous
      - Columnar
      - Cuboidal
      - Glandular

b. Muscular tissue- Study the structure, occurrence and functions

   I. Types of muscular tissues

      - Striated
      - Unstriated
      - Cardiac

c. Connective tissues- Study the structure, occurrence and functions

   I. Types of Connective tissues

      - Blood
      - Bone
      - Ligaments
      - Tendons
      - Cartilage
      - Areolar
      - Adipose

d. Nervous tissue- Study the nature, structure, occurrence and functions

Chapter- VII - DIVERSITY IN LIVING ORGANISMS

1. Classification of living organisms- General concept, definition and its need
2. Basis of classification of living organisms- Study the main characteristics
3. Classification and evolution
4. Nomenclature- Binomial nomenclature

5. The hierarchy of classification – Groups-Taxonomy, classified into five main kingdoms

   a. Monera
   b. Protista
   c. Fungi
   d. Plantae- -General concept and study its classification, structure and their characteristics
      I. Thallophyta
      II. Bryophyta
      III. Pteridophyta
      IV. Gymnosperms
      V. Angiosperms
   e. Animalia-Classification of Animalia, structure and their characteristics
      I. Porifera
      II. Coelenterata
      III. Platyhelminthes
      IV. Nematoda
      V. Annelida
      VI. Arthropoda
      VII. Mollusca
      VIII. Echinodermata
      IX. Protochordata
      X. Vertebrata.- Study the five classes, structure and characteristics
         - Pisces
         - Amphibia
         - Reptilia
         - Aves
         - Mamalia.

Chapter- VIII – MOTION

1. Motion- General concept, definition ,meaning
2. Types of motion
   a. Translatory motion- Meaning and study its type and difference between them
      I. Rectilinear Motion
      II. Curvilinear Motion
   b. Rotatory motion
   c. Vibratory motion
3. Uniform motion
4. Non uniform motion
5. Speed- Study the definition, its formula and its unit
6. Average speed- Study the definition , its formula and its unit
7. Speed with direction-
   a. Velocity
   b. Average velocity
8. Acceleration- Definition, Formula and unit
   a. Uniform acceleration
   b. Non uniform acceleration
9. Derivation of Equation of Motion- Derive the formulas of and understand the graphs
   a. Distance – Time graphs
   b. Velocity – time graphs
10. Study and derive the Equation for velocity – time relation ($v = u + at$)
11. Study and derive the Equation for position – time relation ($s = ut + \frac{1}{2} at^2$)
12. Study and derive the Equation for position – velocity relation ($2as = v^2 - u^2$)

Chapter- IX - FORCE AND LAWS OF MOTION

1. Force- Definition, general concept, meaning , effect and study its type

a. Balanced

b. unbalanced forces

2. Force of friction

3. Galileo's experiment of motion of an object on an inclined plane

4. Newton's laws of motion

   a. Inertia-Definition, meaning and examples

   b. Inertia and Mass- study the relation between two

   c. Momentum of a body- Definition, formula and examples

   d. Newton's second law of motion- Application, Mathematical formulation and examples

   e. Newton's third law of motion- General concept, Application, Mathematical formulation and examples

5. Conservation of momentum- General concept, formula and examples

Chapter- - X – GRAVITATION

1. Gravitation- Definition ,general concept, meaning and examples

2. Centripetal force- Definition ,general concept, meaning and examples

3. Universal law of gravitation- General concept, derivation of formula, study the unit

   a. Importance Of The Universal Law Of Gravitation

4. Free fall- General concept, derivation of formula, study the unit and examples

5. Mass – Definition , unit

6. Weight- Formula and unit

7. Weight of an object on the moon

8. Thrust – Definition, examples

9. Pressure - Definition, examples and relation with thrust, unit

   a. Pressure in fluids (Liquids and gases)

   b. Buoyancy (Up thrust)- Definition and examples

10. Archimedes' principle- study the Uses
11. Study the Density and relative density, their units and formula

Chapter- XI - WORK AND ENERGY

1. Work- - Definition ,general concept, meaning, Formula, unit and examples
2. Study the Definition ,general concept, meaning, Formula, unit and examples of Energy
3. Types of Energy- Study their formula, unit and examples
   a. Kinetic energy
   b. Potential energy
4. Transformation of energy
5. Rate of doing work (Power) - Study the Definition, general concept, meaning, Formula, unit, examples and commercial unit of power.

Chapter- XII Sound

1. Sound- General concept, meaning
2. Study the Production of sound with the help of examples
3. Study the Propagation of sound-with the help of examples
4. Wave – Sound Wave- Definition, meaning, and general concept
5. Types of wave- -Study the definition with the help of examples
   a. Electromagnetic Wave
   b. Mechanical Wave
6. Study the types Of Wave - On The Basis Of Direction
   a. Transverse Wave- Definition , Examples
   b. Longitudinal Wave- Definition, examples
7. Study the concepts of
   a. Compression and Rarefaction
   b. Density, pressure and disturbance
8. Production of sound in laboratory
9. Study the Characteristics of sound wave with the help of graphical representation, formula and their unit

a. Wavelength

b. Amplitude

c. Time period

d. Frequency

e. Velocity (Speed) –Study the factors

I. Nature of the medium

II. Temperature

III. Humidity present in air

10. Study the Quality of Sound

11. Study the Tone and Note of sound

12. Study of Reflection of Sound

13. Use of Reflection of Sound

a. Loudspeaker

b. Megaphone

c. bulb horn

d. Stethoscope

e. Soundboard

14. Echo- Definition, Condition necessary for creation of echo

15. Multiple Echo- Uses of multiple reflection of sound

16. Study of Reverberations- -

17. Study the Range of Hearing or Audible Range

18. Infrasonic Sound or Infrasound- general concept and definition

19. Ultrasound or Ultrasonic Sound- General concept and its uses

20. Human Ear- Structure of human ear , functions and Working of Human Ear

Chapter- XIII WHY DO WE FALL ILL

1. Health and its failure- Study of conditions necessary for good health

a. Physical and social environment.

b. Economic conditions.

c. Social equality and harmony

2. Differences between Healthy and Disease free

3. Types of diseases
    a. Acute diseases- Period and its effect
    b. Chronic disease- Period and its effect
4. Study the Causes of diseases
5. Types of Diseases
    a. Infectious diseases (Communicable diseases)-
        I. Infectious agents- study the structure and its effects
            - Viruses
            - Bacteria
            - Fungi
            - Protozoans
            - Worms
        II. Means of spread of infectious diseases- Study the different means
            - through air
            - water
            - food
            - Vectors
            - physical contact
            - Sexual contact.
        III. Study the Principles of treatment
            - To reduce the effects of the disease
            - To kill the microbes
        IV. Study the Principles of prevention
            - General ways of prevention
            - Specific ways of prevention
    b. Non-infectious Disease

Chapter- XIV NATURAL RESOURCES

1. Study of the different Resources on the Earth
    a. Biosphere – General concept and meaning
    b. Air – General concept and meaning

I. Study of the Carbon Dioxide Fixation

II. Study of the role of the atmosphere in climate control

III. Study of the Movement Of Air: Winds

IV. Study the Air Pollution and its pollutant

2. Rain- General concept and meaning and process

3. Water: A Wonder Liquid—General concept

a. Study of the Importance of Water

b. Study of the Water Pollution, pollutants and its effect

4. Soil- General Concept, Factors that make soil.

a. The Sun

b. Water

c. Wind

d. Living organisms

5. Study of various Biogeochemical Cycles

a. The Water-Cycle

b. The Nitrogen-Cycle

c. The Carbon-Cycle

I. Study of The Greenhouse Effect

d. The Oxygen-Cycle

6. Study of Ozone Layer and its importance

Chapter- XV IMPROVEMENT IN FOOD RESOURCES

1. Study of Need for increasing food production

2. Different types of crops and their requirement

a. Kharif crops

b. Rabi crops

3. Study of Improvement in crop yield and activities

a. Crop variety improvement- Study the important factors

I. Higher yield

II. Biotic and abiotic

III. Change in maturity duration

IV. Wider adaptability

V. Desirable agronomic characters

b. Study of Crop production improvement and important factors

I. Nutrient management

- The macro nutrients:- nitrogen, phosphorus, potassium, calcium, magnesium and Sulphur
- The micro nutrients are: - iron, magnesium, boron, zinc, copper, molybdenum and chlorine.
- Study of Manure, Compost, Green manure, Fertilizers and its effect

II. Study of different ways of Irrigation

- Wells
- Canals
- Rivers
- Tanks
- check dams

III. Study of different kinds of Cropping management

- mixed cropping,
- inter-cropping
- crop rotation

c. Study of Crop protection management

4. Animal husbandry- Study of feeding, breeding and disease control

   a. Cattle farming

   b. sheep farming

   c. goat farming

   d. poultry farming

   e. fish farming.-Types of fish farming

      I. Marine fisheries

      II. Inland fisheries

   f. Study of Bee keeping and its requirement

3.4.0 Screenshots of Researcher Developed Facebook Page

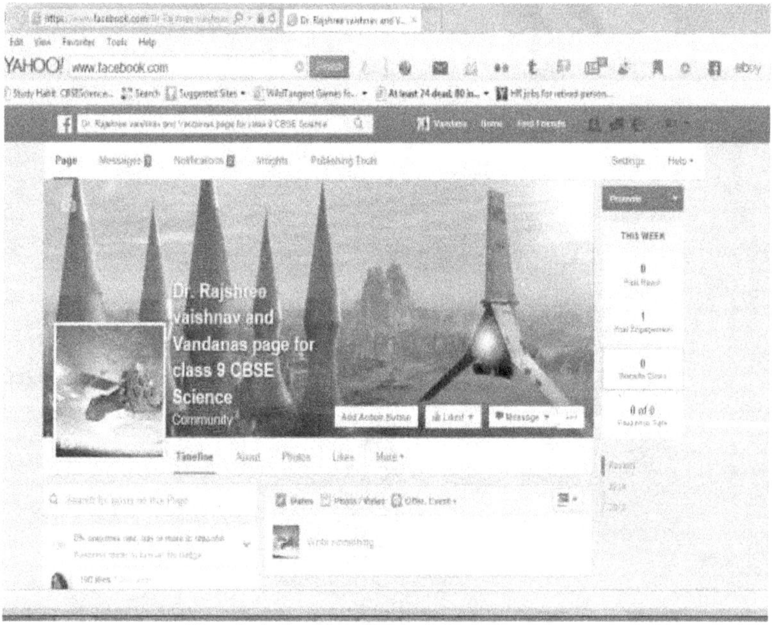

Fig. 3.1 Screenshot of Front page

Fig. 3.2 Screenshot of Content-1

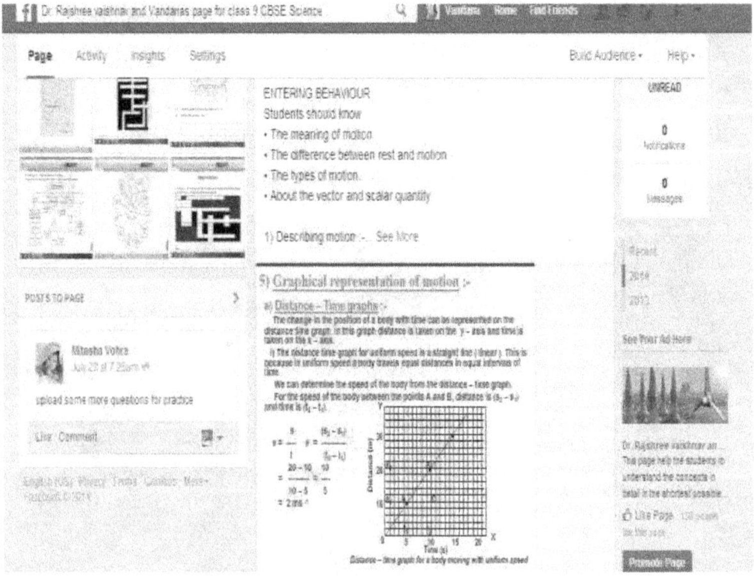

Fig. 3.3 Screenshot of Content-2

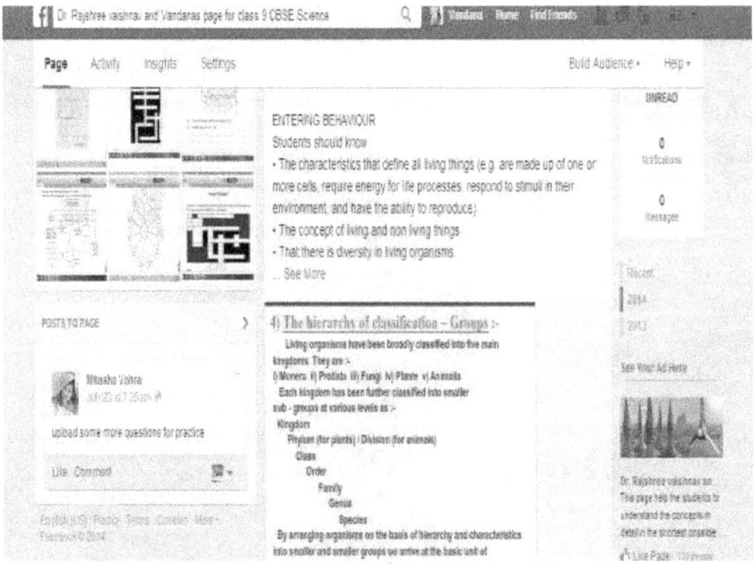

Fig. 3.4 Screenshot of Content-3

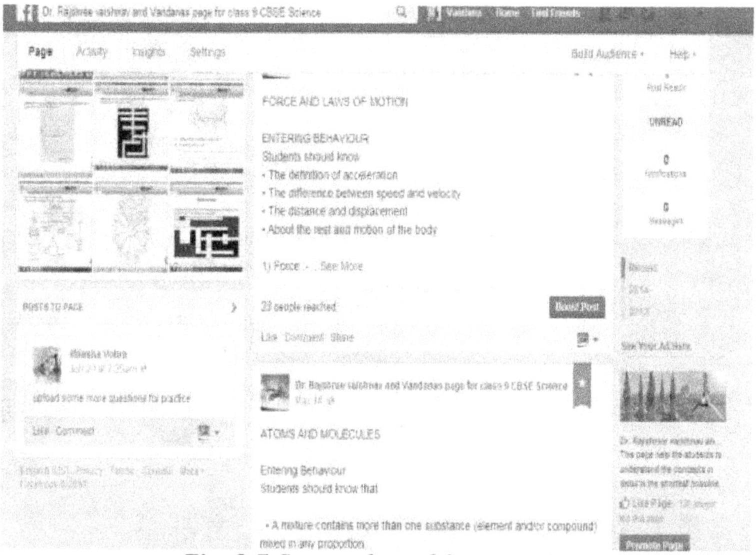

Fig. 3.5 Screenshot of Content-4

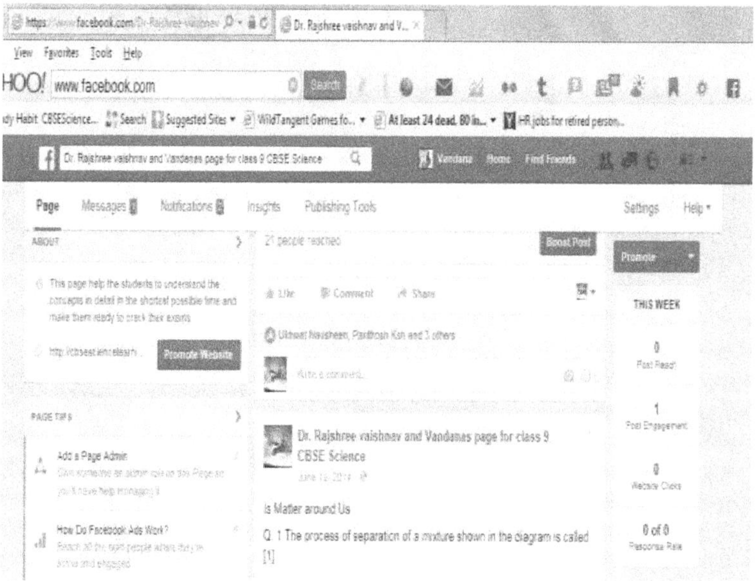

Fig. 3.6 Screenshot of Content-5

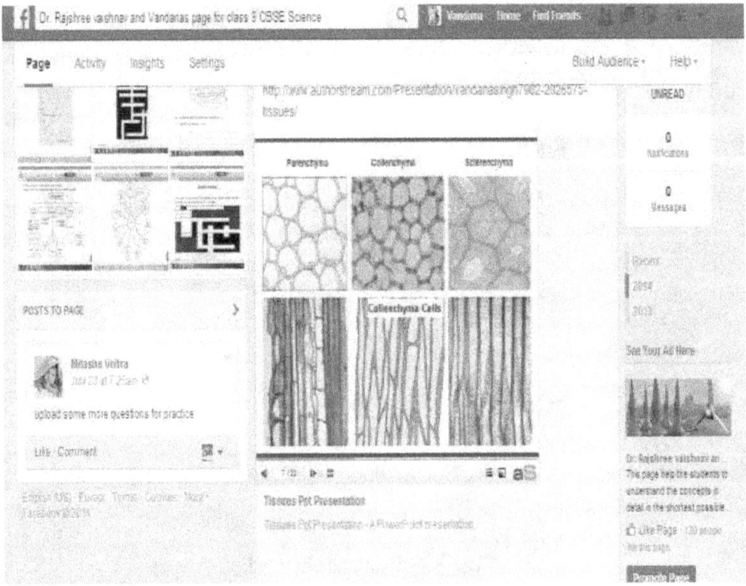

Fig. 3.7 Screenshot of ppt-1

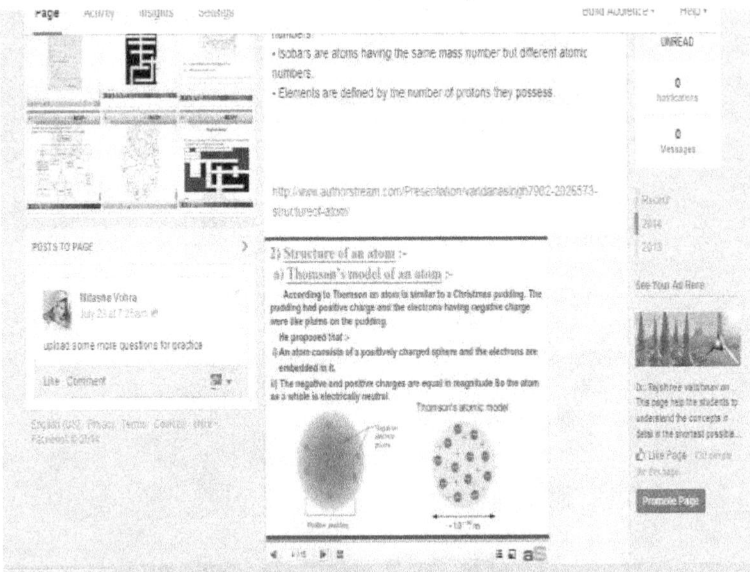

Fig. 3.8 Screenshot of ppt-2

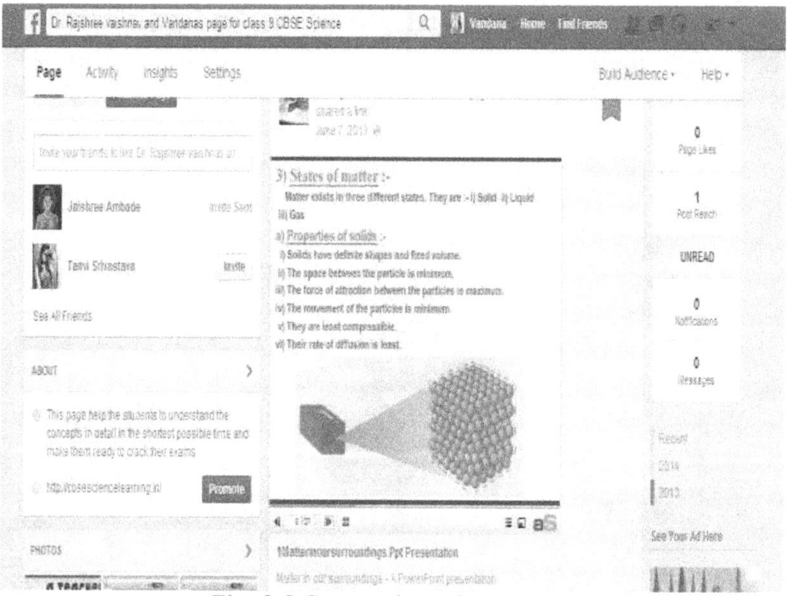

Fig. 3.9 Screenshot of ppt-3

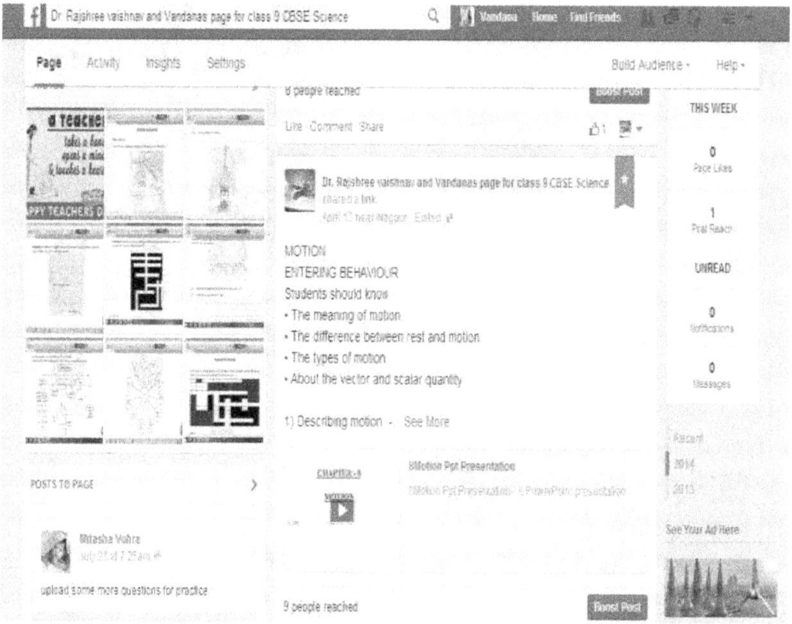

Fig. 3.10 Screenshot of ppt-4

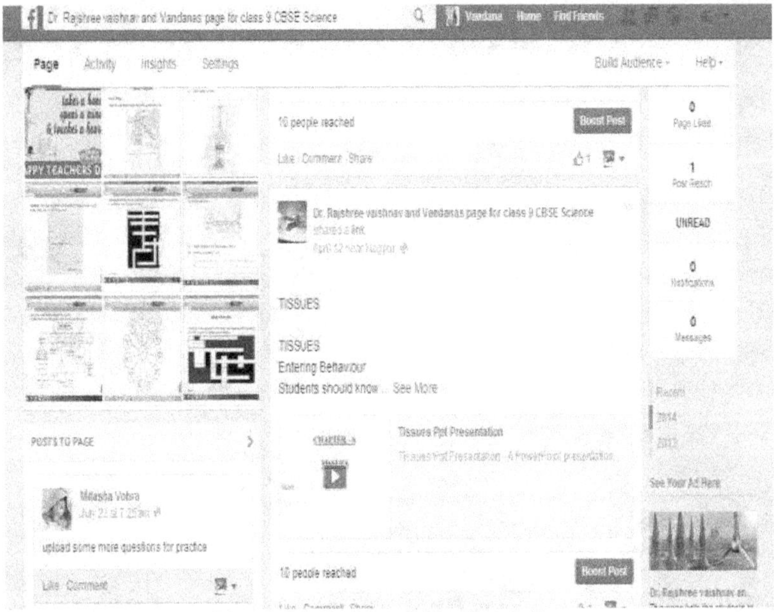

Fig. 3.11 Screenshot of ppt-5

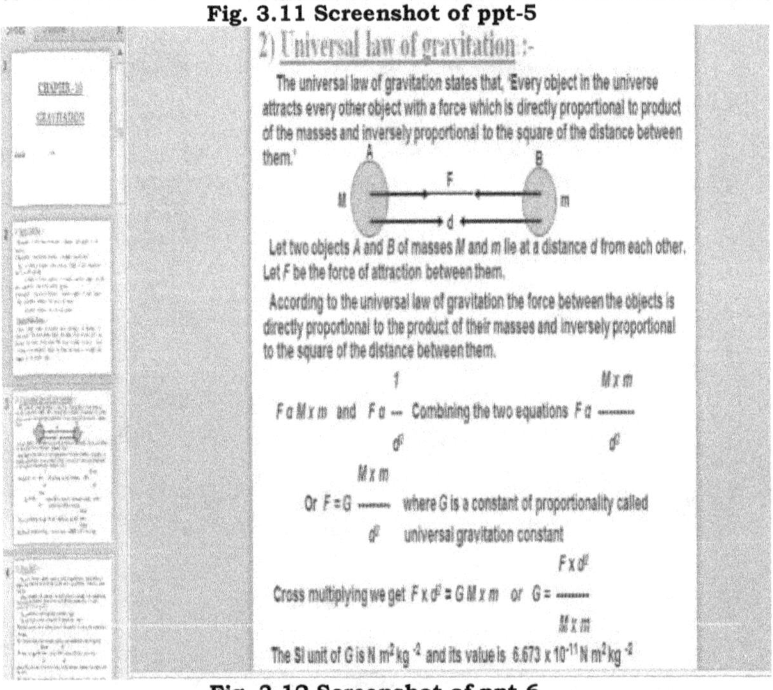

Fig. 3.12 Screenshot of ppt-6

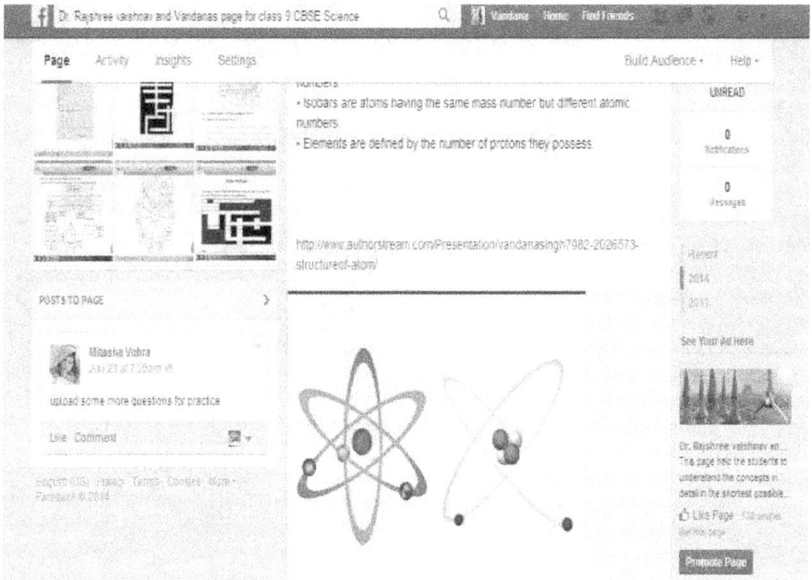

Fig. 3.13 Screenshot of ppt-7

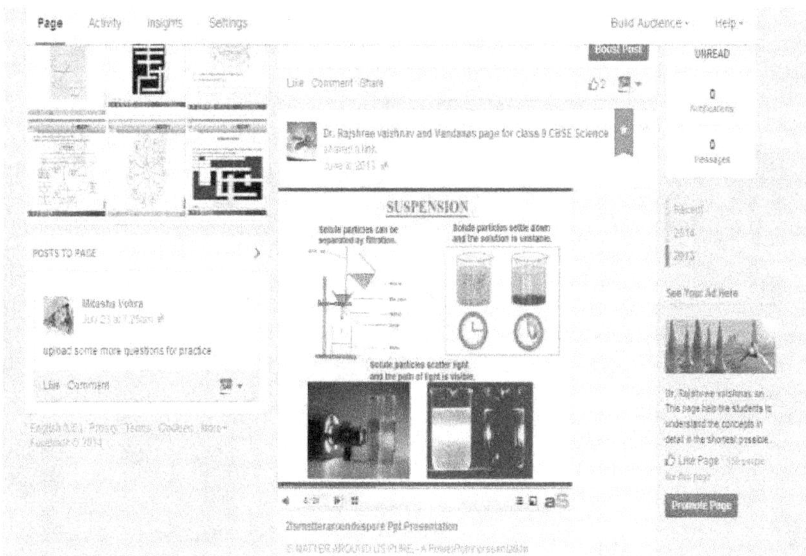

Fig. 3.14 Screenshot of ppt-8

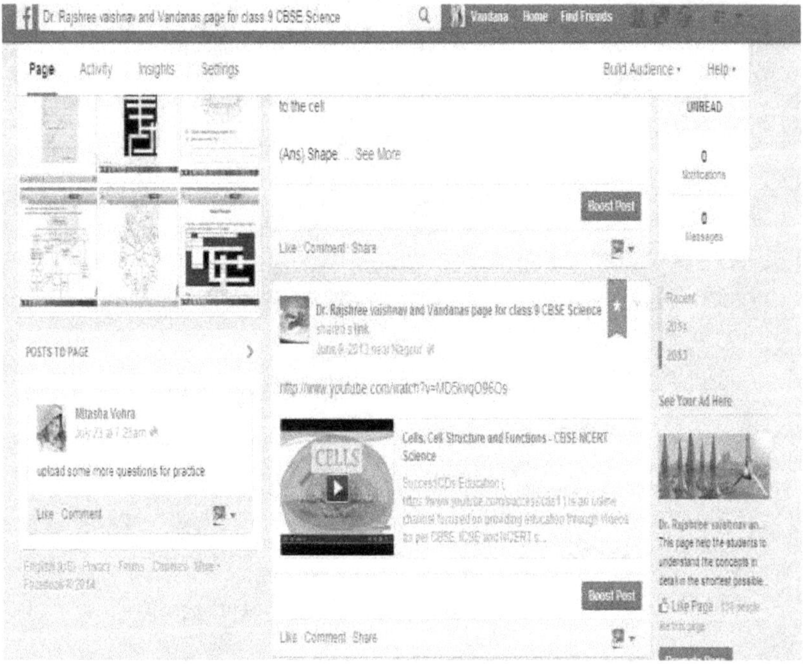

Fig. 3.15 Screenshot of Video-1

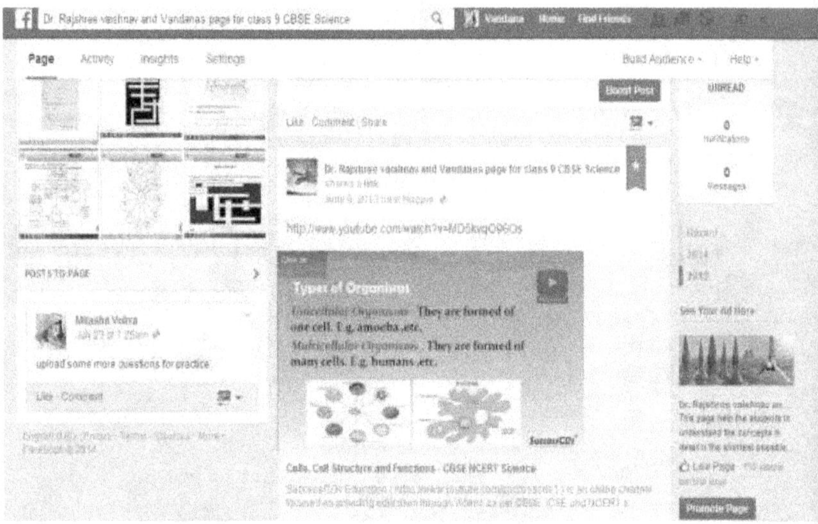

Fig. 3.16 Screenshot of Video-2

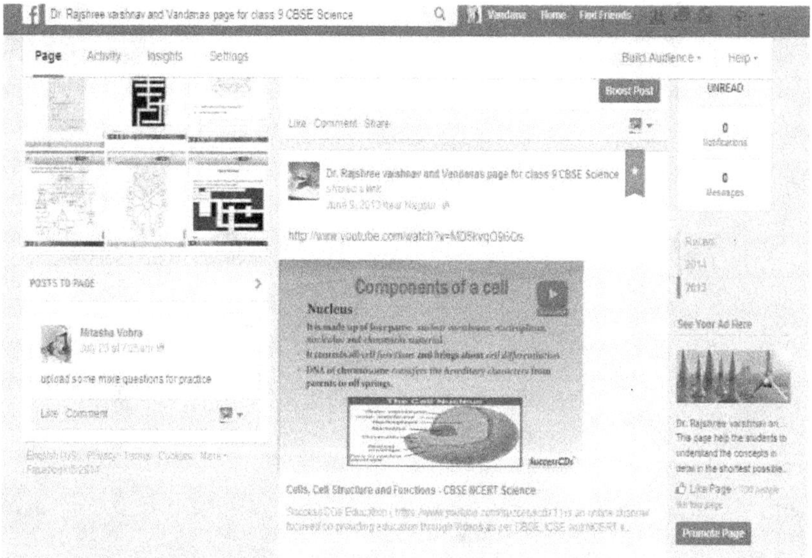

Fig. 3.17 Screenshot of Video-3

Fig. 3.18 Screenshot of Video-4

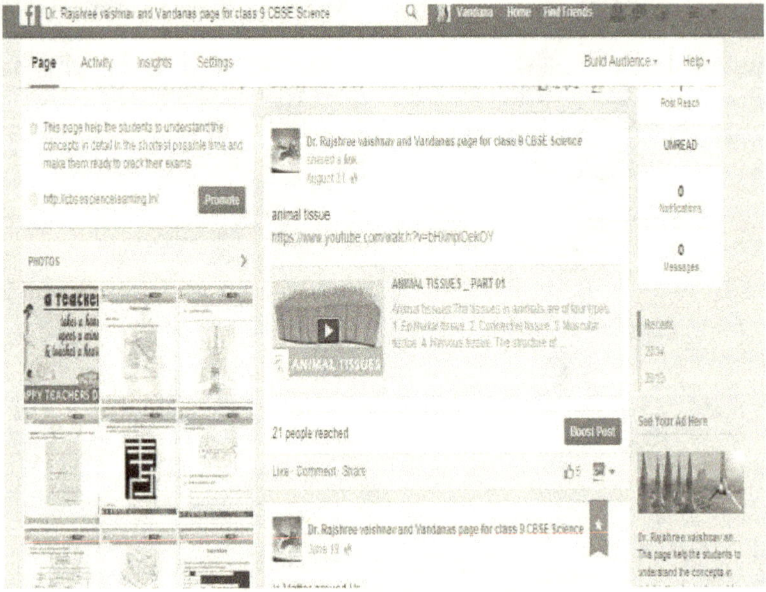

Fig. 3.19 Screenshot of Video-5

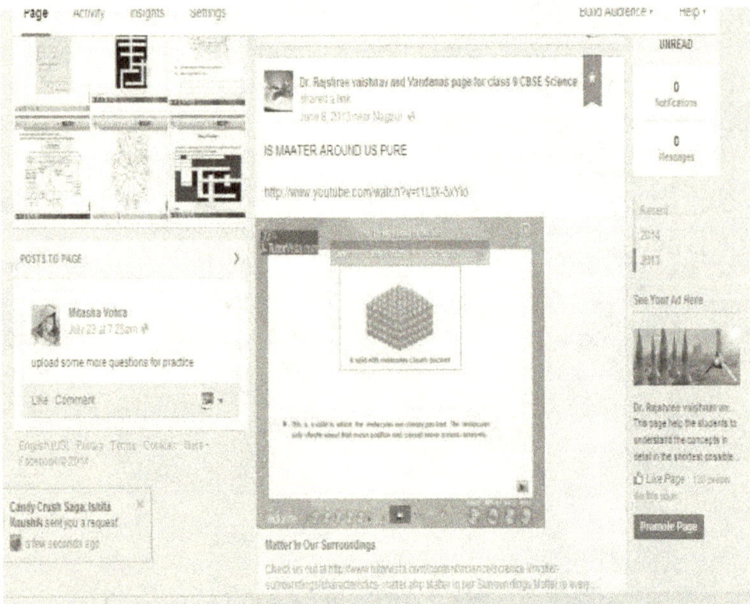

Fig. 3.20 Screenshot of Video-6

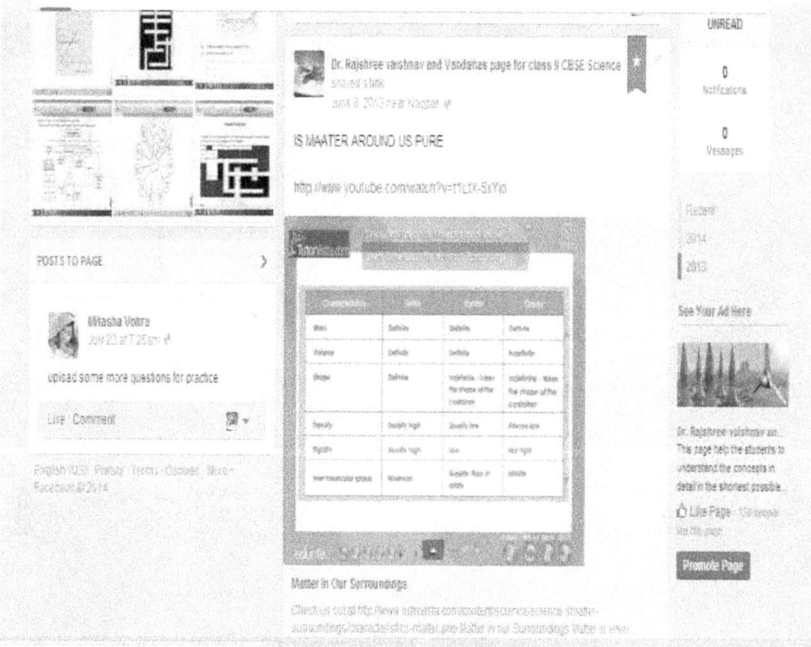

Fig. 3.21 Screenshot of Video-7

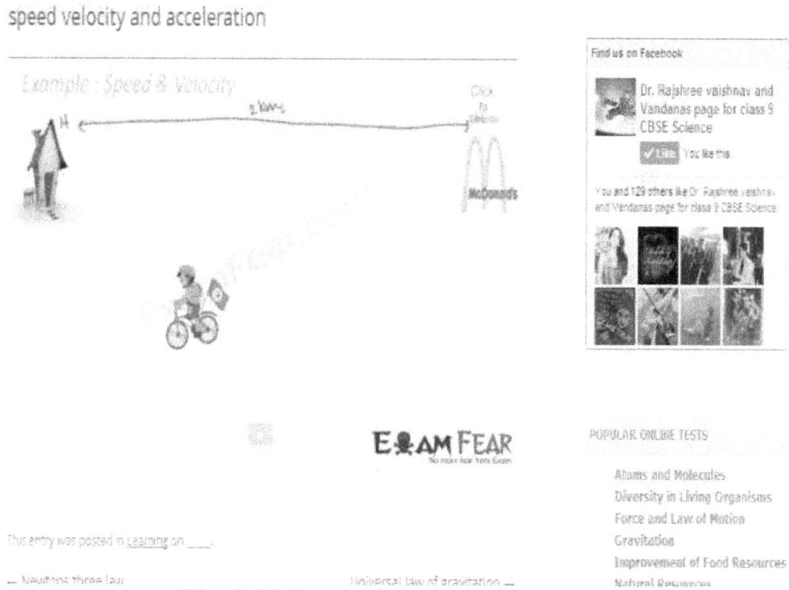

Fig. 3.22 Screenshot of Video-8

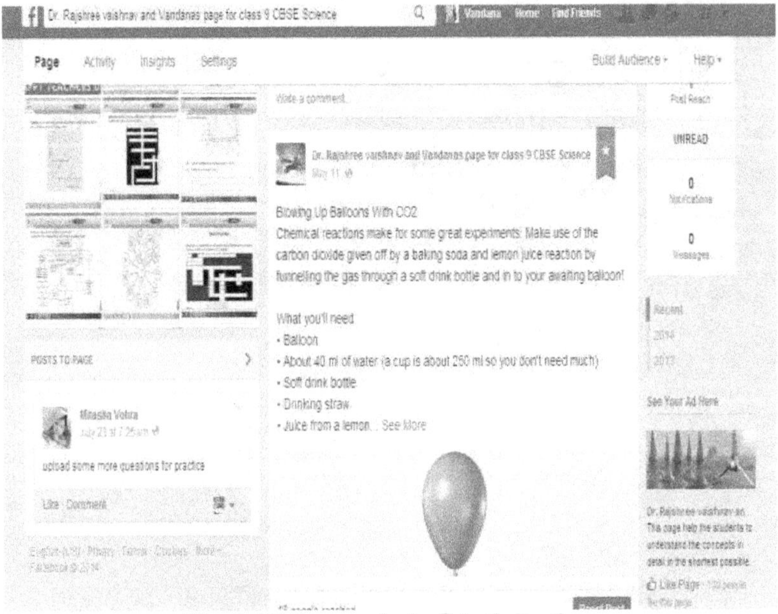

Fig. 3.23 Screenshot of Activity-1

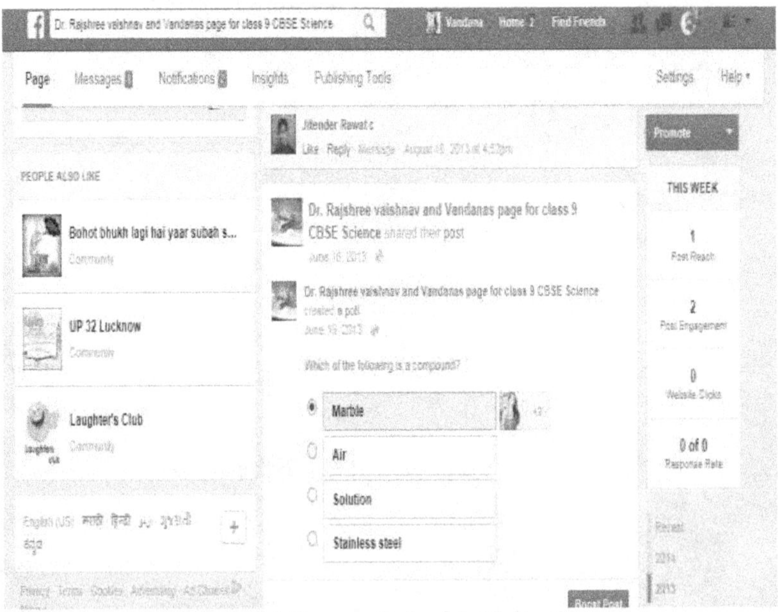

Fig. 3.24 Screenshot of Activity-2

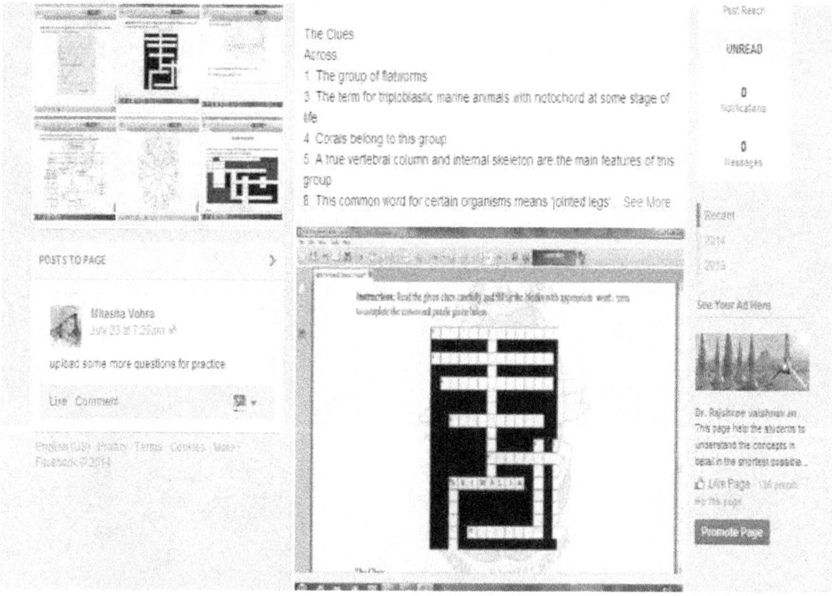

Fig. 3.25 Screenshot of Crosswords-1

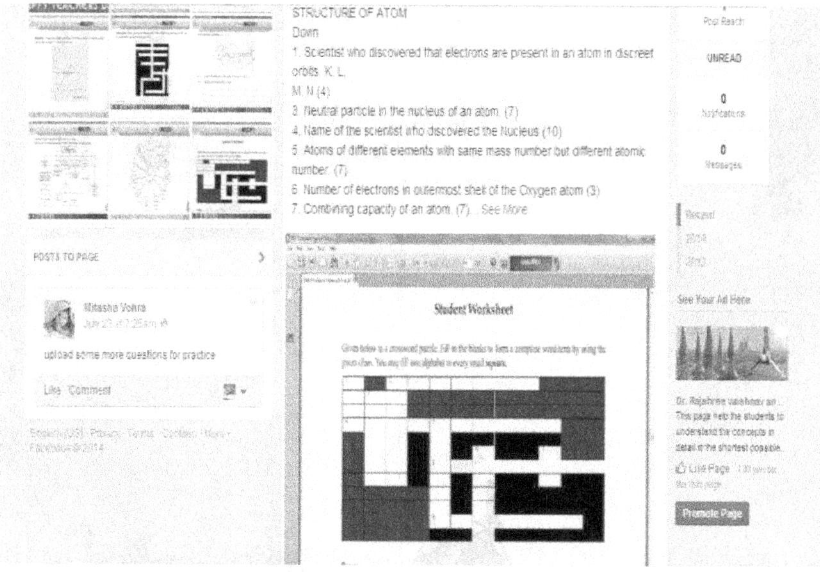

Fig. 3.26 Screenshot of Crosswords-2

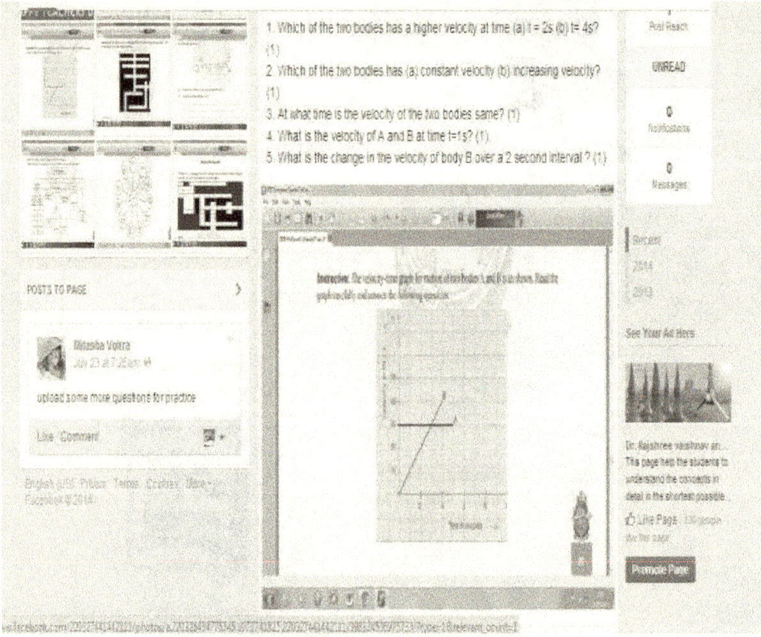

Fig. 3.27 Screenshot of Worksheet-1

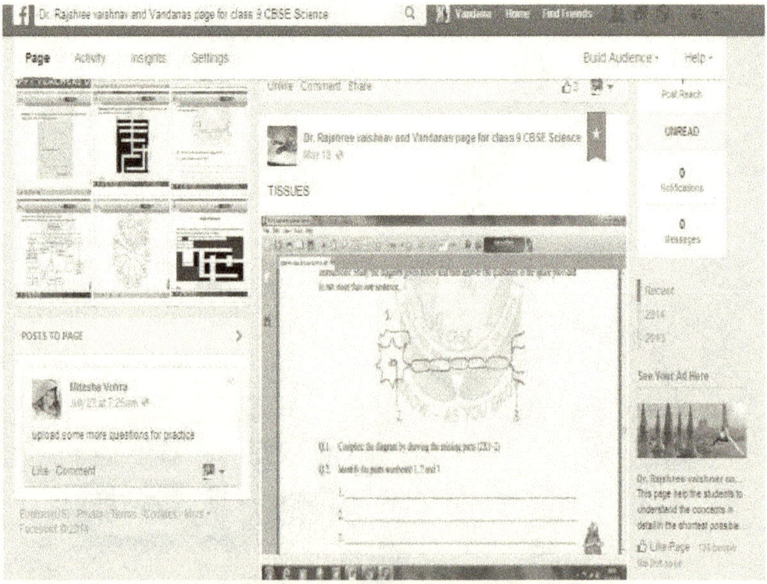

Fig. 3.28 Screenshot of Worksheet-2

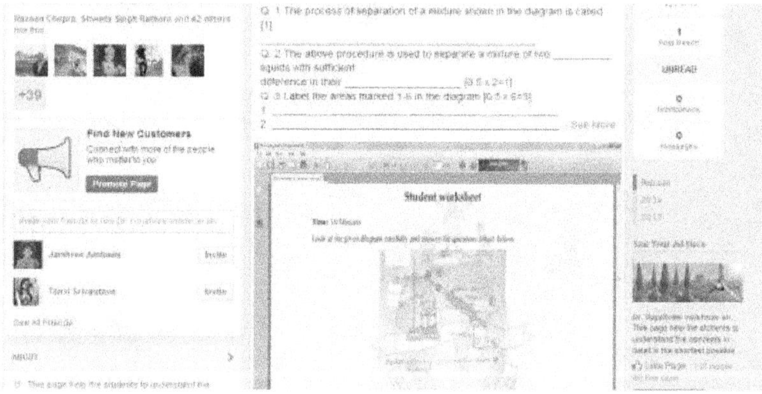

Fig. 3.29 Screenshot of Worksheet-3

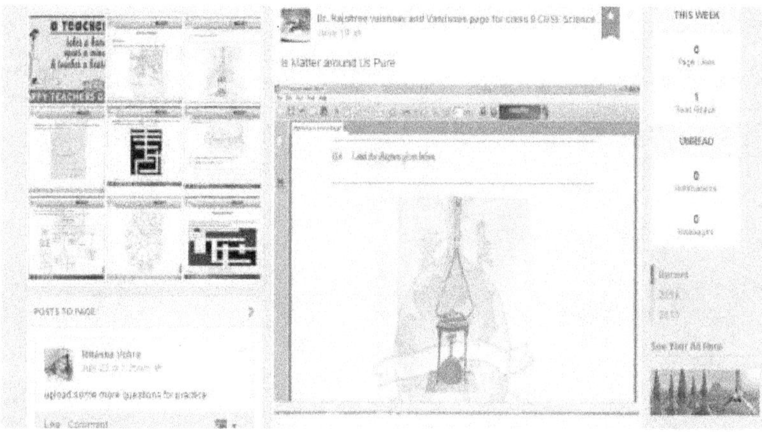

Fig. 3.30 Screenshot of Worksheet-4

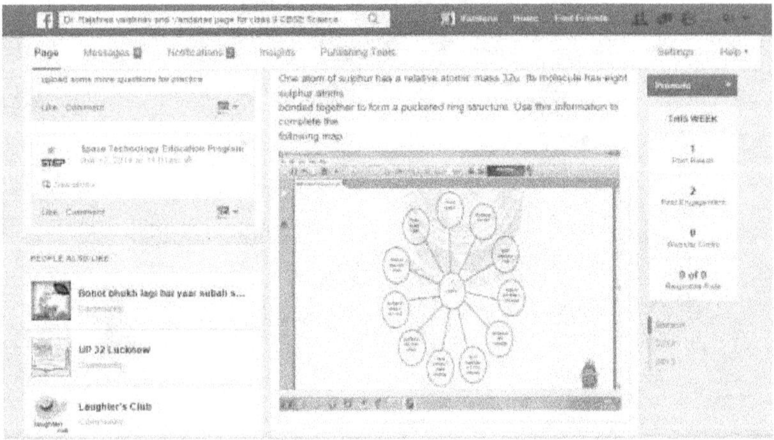

Fig. 3.31 Screenshot of Worksheet-5

Matter In Our Surroundings

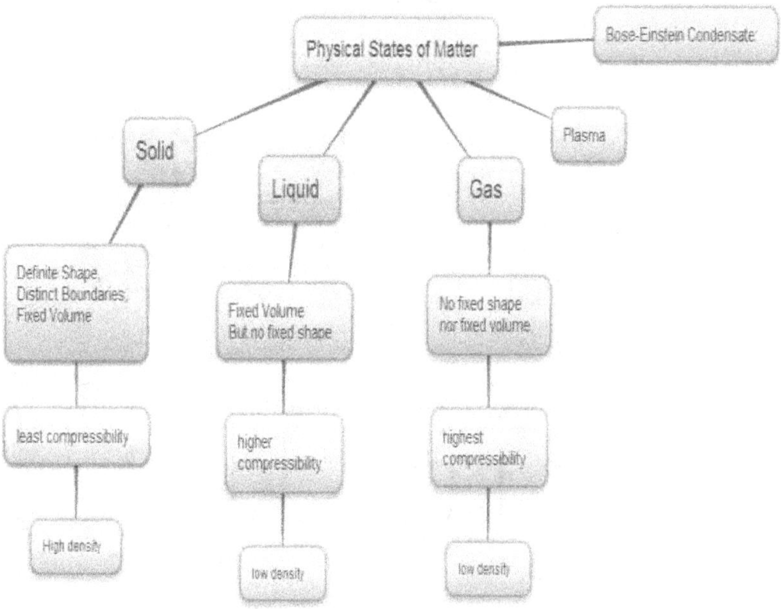

Flow chart 3.2 Physical States of Matter

Is Matter Around Us Pure

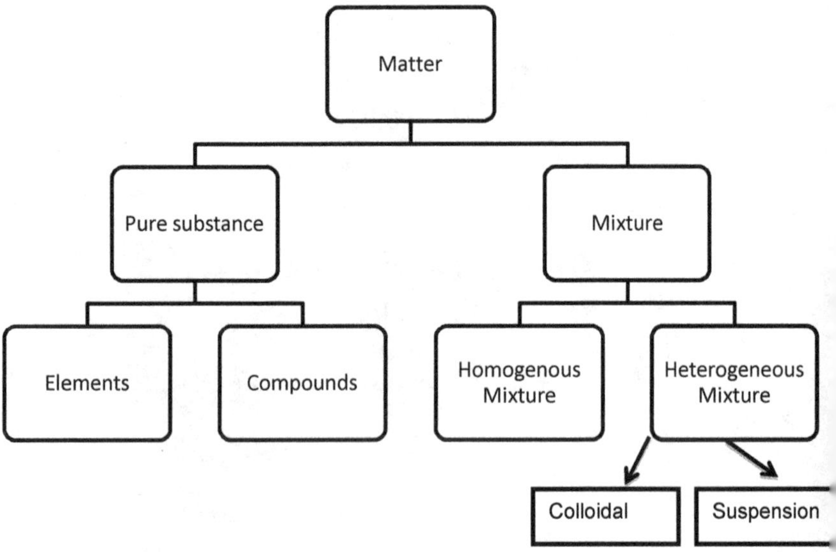

Flowchart 3.3 Classification of Matter

Structure of atoms

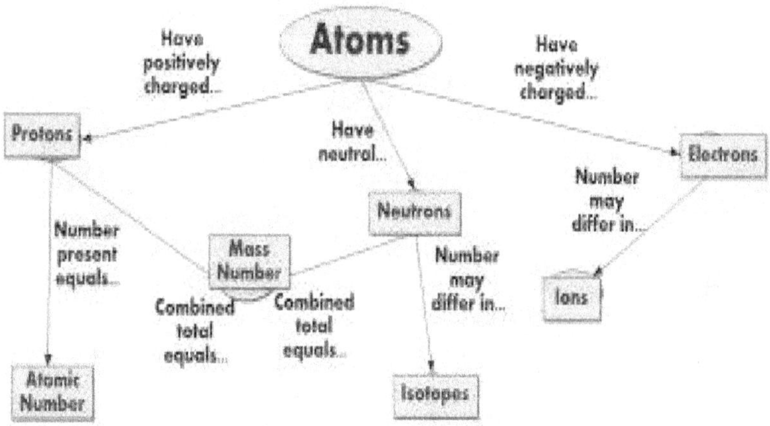

Flowchart 3.4 Atoms

Diversity in living organisms

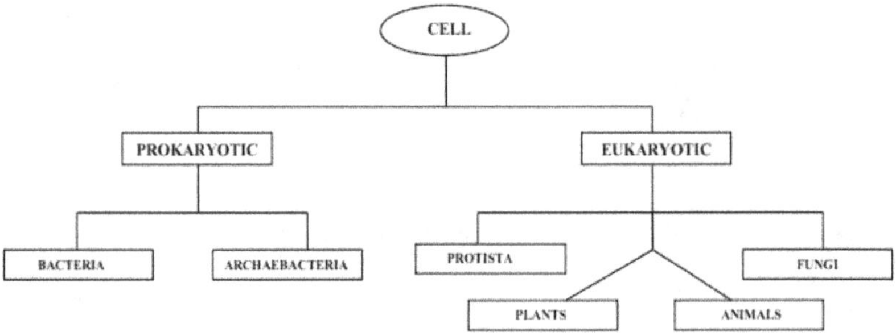

Flowchart 3.5 Division of Cell

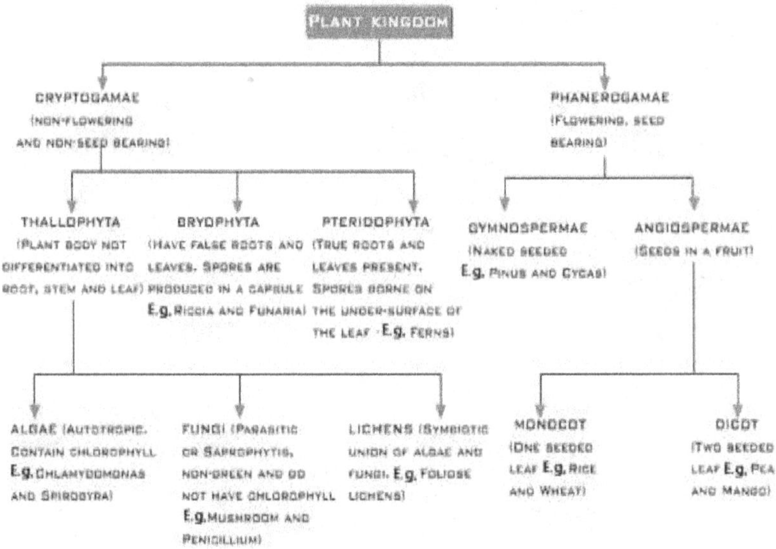

Flowchart 3.6 Classification of plant kingdom

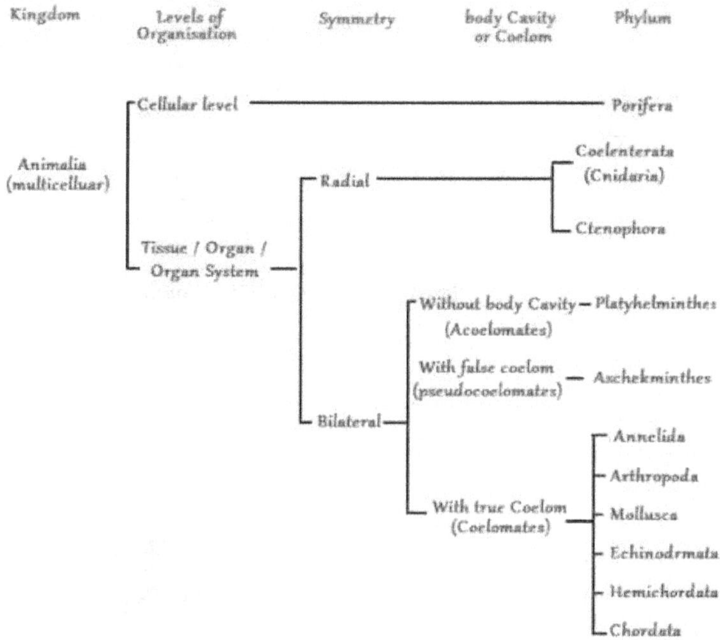

Flowchart 3.7 Classification of Animalia

Tissues

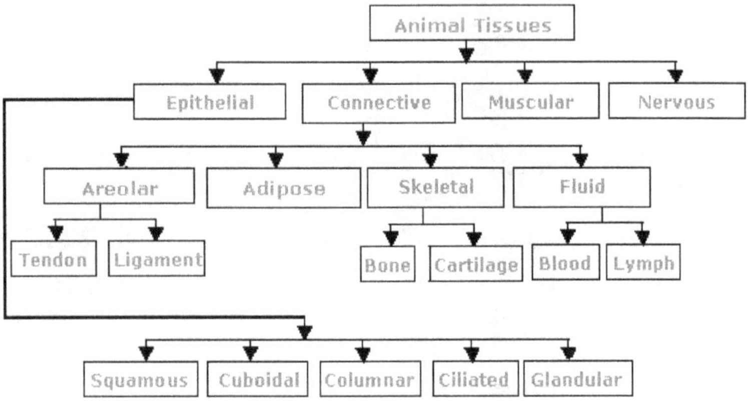

Flowchart 3.8 Animal tissues

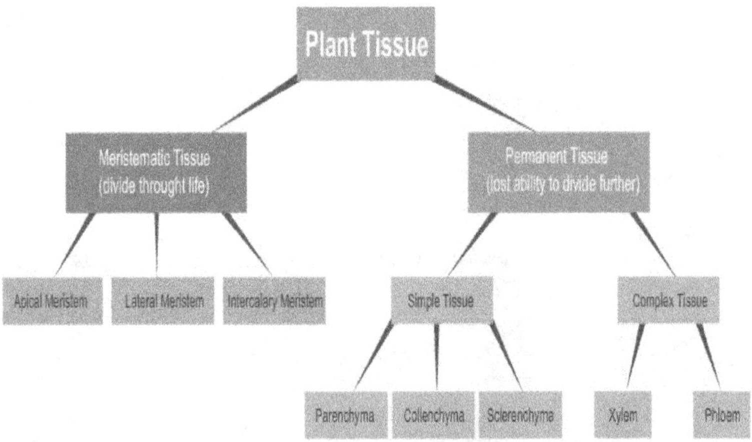

Flowchart 3.9 Plant tissue

CHAPTER- IV
METHODOLOGY

4.0.0. Introduction

The present chapter deals with the details related to sample, design tools procedure of data collection and statistical analysis used for analysing the data.

4.1.0 Sample

In the present study entitled "Effectiveness of social networking site Facebook for teaching science"- A study belongs to the area of educational technology. Facebook was developed for teaching science to class IX C.B.S.E students of Nagpur city (Maharashtra).

The whole syllabus prescribed by C.B.S.E in 2006 for class IX was taken for development of online Facebook page. The study has been conducted in two stages.

In stage one, the empirical validity of the material was established. For this pilot study was conducted on 25 students of class IX C.B.S.E were selected. In the stage two for final study another group of students were selected in this way two samples were used for the study.

4.1.1 Sample for pilot study

Purposive sampling technique was employed to select the sample for pilot study. The sample comprised of 25 students of class IX of Wonderland High School, Nagpur city (Maharashtra). Out of 25 students, 15 were male and 10 were female. The age of the students ranged from 13-15 years. The medium of instruction was English. The school is affiliated to Central Board of Secondary Education, New Delhi.

4.1.2 Sample for Final Study

For the final study, the two school of Nagpur city (Maharashtra) were selected namely Kendriya Vidyalaya Ambazari Nagpur and Kendriya Vidyalaya Vayusena Nagpur.

These schools were selected purposively. These schools were following the C.B.S.E syllabus and they have uniform pattern of curriculum. In Kendriya Vidyalaya Ambazari Nagpur 5 sections of IX class was there. Section A, B and C was selected randomly. From three sections 100 students had taken part in the study Kendriya Vidyalaya Vayusena Nagpur, 4 sections are there, three sections were selected randomly, section A, B and C 100 students of this part in the study.

Thus the sample size for the final study was 200 students, studying in IX class C.B.S.E syllabus. The age of students were ranging from 13 to 15 years.

Both the schools are co-educational Senior Secondary institution affiliated to the Central Board of Secondary Education (C.B.S.E) New Delhi. The medium of instructions in both the schools was English. The students were able to read and write both Hindi and English.

All the schools follow the same pattern having common examination system for IX Class annual examination.

Sampling details are given in able No: - 4.1

Table No. 4.1: Details of Sample

Stage	**Name of School**	**No. of sudents**			**Age Range**	**Group**
		Male	**Female**	**Total**		
Pilot Study	Wonderland High school Nagpur	15	10	25	13-15	Try-out
Final Study	Kendriya Vidyalaya Vayusena	53	47	100	13-15	Experimental
Final Study	Kendriya Vidyalaya Ambazari	53	47	100	13-15	Control

4.2.0 Design of the Study

The present study was experimental in nature. The sample consists of 200 Students divided into two groups, namely the Experimental Group and the Control Group.

The Experimental Group was taught through developed Facebook page along with the regular classroom teaching by their teacher followed by discussion and problem solving and online test .In addition to this, web-based Facebook page was easily accessible to the students so that they can use Facebook at anytime, anywhere whenever they were free.

The Control Group was taught through conventional method by their subject only.

In the present study the dependent variables were achievement, reaction of the students towards Facebook. The independent variables were the Facebook and Sex. The intelligence, study habit was taken as co-variate.

This is the fact that they learned according to their own pace. Similarly they were gone through additional activities like online test, discussion and problem solving session whereas the time taken by control group was according to the time schedule allotted and taken by the subject teacher.

The experimental design employed in this study was pre-test, post-test control group design. The dependent variables are Achievement, Reaction towards Facebook. The two groups were matched with respect to intelligence and study habit with the help of statistical technique namely analysis of co-variance.

The independent variables were the treatment and sex. The whole activity performed by different groups throughout the experimentation is presented in Table no. 4.3. The table reveals all the information about types of treatment, sequence of activity along with variables used.

Table No. 4.2: Activities Performed by Both the Groups at Final Stage

Chapters/ Topic	Activity	Experimental Group	Control Group	Types of Variable
Chapter-I Matter in our surroundings	CRT I (Pre)	Online test on www.cbsesciencelearning.in	Paper Pencil	Dependent
	Instructional Material	Studying through Facebook + Conventional	Conventional Method	Independent
	CRT I (Post)	Online test on www.cbsesiencelearning.in	Paper Pencil	Dependent
Chapter-II Is Matter around us pure	CRT I (Pre)	Online test on www.cbsesciencelearning.in	Paper Pencil	Dependent
	Instructional Material	Studying through Facebook + Conventional	Conventional Method	Independent
	CRT I (Post)	Online test on www.cbsesiencelearning.in	Paper Pencil	Dependent
Chapter-III Atoms and Molecules	CRT III (Pre)	Online test on www.cbsesciencelearning.in	Paper Pencil	Dependent
	Instructional Material	Studying through Facebook + Conventional	Conventional Method	Independent
	CRT III (Post)	Online test on www.cbsesiencelearning.in	Paper Pencil	Dependent
Chapter-IV Structure of the Atom	CRT IV (Pre)	Online test on www.cbsesciencelearning.in	Paper Pencil	Dependent
	Instructional Material	Studying through Facebook + Conventional	Conventional Method	Independent
	CRT IV (Post)	Online test on www.cbsesiencelearning.in	Paper Pencil	Dependent
Chapter-V The Fundamental unit of life	CRT V (Pre)	Online test on www.cbsesciencelearning.in	Paper Pencil	Dependent
	Instructional Material	Studying through Facebook + Conventional	Conventional Method	Independent
	CRT V (Post)	Online test on www.cbsesiencelearning.in	Paper Pencil	Dependent
Chapter-VI Tissues	CRT VI (Pre)	Online test on www.cbsesciencelearning.in	Paper Pencil	Dependent
	Instructional	Studying through Facebook	Conventional	Independent

Chapters/ Topic	Activity	Experimental Group	Control Group	Types of Variable
	Material	+ Conventional	Method	
	CRT VI (Post)	Online test on www.cbsesiencelearning.in	Paper Pencil	Dependent
Chapter-VII Diversity in Living Organism	CRT VII (Pre)	Online test on www.cbsesciencelearning.in	Paper Pencil	Dependent
	Instructional Material	Studying through Facebook + Conventional	Conventional Method	Independent
	CRT VII (Post)	Online test on www.cbsesiencelearning.in	Paper Pencil	Dependent
Chapter-VIII Motion	CRT VIII (Pre)	Online test on www.cbsesciencelearning.in	Paper Pencil	Dependent
	Instructional Material	Studying through Facebook + Conventional	Conventional Method	Independent
	CRT VIII (Post)	Online test on www.cbsesiencelearning.in	Paper Pencil	Dependent
Chapter-IX Force and Laws of Motion	CRT IX (Pre)	Online test on www.cbsesciencelearning.in	Paper Pencil	Dependent
	Instructional Material	Studying through Facebook + Conventional	Conventional Method	Independent
	CRT IX (Post)	Online test on www.cbsesiencelearning.in	Paper Pencil	Dependent
Chapter-X Gravitation	CRT X (Pre)	Online test on www.cbsesciencelearning.in	Paper Pencil	Dependent
	Instructional Material	Studying through Facebook + Conventional	Conventional Method	Independent
	CRT X (Post)	Online test on www.cbsesiencelearning.in	Paper Pencil	Dependent
Chapter-XI Work and Energy	CRT XI (Pre)	Online test on www.cbsesciencelearning.in	Paper Pencil	Dependent
	Instructional Material	Studying through Facebook + Conventional	Conventional Method	Independent
	CRT XI (Post)	Online test on www.cbsesiencelearning.in	Paper Pencil	Dependent
Chapter-XII Sound	CRT XII (Pre)	Online test on www.cbsesciencelearning.in	Paper Pencil	Dependent

Chapters/ Topic	Activity	Experimental Group	Control Group	Types of Variable
	Instructional Material	Studying through Facebook + Conventional	Conventional Method	Independent
	CRT XII (Post)	Online test on www.cbsesiencelearning.in	Paper Pencil	Dependent
Chapter-XIII	CRT XIII (Pre)	Online test on www.cbsesciencelearning.in	Paper Pencil	Dependent
Why do we fall ill	Instructional Material	Studying through Facebook + Conventional	Conventional Method	Independent
	CRT XIII (Post)	Online test on www.cbsesiencelearning.in	Paper Pencil	Dependent
Chapter-XIV Natural Resources	CRT XIV (Pre)	Online test on www.cbsesciencelearning.in	Paper Pencil	Dependent
	Instructional Material	Studying through Facebook + Conventional	Conventional Method	Independent
	CRT XIV (Post)	Online test on www.cbsesiencelearning.in	Paper Pencil	Dependent
Chapter-XV Improvement in food resources	CRT XV(Pre)	Online test on www.cbsesciencelearning.in	Paper Pencil	Dependent
	Instructional Material	Studying through Facebook + Conventional	Conventional Method	Independent
	CRT XV (Post)	Online test on www.cbsesiencelearning.in	Paper Pencil	Dependent
Intelligence test	Test Administration	Intelligence test	Intelligence test	Co-variate
Study Habit	Test Administration	Study Habit	Study Habit	Co-variate
Reaction Scale	Test Administration	Reaction	-----	Dependent

CRT: Criterion reference test

4.3.0 Tools

In the present study, the data were collected pertaining to the following variables namely, Achievement and Reaction of students towards developed Facebook page, Intelligence and Study Habit. The data with respect to intelligence, study habit were collected by administering standardized tests while the data related to achievement and reaction towards the developed Facebook page were collected with the help of tools developed by the investigator. The details of the tools used were given under the following caption.

4.3.1 Achievement

The content on Facebook page was developed for 15 chapters of Science. It covers the whole syllabus prescribed by C.B.S.E. for class IX in science subject. For testing the achievement of students, 15 criterion tests were prepared on all the 15 chapters of science C.B.S.E. syllabus of IX class. The tests mainly consist of multiple choice questions (MCQ) and fill in the blank type of questions. On the basis of the type of questions each criterion test was:

It is a computerized test consisting of multiple choice questions only and true/false. Total 15 items of one mark each are there. The total time allotted to complete the test was 20 minutes.

Thus, the total time allotted to each criterion test was 20 minutes and the total marks allotted for each test was 15 marks for 15 chapters.

The details regarding criterion reference test is already given in chapter III. The scoring was done by following scoring key. The marking scheme/ scoring key are available in Appendix I.

4.3.2 Reaction scale

A reaction scale developed by the investigator was used to collect the reactions of the students towards the developed Facebook page. The scale was developed on the lines of reaction scale developed by Dr. Rajshree S. Vaishnav (2005)

The five point reaction scale was developed on 4 aspects of developed Facebook page namely:

1. Instruction through Facebook
2. Presentation of Content
3. Technical facilities available
4. Evaluation and Feedback

There were 10 items in each aspect for knowing the reactions of the students. The total items in the reaction scale are 40. To avoid guessing some Statements were written in negative form and some in positive form.

1. Instruction through Facebook:

This aspect measured the reaction towards the factors like motivation, learning environment, time factors and suitability of computers in instructional process.

2. Presentation of the Content:

This aspect was mainly related with presentation style of Facebook page. The students reactions towards sequence and presentation of the content, language used, explanation of technical terms, relevant examples graphics used were measured.

3. Technical Facilities Available:

This aspect was mainly concerned with different technical facilities available in the Facebook page. It measured the reactions of students towards the use of different colour, inbuilt mechanism for shifting i.e. Menu choice, concrete presentation of abstract ideas, self-paced learning, time consumes and easily accessible of Facebook page.

4. Evaluation and Feedback:

This aspect measured the reactions towards types of questions, quality of explanation given for wrong answers, use or prompts for initiating correct responses, reasoning based questioning, evaluation facility, assignment and its verification facility, discussion sessions and additional reading references.

In the last, an opportunity was given to the student's face to face conversation with the investigator to express their frank opinion about the Facebook page.

The reaction scale is given in Appendix I

4.3.3 Intelligence

To measure intelligence, verbal intelligence test developed by Ojha and Ray Choudhary was used. Keeping in view the comprehensiveness, time required for completing, reliability of the test and age group, this test was selected.

This test is in Hindi consisted of 112 items, divided into 8 aspects. These aspects are:

1. Classification consists of 15 items, time limit- 3 minutes
2. Analogies consists of 15 items, time limit- 4 minutes
3. Synonyms consists of 20 items, time limit- 4 minutes
4. Number test having 12 items, time limit to complete is 5 minutes
5. Completion Test consists of 12 items, time limit- 5 minutes
6. Paragraph test having 10 items, time limit- 3 minutes
7. Best reason having 10 items, time limit- 4 minutes
8. Simple reason total item 17, time limit- 12 minutes

The total time limit for this test is 40 minutes. Due instructions are given in each subtest for time limit. Maximum score in this test is 112. This test is suitable for age group between 13 to 16 years.

The reliability of verbal intelligence test of Ojha and Ray Choudhary was 0.87 by split half method and 0.91 by Kuder-Richardson formula.

The validity of the test was measured by correlation of scores between all eight parts of the test, he correlation ranging from .574 to .310, thus the test was valid and reliable.

Therefore, in the present study intelligence was assessed by administering a verbal intelligence test developed by Ojha and Ray Choudhary (1958). The scoring of test was done with the help of scoring key provided by the author of test.

4.3.4 Study Habit

The study habit is a very important characteristic of all human beings who are being educated and are educated. Study habit is important for higher academic achievement of students. It has long reaching effects deep into the life of individual.

The study habit of both control and experimental group was measured by using study habit inventory developed by Prof. M. Mukhopadhya and Prof. D.N. Sanswal (1983).

The study habit inventory is divided into 9 different kinds of study behaviours.

Table No. 4.3: Sub- components of Study Habit Inventory

Sr. No.	Sub-Component	Weightage (%)	No. of items
1	Comprehension	28	13
2	Concentration	23	10
3	Task Orientation	18	9
4	Interaction	7	3
5	Drilling	7	3
6	Support	7	3
7	Recording	5	2
8	Language	5	2
9	Sets	---	7

The seven items are related with study sets in which no weightage is given. In all total 52 items are there, the maximum score for the inventory is 208.

The discrimination power of inventory was calculated for all the sub components having value 35.27 which is significant. The internal consistency was measured by coefficient of correlation for all the items ranging from .49 to .87 which is significant at .01 levels.

The reliability of whole inventory was measured by split half method. The reliability coefficient is .91 that indicates that inventory is highly reliable.

All the 52 items are categorised into positive and negative nature. Inventory having 5 point scale i.e. always, frequently, sometimes, rarely and never. Positive items have score value ranging from four for always to zero for never. Negative items were having score value from 0 to 4 i.e. zero for always and four for never. The items are self-explanatory and sufficient instructions are also given in it. Scoring was done with the help of scoring key provided by the author for all the nine sub component items. No time limit is given to answer the items.

4.4.0 Procedure of Data Collection

There were two groups in the study namely, Experimental Group and Control Group. The procedure of data collection for both the group is described here in detail under different captions.

4.4.1 Data Collection from Experimental Group

As stated above 100 students of Kendriya Vidyalaya Vayusena, Nagpur were assigned as experimental group. Before going to take them for experimentation, proper instructions and other details, related with computer and how to access to Facebook page were given by the researcher. All the students had the basic knowledge about computers as well as about login through link to Facebook online website.

Thereafter, the students of Kendriya Vidyalaya Vayusena, Nagpur as per their time and suitability gone through the textual based.

Facebook content along with their regular classroom teaching. Students were free to learn according to their own pace. They could read given information as many times as they wanted and were free to comment or ask queries on the given Facebook contents. The students were very active and were actively asked question through mails, comments, face to face discussion and feedback was taken.

After studying through Facebook as per their time and suitability, 3 days in a week, at least for 25-30 minutes were provided for interaction. During this session difficulties raised by the students regarding Facebook were discussed and solved.

After completion of a chapter, the same criterion test was administered as post- test for that chapter. In the same pattern all the 15 chapters of Science were taught to the students with developed web-based Facebook.

After completing of all chapters intelligent test was administered. After completing of all 15 chapters, intelligent test, study habit inventory and reaction scale was administered to the group. In this way the present study was lasted for months during April 2014 to February 2015.

4.4.2 Data Collection for Control Group

100 students of class IX of Kendriya Vidyalaya Ambazari, Nagpur were considered as control group for the study. The school followed the same CBSE syllabus as experimental group. This group did not receive any special treatment. First the criterion reference test for chapter 1st was administered through paper pencil. The whole chapter was taught by their subject teacher through conventional classroom method, after accomplishment of chapter the same criterion reference test was administered as post-test. In this manner all 15 chapters were completed following the same procedure.

In the last after completion of all chapters, intelligence test, study habit inventory administered to the control group.

4.5.0 Statistical Techniques used for Analysis

Objective wise statistical techniques used for analysis of the data are as follows

1. a) To study the effectiveness in terms of students of achievement on criterion tests, t-test was used between pre and post achievement score.

   b) To study the effectiveness in terms of student's reaction on each aspect of developed Facebook page, chi square for frequencies were computed.
2. To compare the mean overall achievement score of the students studying through Facebook along with conventional teaching method, with those studying through conventional method by taking intelligence as co-variate analysis of co-variance was used.
3. To compare the mean overall achievement score of the students studying through Facebook with those studying through conventional method by taking study habit as co-variate analysis of co-variance was used.
4. To compare the overall achievement of male student with female student studying through Facebook t-test was used.

CHAPTER-V
RESULTS AND DISCUSSION

5.0.0 Introduction

This chapter deals with objective wise results along with discussion. There were 4 objectives in the study. The results are presented here in different captions.

5.1.0 Effectiveness of Developed Facebook Material

The first objective of the present study was development of Facebook page for teaching science to the students of class IX C.B.S.E and to study its effectiveness in terms of student's achievement and reaction towards the developed Facebook page.

Facebook page was developed on 15 chapters of science. It covers the whole syllabus of class IX Science prescribed by C.B.S.E New Delhi in 2006. The effectiveness of Facebook page was studied in terms of:

1. Students achievement on criterion tests.
2. Students reaction towards the Facebook

To study the effectiveness of Facebook material in terms of achievement, data were collected by administering the criterion tests prepared for 15 chapters of Science and to obtain the reaction of the students, a reaction scale prepared by investigator was administered to the students. The results are presented below under different captions.

5.1.1 Effectiveness of Facebook Page in Terms of Achievement

One of the criterions used for studying the effectiveness of developed Facebook page was achievement of students on 15 criterion tests. The present study involved students of class IX studied through developed Facebook page. The pre-test and post-test marks were analysed by employing the correlated t-test for criterion tests. To see the overall effectiveness of Facebook page, the total marks obtained in all criterion tests were taken. The results are summarized in table 5.1.

Table No. 5.1 Mean S.D and t Value for Pre and Post-Test of Experiment Group on 15 Criterion Test

Topic/Chapter	Test	N	Mean	S.D	t-value
CRT 1 **Matter in our surroundings**	Pre test Post test	100 100	6.02 11.47	1.73 1.507	9.23*
CRT 2 **Is matter around us pure**	Pre test Post test	100 100	6.05 11.58	1.75 1.42	6.18*
CRT 3 **Atoms and molecules**	Pre test Post test	100 100	5.99 11.71	1.77 1.31	9.94*
CRT 4 **Structure of the Atom**	Pre test Post test	100 100	5.78 11.12	1.9 1.71	7.91*
CRT 5 **The Fundamental unit of Life**	Pre test Post test	100 100	5.72 11.01	1.94 1.82	6.79*
CRT 6 **Tissues**	Pre test Post test	100 100	5.55 11	2.07 1.82	9.9*
CRT 7 **Diversity in living organisms**	Pre test Post test	100 100	6.38 11.21	1.84 1.73	6.31*
CRT 8 **Motion**	Pre test Post test	100 100	6.23 11.92	1.82 1.44	8.67*
CRT 9 **Force and Laws of Motion**	Pre test Post test	100 100	6.42 12.03	1.78 1.32	8.78*
CRT 10 **Gravitation**	Pre test Post test	100 100	6.2 11.78	1.82 1.6	6.55*
CRT 11 **Work and Energy**	Pre test Post test	100 100	6.03 10.68	1.99 1.93	8.19*
CRT 12 **Sound**	Pre test Post test	100 100	6.14 12.01	1.69 1.08	8.96*
CRT 13 **Why do we fall ill**	Pre test Post test	100 100	5.89 10.66	2 1.95	9.95*
CRT 14 **Natural Resources**	Pre test Post test	100 100	6 10.83	1.89 1.89	7.00*
CRT 15 **Improvement in Food resources**	Pre test Post test	100 100	6.08 11.91	1.77 1.12	9.56*
Overall achievement **(All Chapters)**	Pre test Post test	100 100	90.48 170.92	27.76 23.64	8.26*

* Significant at 0.01 level

** Significant at 0.05 level

NS: Non-significant

From table 5.1, it is evident that:-

1. t-value of 9.23 for achievement on chapter-1, "Matter in our surroundings" is significant at 0.01 level with df. equal to 99. It indicates that the mean achievement scores of students before giving the treatment differ significantly from that after the treatment.

   Further the mean post test score (11.47) of students after the treatment is significantly higher than the mean pre-test score (6.02) of students before the treatment, it indicates that Facebook on topic "Matter in our surroundings" could influence the achievement of students on criterion reference test-1.

2. t-value of 6.18 for achievement on chapter- 2, "Is Matter around us pure " is significant at 0.01 level with df. equal to 99. It indicates that the mean achievement scores of students before giving the treatment differ significantly from that after the treatment.

   Further the mean post test score (11.58) of students after the treatment is significantly higher than the mean pre-test score (6.05) of students before the treatment, it indicates that Facebook on topic "Is Matter around us pure" could influence the achievement of students on criterion reference test-2.

3. t-value of 9.94 for achievement on chapter-3, "Atoms and Molecules" is significant at 0.01 level with df. equal to 99. It indicates that the mean achievement scores of students before giving the treatment differ significantly from that after the treatment.

   Further the mean post test score (11.71) of students after the treatment is significantly higher than the mean pre-test score (5.99) of students before the treatment, it indicates that Facebook on topic "Atoms and Molecules" could influence the achievement of students on criterion reference test-3.

4. t-value of 7.91 for achievement on chapter-4, "Structure of the Atom" is significant at 0.01 level with df. equal to 99. It indicates that the mean achievement scores of students before giving the treatment differ significantly from that after the treatment.

   Further the mean post test score (11.12) of students after the treatment is significantly higher than the mean pre-test score (5.78) of students before the treatment, it indicates that Facebook on topic "Structure of the Atom" could influence the achievement of students on criterion reference test-4

5. t-value of 6.79 for achievement on chapter-5, "The fundamental unit of life" is significant at 0.01 level with df. equal to 99. It indicates that the mean achievement scores of students before giving the treatment differ significantly from that after the treatment.

   Further the mean post test score (11.01) of students after the treatment is significantly higher than the mean pre-test score (5.72) of students before the treatment, it indicates that Facebook on topic "The fundamental unit of life" could influence the achievement of students on criterion reference test-5

6. t-value of 9.9 for achievement on chapter-6, "Tissues" is significant at 0.01 level with df. equal to 99. It indicates that the mean achievement scores of students before giving the treatment differ significantly from that after the treatment.

   Further the mean post test score (11) of students after the treatment is significantly higher than the mean pre-test score (5.55) of students before the treatment, it indicates that

Facebook on topic "Tissues" could influence the achievement of students on criterion reference test-6

7. t-value of 6.31 for achievement on chapter-7, "Diversity in Living Organisms" is significant at 0.01 level with df. equal to 99. It indicates that the mean achievement scores of students before giving the treatment differ significantly from that after the treatment.

   Further the mean post test score (11.21) of students after the treatment is significantly higher than the mean pre-test score (6.38) of students before the treatment, it indicates that Facebook on topic "Diversity in Living Organisms" could influence the achievement of students on criterion reference test-7.

8. t-value of 8.67 for achievement on chapter-8, "Motion" is significant at 0.01 level with df. equal to 99. It indicates that the mean achievement scores of students before giving the treatment differ significantly from that after the treatment.

   Further the mean post test score (11.92) of students after the treatment is significantly higher than the mean pre-test score (6.23) of students before the treatment, it indicates that Facebook on topic "Motion" could influence the achievement of students on criterion reference test-8.

9. t-value of 8.78 for achievement on chapter-9, "Force and Laws of Motion" is significant at 0.01 level with df. equal to 99. It indicates that the mean achievement scores of students before giving the treatment differ significantly from that after the treatment.

   Further the mean post test score (12.03) of students after the treatment is significantly higher than the mean pre-test score (6.42) of students before the treatment, it indicates that Facebook on topic "Force and Laws of Motion" could influence the achievement of students on criterion reference test-9.

10. t-value of 6.55 for achievement on chapter-10, "Gravitation" is significant at 0.01 level with df. equal to 99. It indicates that the mean achievement scores of students before giving the treatment differ significantly from that after the treatment.

Further the mean post test score (11.78) of students after the treatment is significantly higher than the mean pre-test score (6.2) of students before the treatment, it indicates that Facebook on topic "Gravitation" could influence the achievement of students on criterion reference test-10.

11. t-value of 8.19 for achievement on chapter-11, "Work and Energy" is significant at 0.01 level with df. equal to 99. It indicates that the mean achievement scores of students before giving the treatment differ significantly from that after the treatment.

Further the mean post test score (10.68) of students after the treatment is significantly higher than the mean pre-test score (6.03) of students before the treatment, it indicates that Facebook on topic "Work and Energy" could influence the achievement of students on criterion reference test-11.

12. t-value of 8.96 for achievement on chapter-12, "Sound" is significant at 0.01 level with df. equal to 99. It indicates that the mean achievement scores of students before giving the treatment differ significantly from that after the treatment.

Further the mean post test score (12.01) of students after the treatment is significantly higher than the mean pre-test score (6.14) of students before the treatment, it indicates that Facebook on topic "Sound" could influence the achievement of students on criterion reference test-12.

13. t-value of 9.95 for achievement on chapter-13, "Why do we fall ill" is significant at 0.01 level with df. equal to 99. It indicates that the mean achievement scores of students before giving the treatment differ significantly from that after the treatment.

Further the mean post test score (10.66) of students after the treatment is significantly higher than the mean pre-test score (5.89) of students before the treatment, it indicates that Facebook on topic "Why do we fall ill" could influence the achievement of students on criterion reference test-13.

14. t-value of 7 for achievement on chapter-14, "Natural Resources" is significant at 0.01 level with df. equal to 99. It indicates that the mean achievement scores of students before giving the treatment differ significantly from that after the treatment.

    Further the mean post test score (10.83) of students after the treatment is significantly higher than the mean pre-test score (6) of students before the treatment, it indicates that Facebook on topic "Natural Resources" could influence the achievement of students on criterion reference test-14.

15. t-value of 9.56 for achievement on chapter-15, "Improvement in Food Resources" is significant at 0.01 level with df. equal to 99. It indicates that the mean achievement scores of students before giving the treatment differ significantly from that after the treatment.

    Further the mean post test score (11.91) of students after the treatment is significantly higher than the mean pre-test score (6.08) of students before the treatment, it indicates that Facebook on topic "Improvement in Food Resources" could influence the achievement of students on criterion reference test-15.

The overall achievement of students on all 15 criterion tests was calculated by the total score of all criterion tests of each student.

The t-value of 8.26 for overall achievement of students on all 15 criterion tests is significant at 0.01 level of significance with df. Equals to 99. It indicates that the total mean overall achievement score (for all 15 criterion tests) of student before the treatment differ significantly from that after the treatment.

The total mean post test score (170.92) of students on the entire 15 criterion test is significantly higher than the total mean pre-test score (90.48) of student before the treatment.

Further, it indicates that the Facebook page on all the 15 chapters of Science could influence the overall achievement of the students on all the 15 criterion reference tests.

Thus the Facebook was found to be effective in terms of the achievement of students on criterion reference tests. Hence the null hypothesis that there will be no significant difference between the pre-test and post-test achievement score of students studying through Facebook page is rejected.

5.1.2 Effectiveness of Facebook Page in Terms of Reaction of Students

The second criteria used for studying the effectiveness of Facebook page in term of reaction of students towards developed Facebook material.

The student's reactions were obtained by administering a reaction scale developed by investigator. The obtained data were analysed for each statement separately by computing chi-square for frequencies. Learning through Facebook was followed by objectives and Fill in the blank type of questions with discussion sessions. Therefore, the reaction of students was taken against the four different aspects of developed Facebook page.

The reaction scale was consisted of 40 items divided into 4 major categories based on 4 different aspects of Facebook material. There were five options against each item. Scoring procedure.

The scale was comprises 40 items pertaining to line sub-components namely

a. Instruction through Facebook

b. Presentation of the Content

c. Technical facilities available

d. Evaluation and feedback

The items have been drafted in Affirmative (36 items) and negative (4 items) forms.

Affirmative (+) items

1,3,4,7,9,10,11,12,13,14,15,16,18,19,20,21,22,23,24,25,26,27,28, 29,30,31,32,33,34,35,36, 37,38,39,40

Negative (--) items

2,5, 6,8,17

Positive item should be given - 5, 4,3,2,1. Whereas the scoring process should be reversed as 1, 2,3,4,5 for negative items. Maximum total score 200 and minimum total score 0.There were five options against each item.

1. Strongly Agree (SA)
2. Agree (A)
3. Undecided (U)
4. Disagree (D)
5. Strongly Disagree (SD)

Students were asked to put a tick mark on one of the option, data were analysed for each statement separately by computing percentage and chi square for frequencies. The results are presented in table 5.2.

Table 5.2 Reaction of Students

(in percentage and chi square value)

A) Instruction through Facebook

Sr. No.	Statement	SA	A	U	D	SD	Chi Square
1	I enjoyed the learning through Facebook as compared to traditional classroom teaching.	30	45	25	0	0	57.5*
2	Reading of subject matter through computer medium is not very easy	0	3	5	22	70	170.9*
3	Sufficient instructions given about how to use the Facebook page were easy and clear to follow.	23	71	5	1	0	179.5*
4	There is sufficient interaction between student and Facebook.	43	31	15	11	0	57.8*
5	Interaction with teacher is not possible while using this Facebook.	0	1	26	28	45	74.3*
6	It is very time consuming to learn through Facebook. It is wastage of time.	0	13	15	51	21	41.8*
7	I feel motivated while learning through Facebook.	31	53	15	1	0	93.8*
8	Sometimes it is very boring to learn through Facebook.	0	12	16	34	38	50.0*
9	It was quite at ease while interacting with the Facebook.	30	33	15	11	11	22.8*
10	It will be enjoyable and helpful to study other subjects also using Facebook.	36	42	20	2	0	73.2*

* Significant at 0.01 level

** Significant at 0.05 level

NS: Non-Significant.

B) Presentation of the Content

Sr. No.	Statement	SA	A	U	D	SD	Chi Square
11	The subject matter presented in Facebook was logically arranged.	52	32	15	1	0	97.7*
12	Text cum graphic presentation for each chapter was balanced.	30	34	26	10	0	41.6*
13	The language used in Facebook is simple and easy to understand.	22	41	15	`12	11	30.75*
14	Selection of file type (PDF, PPT, and Video) was easy.	33	40	15	12	0	50.95*
15	Animations are helpful to make the chapter's learning easy.	61	22	15	1	1	121.6*
16	Power point presentations and Videos for each chapters help in understanding the difficult concepts.	21	52	15	12	0	75.7*
17	Exercises given in each chapter are not adequate.	1	2	15	51	31	89.6*
18	Exercises given in each chapter helps in understanding the chapter in depth.	51	21	16	12	0	72.1*
19	Test questions were based on knowledge, understanding and application.	20	45	5	29	1	64.6*
20	Detail analysis of the result (numerically and graphically) helps to get the proper feedback about learning.	21	61	16	2	0	121.1*

* Significant at 0.01 level

** Significant at 0.05 level

NS: Non-Significant.

C) Technical facilities available:

Sr. No.	Statement	SA	A	U	D	SD	Chi Square
21	Different instructions given on web pages help to use the Facebook.	51	21	16	11	1	71.00*
22	Navigation (moving) from one topic to another is easy.	20	58	9	8	6	95.22
23	Menu choices and icons save the time to learn.	22	52	15	11	0	76.7*
24	Learning according to own choice develops proper understanding.	70	22	7	1	0	171.7*
25	Multimedia effects, PPTs and videos make difficult concepts easy.	22	51	10	12	5	67.7*
26	The hyperlinks provided to each topic helps in moving to required topic and saves the time.	50	32	10	5	3	82.9*
27	Abstract ideas have been presented in concrete form in natural way.	21	42	16	11	10	34.1*
28	I can learn with my own speed.	22	60	10	5	3	110.9*
29	Speed of Internet is no barrier while learning.	25	53	10	6	6	80.3*
30	Anytime, anywhere learning is possible with the Facebook.	22	61	15	12	0	108.7*

* Significant at 0.01 level
** Significant at 0.05 level
NS: Non-Significant.

D) **Evaluation and feedback:**

Sr.No.	Statement	SA	A	U	D	SD	Chi Square
31	Questioning style was appropriate.	30	41	17	6	6	47.1*
32	Immediate confirmation of result helps to understand the content.	27	50	13	5	5	72.4*
33	Numerical problems help in understanding the related concept.	20	39	11	10	10	32.1*
34	Tests on each chapter help in fixing the knowledge.	28	50	13	5	4	74.7*
35	Intelligence test and Study habit test were useful in measuring Intelligence, and Study habit.	17	65	12	5	1	140.55*
36	Questions are quite helpful in developing reasoning ability.	67	26	7	0	0	160.7*
37	I like inbuilt evaluation facilities.	27	34	19	10	10	32.05*
38	Graphical representation makes the result analysis more clear.	40	41	16	2	1	79.7*
39	Provisions for answer given and correct answer helps in understanding the concept.	55	22	9	8	6	84.5*
40	Feedback form was helpful in solving the difficulties and getting suggestions.	27	53	16	4	0	90.5*

* Significant at 0.01 level

** Significant at 0.05 level

NS: Non-Significant.

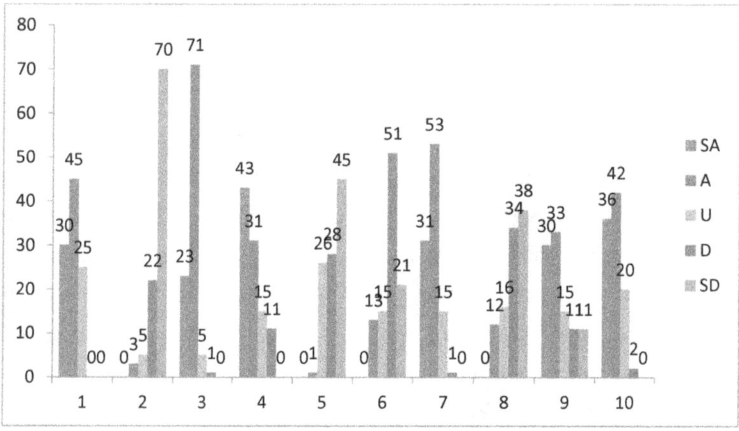

Graph No 5.2.0: Instruction through Facebook

The first part of the reaction scale collected the reactions from the students related with their liking towards part- A of the reaction scale namely "Instruction through Facebook". This part contains 10 statements from table 5.2. It is revealed that the Chi Square value for statement No. 1,2,3,4,5,6,7,8,9,10 is significant at 0.01 level of significance. The students reacted favourably towards this aspect of Facebook material.

In the statements numbering one to four, 75 percent students found that the learning through Facebook as compared to traditional classroom teaching is more enjoyable, 25% percent students were unable to comment. 92 percent students did not find any difficulty in reading through computer medium, whereas 5 percent students were unable to comment. Only 3 percent students found difficulty in reading through computer. 94 percent students were agreed that sufficient instructions were given to learn through Facebook, whereas 5 percent students were unable to comment. Only 1 percent student was disagreed. 74 percent students also agreed that there is ample interaction between student and Facebook. 11 percent students disagree with this whereas 15 percent students were unable to comment.

In statement no. 5 to 10, 1 percent of students felt not comfortable while interacting with teacher through Facebook, 26 percent students were unable to comment and the remaining 73 percent students disagreed with this.13 percent students agreed that it is very time consuming to learn through Facebook 15 percent students were unable to comment and the remaining 72 percent students disagreed with this. 84 percent students felt motivated while learning through Facebook 15 percent students were unable to comment and the remaining 1 percent students disagreed with this. 12 percent students agreed that sometimes it is very boring to learn through Facebook, whereas 16 percent students were unable to comment and the remaining 72 percent students disagreed with this. 63 students agreed that it was quite at ease while interacting with the Facebook, whereas 15 percent students were unable to comment and the remaining 22 percent students disagreed with this. They wanted to learn other subjects also through Facebook page.

There were four statements like interacting with teacher through Facebook is difficult, it took so much time to learn through Facebook there is wastage of time and sometimes it is boring to learn through Facebook. These items were framed negatively. 72 to 73 percent of students were disagreed with these statements. The students did not find any difficulty in learning, they do not feel that there is wastage of time in learning through Facebook, they found it very interesting. The Chi square values for the above statements are significant at 0.01 level of significance. This indicates that the group really favoured the instructions through Facebook.

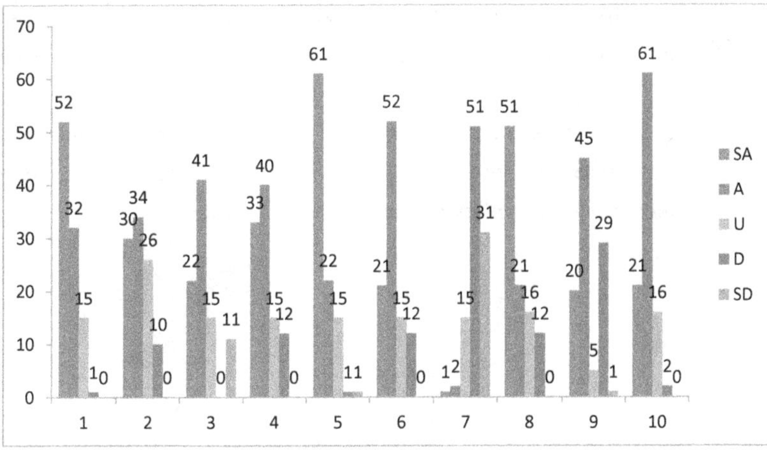

Graph No 5.2.1: Presentation of the content

The second aspect, part B of reaction scale was related with the arrangement of subject matter, graphics, language, selection of file, animations, PPTs and videos, exercises, questions, detail analysis of the result. The Chi square value for all these statement is significant. The 64 to 84 percent students reacted in favour of this aspect like they found logically arranged subject matter, balanced text cum graphic presentation, easy selection of file type etc.

Majority of students 73 to 83 percent students found animations; ppt and videos are helpful to understand the difficult concepts. 72 percent of students agreed with the statement that exercise and graphics given with concepts helped them in understanding the concept. They also liked detail analysis of the result about learning and majority of students agreed that Test questions were based on knowledge, understanding and application. 63 percent students found language simple and easy to understand. 23 percent students disagreed with it, remaining percent were in the state of indecision. The Chi square value is significant.

There was one statement like exercise given in each chapter is not adequate. This item was framed negatively. 82 percent of students were disagreeing with this statement. The Chi square value for above statement is significant at 0.01 level of significance. Thus the majority of students reacted favourably towards the aspect. They liked presentation style of instructional matter.

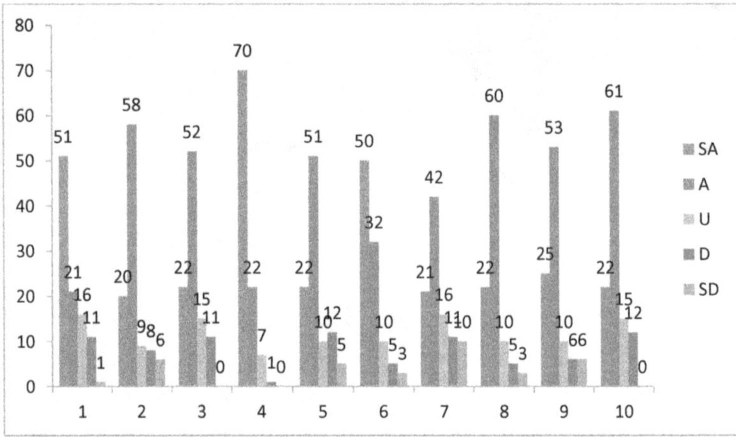

Graph No 5.2.2: Technical facilities available

The third aspect of reaction scale collected reaction of students towards technical facilities available. The reaction of students towards this aspect was collected through to statements numbered 21 to 30. The 72 to 78 percent of students found that various instructions given on web page help to use the Facebook, also agreed that moving from one topic to another is easy and menu choices save the time to learn. The 73 percent students reacted that use of ppts; videos make difficult concepts easy.10 percent students were unable to decide whereas remaining 17 percent students disagreeing with this.

63 to 92 percent students found that learning according to own choice help in proper understanding, abstract idea presented in concrete form in natural way and speed of internet is not a barrier

while learning. 82 to 83 percent students learn anytime, anywhere with their own speed. 82 percent students found the hyperlinks save the time. The students like the technical facilities available in the package. They reacted favourably towards this aspect of reaction scale.

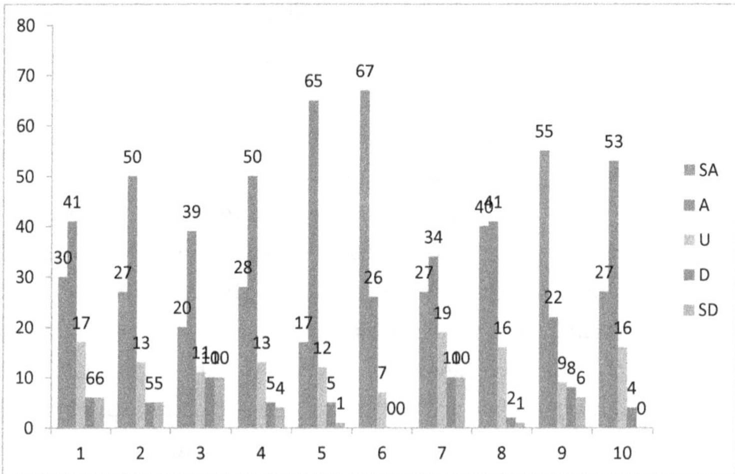

Graph No 5.2.3: Evaluation and feedback

The fourth and last aspect of reaction scale collected information regarding evaluation, feedback and follow up activities. Ten statements numbered 31 to 40 were there. These statements were related with various activities like questioning, immediate confirmation of answer etc. The 59 to 78 percent students were agreed that questioning style was quite appropriate. They found immediate confirmation of answer and numerical problems helpful in understanding the content. They also found tests on each chapter helpful in fixing the knowledge.

61 to 82 percent students were agreed intelligence tests and study habit tests were useful in measuring intelligence and study habit, they found graphical representation makes the result analysis

more clear. They liked inbuilt evaluation facilities and feedback from was helpful in solving the difficulties and getting suggestions to learn more clearly. 93 percent students reacted that question are helpful in developing reasoning ability whereas 14 percent students disagreed with this and the Chi square value is significant at 0.01 level of significance 77 percent of students agreed that the provisions for answer given and correct answer helps in understanding the concept.

The Chi square values for all the ten statements are significant at 0.01 level of significance. The student's reaction was favourable towards the aspect of reaction scale. They like evaluation, feedback and follow-up activities very much.

At the end of reaction scale, face to face discussion as well as the investigator contacted through the e-mails, messages and phone with the students to know the opinion and suggestions for improvement of the Facebook material. It has been found that 20% students required more pictures and videos. 15 % students wanted more clarification for some concepts. Eighteen percent students require advance technical facilities like sound, verbal instructions and animation effects, similar to that which they found in other computer games and multimedia CDs. 12 percent students require more time allocation in school. Thus the majority of students reacted favourably towards majority of items of reaction scale. They showed positive attitude towards Facebook textual content.

From table 5.2 it is evident that out of 40 students of reaction scale the chi square value of all statements are significant at 0.01 level of significance. Looking at the majority of favourable responses, it may be said that developed Facebook textual content was effective in terms of the reaction expressed by the students. Thus it is concluded that the developed Facebook text based content was found to be effective in terms of student's reaction.

Findings

The developed Facebook content was found to be effective in terms of:-

a. Achievement of students on criterion reference tests.

b. Reaction of the students towards Facebook content.

5.2.0 Comparison of developed Facebook page with conventional method in terms of overall achievement by taking intelligence as co-variate

The second objective of the present study was to compare the adjusted mean overall achievement scores of the students studied through developed Facebook page with those taught through conventional method by taking intelligence as co-variate.

The Facebook was developed for the whole IX class CBSE syllabus of Science. The developed Facebook page was for all 15 chapters of the Science, so the number of criterion tests was 15. To get the overall achievement scores of the students the total scores for each student on 15 criterion tests were calculated.

The data were analysed by using the analysis of co-variance where intelligence was taken as co-variate. The results are presented in table 5.3

Table 5.3

Summary of Ancova for overall achievement by taking intelligence as a co-variate

Source of variance	Df	SS Y.X	MSS Y.X	F(Y.X)
Between	2	18961.75	9480.875	
within	197	72125.64	366.12	25.895*
Total	199			

*Significant at 0.01 level
** Significant at 0.05 level
NS: Non-significant

From the table 5.3, it can be seen that the F value of the overall achievement for the two groups is 25.895 which is significant at 0.01 level with df. equal to 1/197.

It shows that the adjusted mean overall achievement score of the students studied through developed Facebook page is significantly different from those taught through conventional method when intelligence was taken as co-variate.

Thus the null hypothesis namely there will be no significant difference between the adjusted mean overall achievement scores of the students studied through developed Facebook page with those taught through conventional method when intelligence was taken as co-variate is rejected. The adjusted mean overall achievement of the student studied through developed Facebook page was significantly higher than those who were taught through conventional method (table 5.4). It may therefore be said that the developed Facebook was superior to conventional method.

Table No. 5.4

Adjusted mean overall achievement scores of experimental and control groups

Group	N	Mx	My	M(y.x)
Experimental	100	153.58	100.12	100.01
Control	100	74.06	79.28	78.18

Finding

The developed Facebook was found to be superior to conventional method in terms of overall achievement when intelligence was taken as co-variate.

5.3.0 Comparison of developed Facebook with conventional method in terms of overall achievement by taking study habit as co-variate

The third objective of the present study was to compare the mean overall achievement scores of the students studied through developed Facebook page with those taught through conventional method by taking study habit as co-variate.

The Facebook was developed for 15 chapters of the Science so the number of criterion tests was 15.To get the overall achievement scores of the students, the total score for each student on 15 criterion tests were calculated.

The data were analysed by using analysis of co-variance where study habit was taken as co-variate. The results are presented in table.

Table No. 5.5

Summary of Ancova for overall achievement by taking study habit as co-variate

Source of variance	Df	SSY.X	MSS Y.X	F(Y.X)
Among group	2	562344.0	281172	59.209*
Within group	197	935513.6	4748.8	
Total	199			

*Significant at 0.01 level
**Significant at 0.05 level
N.S: Non- Significant

From the above table 5.5, it can be seen that the F-value of the overall achievement for the two groups is 59.209 which is significant at 0.01 with df equal to 1/197.

It indicates that the adjusted mean overall achievement scores of the students studied through developed Facebook page is significant different from those taught through conventional method when study habit is taken as co-variate.

Thus the null hypothesis that there will be no significant difference between the adjusted mean overall achievement scores of the students studied through developed Facebook page with those students studying through conventional method when study habit was taken as co-variate is rejected.

The mean overall achievement of the students studied through developed Facebook page was significantly higher than those who were taught through conventional method. From table 5.6 it can be revealed.

It may therefore, be said that the developed Facebook page was superior to conventional method.

Table No. 5.6

Adjusted mean overall achievement scores of Experimental Control group

Group	N	Mx	My	M (y.x)
Experimental	100	153.58	153.48	152.28
Control	100	74.06	119.27	119.10

Finding

The developed Facebook page content was found significantly superior to conventional method in terms of overall achievement when study habit was taken as co-variate.

5.4.0 Comparison of mean overall achievement of male and female students studied through Facebook

The fourth objective of the present study was to compare the mean overall achievement of male and female students studied through Facebook.

To get the overall achievement scores of the students, the total post test scores for each student of experimental group on 15 criterion tests were calculated. The data were analysed by using t test. The results are presented in table 5.7

Table 5.7

Summary of t-test for overall achievement of male and female students of experimental group

Group	N	Test	Mean	SD	t- value
Male	53	Post	149.3585	14.98216	0.013919 (N.S.)
Female	47	Post	138.9574	24.54008	

*Significant at 0.01 level
**Significant at 0.05 level
N.S: Non- Significant

From the above mentioned table no 5.7, it can be seen that the t-value of male students and Female students of experimental group is 0.0139 which is not significant at 0.01 level of significance. It means that the mean overall achievement score of male students is not significantly different from female students studied through developed Facebook.

Thus the null hypothesis that there will be no significant difference between the mean overall achievement score of male students and female students studied through developed Facebook page is not rejected.

It may therefore be said that there will be no significant difference between the performance of male students and female students on achievement test studied through developed Facebook page. Both the group performed equally well. Gender does not affect the performance of students studied through Facebook.

Finding

There was no significant difference between the achievement of male students and female students studied through Facebook, when assessed in terms of overall achievement on criterion reference tests.

5.5.0 Findings of the study

From the analysis of results given in this chapter the following findings have come out

1. The Facebook was found to be effective in terms of:-
    a. Achievement of students on criterion tests.
    b. Reaction of students towards the different aspects of developed Facebook.
2. The Facebook was found to be superior to conventional method in terms of overall achievement of students when intelligence was taken as co-variate.
3. The Facebook was found to be superior to conventional method in terms of overall achievement of students when study habit was taken as co-variate.
4. There was no significant difference between the overall achievement of male student and female students, studied through Facebook when assessed in terms of overall achievement on criterion reference tests.

5.6.0 Discussion of Result

As per the objectives given in chapter 1, the data pertaining to these objectives were analysed by using appropriate statistical techniques as mentioned above. Objective wise discussion of result is presented below under different captions.

5.6.1 Effectiveness of Facebook content in terms of achievement

The developed Facebook was found to be effective in terms of achievement of students at the pre-test and post-test stage on criterion tests. This effectiveness may be because of the following reasons.

1. The students were free to work on the computer for suffering an online web-based material i.e. Facebook textual content at their own pace. They were also free to take their own time while working with the Facebook.
2. The developed Facebook page for Science included the content which had a simple and lucid language a text was supported with different eye catching pictorial. It is very obvious that this visual stimulus might have stimulated learning and holds the students concentration.
3. The Facebook content was developed for teaching Science. The study of Science deals with the Scientific issues related to Matter, Cells ,Tissues, Motion, Gravitation, Diversity in living organisms, Structure of atom, Natural resource etc. It requires presentation of abstract idea in concrete form. Facebook was supported with luci text, loads of pictures to make the text understood in clear terms and content related videos and concrete examples that might have helped in proper understanding of concepts.
4. Some students hesitate to participate freely during the conventional teaching learning process, as in responding to the teachers question and in various classroom activities, hence such students do not get reinforcement in the conventional classroom setting. However working with the Facebook every student was forced to respond, they used to get immediate confirmation, feedback and reinforcement.
5. The main component of the developed Facebook page, there were many facilities incorporated with the material like sufficient instructions for students to learn, confirmation of

responses, active learning, explanation for their questions or doubts etc. due to these facilities student might have achieved higher score.

6. To felicitate learning certain activities like question-answer dialogues among the students and teachers, time to time discussion on the Facebook content to clarify doubts. To develop self-learning habit, additional videos were also provided. All these facilities and activities were responsible for the higher achievement of the students.

7. The Facebook was developed according to the psychological principles of controlled learning. The text presented in controlled increments, one concept at a time with an opportunity for interaction and reinforcement before the next concept is introduced. Such type of planned presentation of content might have yield higher achievement.

5.6.2 Effectiveness of Facebook in Terms of Reaction of Students

The next finding of the study was the reaction of students towards developed Facebook textual content. It has been found that the developed Facebook content was effective in terms of student's reaction. Majority of students reacted positively towards various aspects of Facebook. Many facilities were available to the students in the Facebook like self-paced individualized learning, sequential presentation of content, coloured pictures, videos, feedback, questions- answer dialogues etc.

Inspite of all these facilities the learning through Facebook (web based technology) was a new experience to learners. Favourable reactions of the students indicated that they liked the Facebook as it was a new avenue for the students to go through their learning process and they want to read other subjects also through Facebook. It means that the students felt that the Facebook was useful for them. They found it motivating and helpful in learning. These might be the reason that students reacted favourably towards the developed Facebook.

5.6.3 Comparison of Facebook with conventional method in terms of overall achievement by taking intelligence as co-variate.

The next finding of the study was that the developed Facebook content was found to be superior to conventional method in terms of overall achievement when intelligence was taken as co-variate. This may be because of the following reasons-

1. The conventional class room teaching is mostly stereotyped and does not cater to the individual differences found among the students. It is not possible to take care of individual student understanding through conventional method. Moreover, the students are hesitant in asking questions whenever there is any doubt in their minds. Most of the conventional classroom teachers believe in verbalism and there is hardly any scope for providing visual stimulus to the students.
2. In a conventional classroom setting very little provision is made for the students to respond actively to the information presented before them hence the question of active responding and reinforcement does not arise. All these points are considered during the development of Facebook content. Therefore, the developed Facebook was found to be more effective than the conventional method of teaching.

5.6.4 Comparison of Facebook with conventional method in terms of overall achievement by taking study habit as co-variate.

Study habit plays an important role in higher achievement score of the learner to see the effectiveness of Facebook over conventional method, both the groups were matched with respect of study habit score. The analysis of data reveals that Facebook was found to be superior to conventional method in terms of overall achievement by taking study habit as co-variate. There are some reasons responsible for this finding.

1. The Facebook Page was developed with facility of feedback. Facility providing explanation for their queries, it means it keeps students busy and active in learning, such individualized feedback with explanation is not possible in conventional method of teaching.
2. The Facebook had self-pacing facility; it means each and every student read the topics according to their own pace. There is sufficient scope to think rationally over the content they have read while in conventional teaching, the students are forced to learn according to teacher, so the students some time miss the content or unable to understand and think.
3. To solve the difficulties of the student's discussion and problem solving sessions were organized. During this session, many opportunities were given to discuss the learning difficulties with classmates as well as investigator. To promote self-learning and good study habit additional current topic based videos were also provided. This might have encouraged students to take interest in learning which resulted in higher achievement score by experimental group, as compared to control group.

These might be the reasons that the developed Facebook content found to be significantly superior to conventional method when study habit was taken as co-variate.

5.6.5 Comparison of achievement of male students with female students studied through Facebook.

The fourth objective of the present study is to compare the overall achievement of male students with female students taught through developed Facebook. It was found that the mean overall achievement score of male students did not differ significantly with female students studied through developed Facebook. The reason for such finding was that the developed. Facebook was suitable for both the sexes. Both groups, male students and female achieved higher score on criterion test. It may be because of the fact that biologically there is no difference between their thinking and intelligence. Both are capable to perform same intellectual duties in all the work fields as far as mental approach is concerned we hardly find any marked difference between the two. Hence the achievement score of both the groups were the same.

1. The developed Facebook content has incorporated certain features. Self-paced learning ,active responding, confirmation of response, videos, pictures with text, simple and lucid language etc. which might have suitable for both the group of students hence they achieved higher on criterion tests but did not differ in their achievement score.
2. The interactive nature of developed Facebook content has ability to mediate learning because both passive and active aspect of learning were well integrated in developed Facebook content a detailed description of all the resource material available for the course helped them in solving the queries as well as in achieving higher score by both the group of students.
3. During discussion session, the students were free to discuss with both the teacher and their peers. In a conventional classroom, number of students coming from disadvantaged background or have problems with the language or afraid in asking questions or being in danger of giving an incorrect

answer in class. Students of these categories benefit from Facebook in two ways, first they have freedom of asking different types of questions, secondly they were able to repeat lesson as often as required. This builds a degree of self-confidence among them.

This might have resulted in higher achievement score by both male students and female on criterion tests. Hence it can be calculated that sex did not affect the achievement of student studied through Facebook. The mean overall achievement score of male students and female studied through Facebook did not differ significantly on criterion tests.

Chapter VI

SUMMARY IMPLICATION AND SUGGESTION

6.0.0 Introduction

The present study entitled " Effectiveness of social networking Facebook for teaching science"- A study, belongs to the area of educational technology i.e. use of social networking (Facebook) for creating a rich content for the 21st century students, so that they are free to access it as per their own pace, time suitability.

Facebook is now one of the most common types of online website found on the internet. The accessibility and the reflective nature of Facebook are appropriate to many learning and teaching application and convenient for the learners as well as for the teacher educators to use the website anytime and anywhere.

In the developed Facebook content certain features have been incorporated to make it more users friendly and convenient to achieve the multi-dimensional objectives of education.

Facebook page was developing for the fifteen chapters of science of class IX for CBSE syllabus. It is an attempt to find out the effectiveness of Facebook in terms of achievement and as well as the reaction of learner. The effectiveness of developed Facebook is determined on the basis of comparison between the achievement score of students studying with only conventional method of teaching with those studying through Facebook with regular classroom teaching by taking intelligence and study habit as co-variate. The comparison between overall achievement of male and female students studying through Facebook along with conventional method was also done.

6.1.0. Statement of the Problem

"Effectiveness of social networking Facebook for teaching science"-A study

6.2.0. Objectives of the Study

Objectives of the present study are set out as follows

1. To develop learning material using Facebook pages for teaching science to students of class IX CBSE and study its effectiveness in terms of:

   a. Achievement of students

   b. Reaction of students towards developed Facebook page

2. To compare the mean overall achievement score of the students studying through Facebook along with conventional teaching method, with those studying through conventional method by taking intelligence as co-variate.
3. To compare the mean overall achievement score of the students studying through Facebook with those studying through conventional method by taking study habit as co-variate.
4. To compare the overall achievement of male student with female student studying through Facebook.

6.3.0. Hypothesis

1. There will be no significant difference between the pre and post-test mean overall achievement score of students studying through Facebook.
2. There will be no significant difference between the adjusted mean overall achievement score of students studying through Facebook with those studying through conventional method by taking intelligent as co-variate.
3. There will be no significant difference between the adjusted mean overall achievement score of students studying through Facebook with those studying through conventional method by taking study habit as co-variate

4. There will be no significant difference between the overall achievement score of male & female studying through Facebook.

6.4.0. Scope and Delimitation of the Study

The present study is delimited to the following areas

1. The study will be limited to students of CBSE class IX only.
2. This study will evaluate the impact of only those students who are studying through English medium.
3. This study is limited to Nagpur area of Maharashtra state only.
4. This study is limited for teaching science subject only.
5. Central Board of Secondary Education syllabus will be taken for development of Facebook page.

6.5.0. Sample

In the present study, Facebook page was developed for teaching Science to class IX C.B.S.E. students of Nagpur (Maharashtra). The whole syllabus prescribed by C.B.S.E in 2006 for class IX was taken for development of online Facebook page. The study has been conducted in two stages.

In stage one, the empirical validity of the material was established. For this pilot study was conducted on 25 students of class IX C.B.S.E were selected. In the stage two for final study another group of students were selected in this way two samples were used for the study.

6.5.1 Sample for pilot study

The sample comprised of 25 students of class IX of Wonderland High School, Nagpur city (Maharashtra). Out of 25 students, 15 were male and 10 were female. The age of the students ranged from 13-15 years. The medium of instruction was English. The school is affiliated to Central Board of Secondary Education, New Delhi.

6.5.2 Sample for Final Study

For the final study, the two school of Nagpur city (Maharashtra) were selected namely Kendriya Vidyalaya Vayusena, Nagpur, Kendriya Vidyalaya Ambazari Nagpur

These schools were selected purposively. These schools were following the C.B.S.E syllabus and they have uniform pattern of curriculum. In Kendriya Vidyalaya Vayusena Nagpur 5 sections of IX class was there. Section A, B and C was selected randomly. From three sections 100 students had taken part in the study. Kendriya Vidyalaya School Ambazari Nagpur, 4 sections are there, three sections were selected randomly, section A, B and C 100 students of this part in the study.

Thus the sample size for the final study was 200 students, studying in IX class C.B.S.E syllabus. The age of students were ranging from 13 to 15 years. The medium of instructions in both the schools was English.

6.6.0. Design of the Study

The present study was experimental in nature. The sample consists of 200 Students divided into two groups, namely the Experimental Group and the Control Group.

The Experimental Group was taught through developed Facebook page along with the regular classroom teaching by their teacher followed by discussion and problem solving and online test. In addition to this, web-based Facebook page was easily accessible to the students so that they can use Facebook at anytime, anywhere whenever they were free.

The Control Group was taught through conventional method by their subject teacher only.

In the present study the dependent variables were achievement, reaction of the students towards Facebook. The independent variables were the Facebook and Sex. The intelligence, study habit was taken as co-variate.

6.7.0. Treatment

The Facebook page was developed on IX class Science syllabus of Central Board of Secondary Education, New Delhi (C.B.S.E) supported by variety of tools with which include videos and photos and discussion session were used as a treatment for experimental group.

6.8.0 Tools

Following tools were used in the study

1. Self-developed fifteen criterion reference tests for measuring the achievement on fifteen chapters of IX class Science syllabus.
2. Self-reaction scale for measuring reaction of students towards developed Facebook page.
3. Intelligence test developed by Ojha and Ray Choudhary was used to measure the study habit of the student.
4. Study habit inventory developed by Mukhopadhyay and Sansanwal (1983) was used to measure the study habit of the student.

6.9.0 Procedure of Data Collection

There were two groups in the study namely, Experimental Group and Control Group. The procedure of data collection for both the group is described here in detail under different captions.

6.9.1 Data Collection for Experimental Group

As stated above 100 students of Kendriya Vidyalaya Vayusena, Nagpur were randomly assigned as experimental group. Before going to take them for experimentation, proper instructions and other details, related with computer and how to access to Facebook page were given by the researcher. All the students had the basic knowledge about computers as well as about login through link to Facebook online website.

Thereafter, the students of Kendriya Vidyalaya Vayusena, Nagpur as per their time and suitability gone through the textual based.

Facebook content along with their regular classroom teaching. Students were free to learn according to their own pace. They could read given information as many times as they wanted and were free to comment or ask queries on the given Facebook contents. The students were very active and were actively asked question through mails, comments, face to face discussion and feedback was taken.

After studying through Facebook as per their time and suitability, 3 days in a week, at least for 25-30 minutes were provided for interaction. During this session difficulties raised by the students regarding Facebook were discussed and solved.

After completion of a chapter, the same criterion test was administered as post- test for that chapter. In the same pattern all the 15 chapters of Science were taught to the students with developed web-based Facebook.

After completing of all 15 chapters, study habit inventory, intelligent test and reaction scale was administered to the group. In this way the present study was lasted for months during April 2014 to February 2015.

6.9.2 Data collection for Control Group

100 students of class IX of Kendriya Vidyalaya Ambazari, Nagpur were considered as control group for the study. The school followed the same CBSE syllabus as experimental group. This group did not receive any special treatment. First the criterion reference test for chapter 1st was administered through paper pencil. The whole chapter was taught by their subject teacher through conventional classroom method, after accomplishment of chapter the same criterion reference test was administered as post-test. In this manner all 15 chapters were completed following the same procedure.

In the last after completion of all chapters, intelligence test, study habit inventory administered to the control group.

6.10.0 Data Analysis and Interpretation

Objective wise statistical techniques used for analysis of the data are as follows:

1. a) To study the effectiveness in terms of students of achievement on criterion tests, t-test was used between pre and post achievement score.

   b) To study the effectiveness in terms of student's reaction on each aspect of developed Facebook page, chi square for frequencies were computed.
2. To compare the mean overall achievement score of the students studying through Facebook along with conventional teaching method, with those studying through conventional

method by taking intelligence as co-variate analysis of co-variance was used.

3. To compare the mean overall achievement score of the students studying through Facebook with those studying through conventional method by taking study habit as co-variate analysis of co-variance was used.
4. To compare the overall achievement of male student with female student studying through Facebook t-test was used.

6.11.0 Findings

1. The studying through Facebook along with conventional method was found to be effective in terms of:-
   a. Achievement of students on criterion reference tests.
   b. Reaction of students towards the different aspects of developed Facebook material.
2. The studying through Facebook along with conventional method was found to be superior to only conventional method in terms of overall achievement of students when intelligence was taken as co-variate.
3. The studying through Facebook along with conventional method was found to be superior to only conventional method in terms of overall achievement of students when study habit was taken as co-variate.
4. There was no significant difference between the overall achievement of male student and female students, studied through Facebook along with conventional method when assessed in terms of overall achievement on criterion reference tests.

6.12.0 Conclusion

The developed Facebook has proved effective which is evident from the achievement of the students of the sample. They had high positive reaction towards the developed Facebook page. This proves that the study through Facebook along with conventional method is more interesting, useful, easily assessable and compatible than the only conventional method normally used in the classroom.

The sex did not influence the achievement of students studied through developed Facebook page. It is equally compatible for both the sexes. Students studying through Facebook have a positive and favourable reaction. This proves that the developed Facebook page is effective and motivating for the students.

6.13.0 Education Implication

The educational implications of the findings are given under the following headings

1. Students
2. Parents
3. Teacher
4. Teacher Educators
5. Administrators
6. Software designers

6.13.1 Students

In the past, learning and education simply meant face-to-face lectures, reading books or printed handouts, taking notes and completing assignments generally in the form of answering questions or writing essays. Today, education and training have taken on a whole new meaning. Computers are an essential part of every classroom and teachers are using DVDs, CD-ROMs and videos to show students how things work and operate. So it is impossible to achieve the multifaceted objective of education by single source of learning.

Since studying through Facebook along with conventional method has proved its effectiveness in improvement of achievement score, hence students should take interest in learning through computers via to web based educational website.

Facebook can be the catalyst that has students analysing and synthesizing course materials. With proper planning and appropriate curriculum, individual students may also use a Facebook i.e. class page to find ways to apply new ideas, share their work and thoughts on Facebook.

6.13.2 Parents

Social media tools, such as Facebook, blogs and twitter are helping teachers to keep parents and other community members informed by posting important information like homework assignments and test dates. Today's teachers are increasingly turning to a variety of digital technologies to make communication with parents easier and more current.

With a Facebook parents can visit the classroom virtually at their convenience. Facebook attracts parent's attention with the aim of sharing knowledge with parents and can deal with issues that affect their children.

Parents appreciate getting to know their child's teacher as a person and it helps to build rapport and establish a closer relationship.

6.13.3 Teacher

With technology, educators have a variety of learning tools at their fingertips. Teachers can collaborate to share their ideas and resources online. They can communicate with others across the world in an instant, meet the shortcomings of their work, refine it and provide their students with the best. This approach definitely enhances the practice of teaching.

School teacher should acquaint themselves with new web tool and educational websites. Since Facebook along with conventional method has proved its superiority over the conventional method of teaching in terms of achievement of students, therefore teachers can use this Facebook page for their effective classroom teaching. Those teachers who are well versed with web 2.0 tools should try to develop software in their respective subjects, by following the principles of development of Facebook page.

By using different readymade packages, teachers can also achieve the teaching objectives an fulfil the present requirement of effective classroom teaching and can also improve their teaching efficiency by using such pages (Supporting) as supporting system.

By utilizing free Facebook page along with their regular classroom teaching, teachers are capable of creating and storing online supplemental materials for students, post class notes for student review and give general feedback to the class as a whole and individually.

Facebook provide a communication space that teachers can utilise with students whenever there is a curriculum need to develop writing, share ideas and reflect on work being undertaken in the classroom. Teachers can simply create, manage and moderate Facebook page for all their students, with a minimum of fuss. The interface makes it easy to add videos, photos and other Web 2.0 tools, and the customizable features and range of widgets make it a useful tool for many different level of student.

6.13.4 Teacher Educators

The current generation of youth often described as digital natives, may be resistant to traditional methods of teaching and learning in India still the use of Web 2.0 tools in education field is still in the stage of infancy. But if we have to transform our generation towards a techno than technology based education should be incorporated in teacher education programme.

In order to use the web 2.0 tools in the teaching learning process, the teachers both pre service and in service must be trained in the teacher teaching institution. The teacher training institute must offer techno based education as compulsory or elective papers in their B.Ed.,M.Ed. syllabus. This well help in increasing the trained manpower; Orientation of in -service teachers should be arranged.

The teacher educators should promote researchers in the field of web 2.0 integration of Facebook with other methods of teaching, intelligent tutoring system, online based examination/assessment system. Share your lesson plans can enhance the effective classroom learning.

6.13.5 Administrators

The administrator of educational institutions should try to provide computer with internet facilities for the use of multimedia web 2.0 tools in the schools and colleges to keep teachers and students in touch with the latest gadgets. Provision should be made for training of teachers in the various technological field of education. Curriculum must be designed keeping in view of the latest technological developments in the field computers. The administrators should try to procure computer software in different subjects and for different levels.

Now a days many institutions are exploring distance education, either as a component of their regular class teaching program or as an outreach to students who will not be able to attend on campus classes regularly. Facebook combined with a good course management system and access to a tutor through teleconferencing or E-mail can be major components of such courses.

6.13.6 Software Designers

Software designers are playing a key role in the design, installation, testing and maintenance of software systems. Currently about one third of IT jobs are in development and programming. Software designer are making the development of computer software in any subject requires two main things; first the person having mastery over the subject matter an second the person having knowledge of computer programming. Generally the software developers have mastery over programming but they do not know how to analyse an arrange content.

So it requires a fine co-ordination between subject expert and computer programmer. They must take genuine interest in developing computer software in various school subjects. This software must be made available to the schools at cheaper rate.

Facebook is an international website and the above research has shown its effectiveness in enhancing teaching and learning and for the development of web based page in different subjects.

The above develop Facebook page will be a guideline for the Indian software designer, so they can develop a page by using the principles of controlled and effective learning.

6.13.7 Suggestions for further research

The suggestions for further researches in the area of social media in education are given below

1. Facebook page may be developed for teaching other subjects at different levels.
2. Facebook page may be compared with traditional method of teaching by considering some other variable like different dimension of personality, anxiety, span of attention of the students, higher mental abilities etc. as co-variate.
3. Facebook may be supported with other advance facility like online help, problem solving by teacher through internet, e-

mail teleconferencing, on line virtual libraries, virtual classrooms etc.

4. Computer software can be developed in more interactive mode, so that learner can use independently.

6.13.8 Recommendations

1. Taking the advantages of the Web 2.0 technology can help in designing the e-learning courses.
2. Train the students to use the applications of social media in learning.
3. Linking the social media applications with Learning Management System (LMS) used in universities.
4. Supporting the researches in the field of e-learning and distance education.

CPSIA information can be obtained
at www.ICGtesting.com
Printed in the USA
LVHW041613220423
745024LV00001B/23

9 781805 254522